TRAVELS WITH
ROSINANTE
—5 years' cycling round the world—

BY BERNARD MAGNOULOUX

The Oxford Illustrated Press,

The Oxford Illustrated Press

© 1988, Bernard Magnouloux

ISBN 0 946609 70 5

Published by:
The Oxford Illustrated Press Limited, Haynes Publishing Group,
Sparkford, Nr Yeovil, Somerset BA22 7JJ, England.

Haynes Publications Inc., 861 Lawrence Drive, Newbury Park,
California 91320, USA.

Printed in England by:
J.H. Haynes & Co Limited, Sparkford, Nr. Yeovil, Somerset.

British Library Cataloguing in Publication Data
Magnouloux, Bernard
    Travels with Rosinante: 5 years' cycling
    round the world.
    1. Journeys around the world by bicycles
    I. Title
    910.4'1
    ISBN 0-946609-70-5

Library of Congress Catalog Card Number 88-82573

All line illustrations by Bernard Magnouloux.

Contents

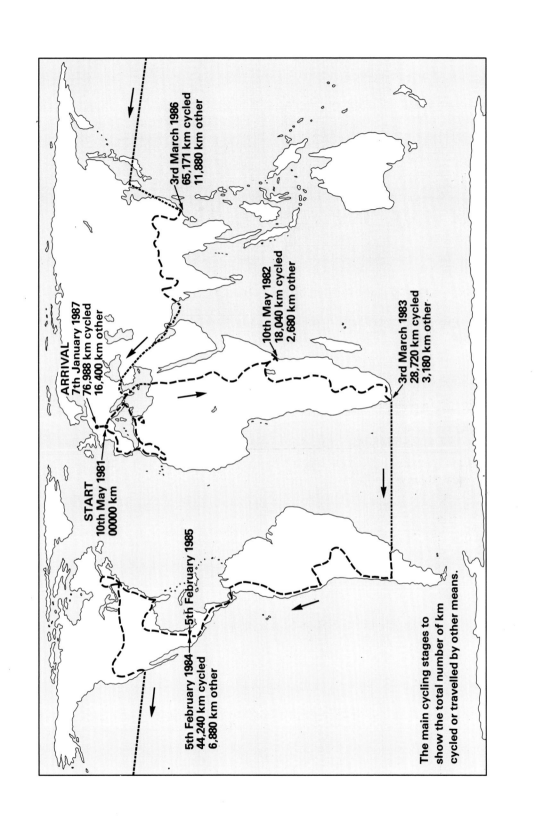

3rd March 1986
65,171 km cycled
11,880 km other

10th May 1982
18,040 km cycled
2,680 km other

3rd March 1983
28,720 km cycled
3,180 km other

ARRIVAL
7th January 1987
76,988 km cycled
16,400 km other

START
10th May 1981
00000 km

5th February 1985

5th February 1984
44,240 km cycled
6,880 km other

The main cycling stages to
show the total number of km
cycled or travelled by other means.

Acknowledgements

To the Malawian bicycle dealer who, in the bush, when I bought a complete Indian brake from him, charged for the handle only and said, 'the cable is for free, I am sponsoring you'.

To Peugeot South Africa for the good job they did on poor Rosinante in Johannesburg.

To Peugeot St Vallier/Rhône, Sonnier Ets, who donated Rosinante II and the Municipality of St Vallier who organized the welcome back reception.

To Radio-France-Drôme and Cattin Cycles for the luxurious gift of Rosinante III.

To my family and Françoise for their love and help.

To the reader: the witch doctor dance in southern Sudan is nothing but . . . a football match.

To Sir Henry Morton Stanley for passages of my Tanzania chapter inspired by his famous meeting in *In The Dark Continent*.

To Jack Kerouac for the beginning of chapter 'Across the USA' inspired by a passage in *On the Road*.

To John Steinbeck for a few lines in my last chapter, inspired by his reflections in *Travels with Charley,* in which his car is nicknamed . . . Rocinante.

Bernard Magnouloux 1988

Foreword by Nick Crane

The thunder cracked once, then again with a double boom that made the mountain shudder as if it had been hit by a meteorite. Nothing moved on the Kamba La. The bikes began to roll, and as they rolled the first spots of rain fell, borne on a new, untidy wind.

During the previous night we had been attacked by dogs, shivered in two different caves then pushed the bikes through falling snow for three hours before finding the road. The night before that we had slept in a gully in the gorge of the Brahmaputra; the night before that another gully on a lonely hillside somewhere on the road to Xigatse; before that . . . the town of Lhatse, where we slept indoors, in the lodging compound in a small room we shared with a kind Chinese man whose trousers were hanging from the ceiling and who lent us his soap, towel and face cream. Since then we had cycled and walked 380 kilometres. All of it had been on dirt roads, or worse, tracks. Some of the time we had been lost.

The rain came thick like freezing steel needles. It forced its way up my sleeves; it somehow found a way round the neck of my hood so that it ran as slow as fear down my spine. The bike wanted to run away, to pull free of my grip and hurtle off the edge of one of the potholed hairpins. Far below the silvery snake of the Yarlung Tsangpo—the Brahmaputra—mocked our fragile flight. We twisted and turned down—mud splashing wheels, jarring handlebars—lusting for that extra degree of warmth that must come with the drop in altitude. We would reach Lhasa next day, for sure.

On the other side of the river, we reached a village, and on the next day rode up the Lhasa valley.

The Potala Palace rose from a dash of white between the peaks ahead, growing to a gleaming cube and then a complex stack of interlocking rectangles, tapered and staired. The streets were full: of Chinese in uniforms, of Tibetans in thick skin coats, some with wild Kampa hair-dos of red wool tied round black manes above strong bones. There were motorbikes, jeeps, trucks. And noise.

The travellers that year—1986—were staying either at the Kirey Hotel (also known as 'The Taxi Stand') or at the Snowlands. The Kirey was full. The Snowlands has a sun-filled courtyard surrounded by balconies off which run the rooms. Pinned to the wall of the hotel's entrance arch were a number of notices penned by Western travellers; pleas for information on how to reach Golmud up north; a doctor wanting to hire a jeep to cross to Kathmandu, and needing three other riders; and in blue biro a man with a French-sounding name enquiring eloquently whether anybody in Lhasa had a spare derailleur mechanism for a bicycle.

On the road from Kathmandu, Dick and I had already met several cyclists; near Tingri we had asked the way of a Tibetan on a huge black roadster; earlier, just a day out of Kathmandu we had come upon two Americans, Peter and Janet, who were pedalling up to the border to see what Tibet looked like. And on a wild stretch of gravel north of Mount Everest we'd overtaken Eamonn Wallace, an Irishman on an overloaded bike who had shared with us a piece of cherry cake some German tourists had given him. We sometimes talked about Eamonn; he had cycled all the way from Ireland to Tibet. It made our own 5,000-kilometre dash across central Asia seem like a short package holiday.

The few overland cyclists who had made it to Lhasa that May were regarded as slightly freakish by most of the other travellers. In a room three doors along the balcony from our own was Brian Williamson—a New Zealander who had bought a secondhand mountain bike in Kathmandu and made a spur of the moment decision to cycle through the Himalayas to the Tibetan capital. Brian was carrying enough bike tools to build a bridge over the Yangtze. He had a Swiss Army knife with a serrated blade that would cut aluminium; we borrowed it to saw the zip pullers off our panniers so that we could save a bit more weight. Then we met Robert Goo, a Chinese-American who had brought *his* mountain bike from Kathmandu on the roof of a bus. And there was Marc Noël, a Belgian who had ridden into Tibet the long way, from Chengdu, and who departed for Nepal the day after we arrived. (You will read more of him later . . .)

But the cyclist who everybody was talking about was the Frenchman. He too had reached Lhasa the hard way, from the east along the saw-tooth trail that clambers up and down between the mighty rivers of the Yarlung, Yangtze, Mekong and Salween. Everybody knew his first name—Bernard—but always tripped over his surname. He was variously called Mongiloo, Mingaloo or Manginoo.

It was two days before we met him, a tall, thin man with a thatch of red hair and a face that looked as if it had been out in the cold too long. He came along the balcony of the Snowlands to the corner where Dick and I were engaged in the final stages of removing shims from a freewheel block.

'Hello,' he said, 'Do you have a spare derailleur?'

'Ah, you must be Bernard Mag . . .' we said, hesitating over that tricky syllabic doublet.

'. . . nouloux,' said Bernard.

We all leaned back in the thin sun. In the courtyard below, the woman who brought the yoghurt each morning was packing her basket. In the Jokhang Temple the red-robed monks would be chanting their deep, bass mantra that sounded like the drone of so many Lancaster bombers. Bernard's mechanical problem was unenviable. He had only one working gear on his bicycle; we had ten; Brian Williamson had eighteen. Only having one gear on your bicycle in the middle of Tibet is as close as you can get to being up a creek without a paddle.

Bernard was not in a rush. It had taken him five years to cycle to Lhasa. He was on his second bicycle. It is difficult to know where to start the questions when faced by someone who has pedalled the length and breadth of the world; all those stories! Dick and I had to leave Lhasa that day, pressed by the urgency of a ride that could not have been more different in nature to that of Bernard's. We did not have time to hear the stories.

'When are you leaving Lhasa?' we asked him. Bernard replied with a wonderfully unhurried shrug: 'In a short while; when it feels right. Maybe I can make my bicycle work with two gears.'

That was two years ago this month. It wasn't until I read the manuscript of *Travels with Rosinante* that I found out how much we had missed by rushing away from the tall Frenchman that sunny day in Lhasa. This book has two gears too. First there is the leg-spinning up and down of everyday anecdotes: eating a whole, boiled rat ('like a sausage . . . a furry sausage'), snowstorms and dysentery, a mugging in Mexico, love on the Indian Ocean. And second there is the high gear; the story of the unstoppable rolling nomad who will always have to move on because he has to see what is around the next corner.

There is all the difference in the world between a short, sharp adventure and an open-ended journey. Most of us have tried the former, be it a weekend's cycle-camping or a mountain climb, but few have the courage to pack up home and comfort and settle into life as a wanderer.

The scale of Bernard's ride is awesome; by the time Dick and I met him in Lhasa, he had cycled over 70,000 kilometres—equivalent to pedalling the length of Britain 52 times. His five years of pedalling had taken him through four continents; on his ride from China to Lhasa he had taken 33 days and covered 2,400 kilometres. All of it had been on dirt roads. On this section alone he had cycled over 18 passes at heights of between 3,500 and

4,000 metres. But this is not a book about physical feats—though there are plenty of remarkable examples; more it is an odyssey through a world that has never presented the traveller with such extremes. From the cosiness of a Greek village where he worked temporarily as a plasterer, Bernard sets off through civil wars and superpowers; sleeps with both the humble and the have-everythings. It is his varied companions and his reaction to them that brings such riches.

How does Bernard manage to strike up such vivid relationships with people he meets along the way? Part of the answer can be found in the chapter on Chile. When picked up by the police he has a length of string between one side of his moustache and a bicycle spoke nipple which is pressed through his ear lobe. The reason? The strong side-wind kept blowing his moustache into his mouth. This is an astonishing story from an unusual teller.

Nick Crane
May 1988

Introduction
Mexico: The Cold Gun Barrel

It was a small pistol but no less terrifying than a big one: it too had an evil eye. However it provoked in me an unexpected thought: 'At last! It's happening—a real mugging! And among cactuses and rocks, just like in the Westerns! What luck!'

This would make a good story, a better story than the stoning in North Africa, the tsetse fly attack in Zambia, the scorpion sting in Costa Rica or the tribal war which marked my arrival in Kenya . . .

When a traveller embarks on a journey, he knows that attacks are part of the game: a round-the-world bicycle adventure without bad experiences would not be regarded as serious. That's why, confronted with this small pistol, I was delighted. My only concerns were 'don't miss a detail of it' and 'don't lose your life in the process as you'll need it to tell the story'.

When I had entered Mexico, I hadn't changed my routine: at midday, every day, I left the road to find a place to rest near a stream. Streams are good picnicking places: there is water and generally there are trees for firewood and shade. So, even though I was still near Acapulco and in the state of Guerrero—reputedly the most dangerous state in the country—I stuck to my routine and began to cook my daily rice; my twice daily rice. I only ever changed the seasoning: one day it was Maggie's chicken soup, next day it was Maggie's beef soup, next day chicken and so on; that's all my French culinary skills amounted to.

I had been sitting next to Rosinante, my old companion, the bicycle with a soul, when the small Indian, stripped to the waist and sporting a pair of bright yellow shorts, had come over to me. I thought he had wanted a chat, but instead he had pulled the gun on me and had demanded *'La radio y tu dinero* (your radio and your money)'.

This radio had brought me nothing but trouble. At the beginning of my journey the aerial I had erected at the back of Rosinante together with the telephone wire I had rigged up to carry electricity from the dynamo to the front lamp (so I could hold the lamp in my hand while I was riding and

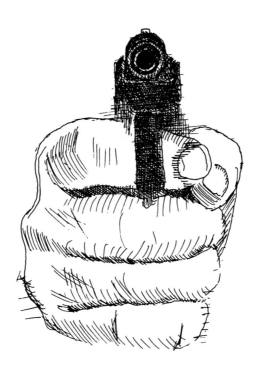

point it in any direction I wanted) had convinced the Moroccans that I was a spy for the Polisario. In the Sudan it was the aerial itself that had given me trouble. In the deep and primitive south, I had met a convoy of three jeeps driven by Italian tourists, one of whom was a radio ham and had equipped his car with a powerful transmitter. As I leant Rosinante against his car, when he called his wife on the phone that evening, very mysteriously, every time he spoke, Rosinante's lights lit up! This so impressed the Shilluks who were standing nearby, that they wanted to adopt Rosinante as their new totem. Fortunately the radio ham was able to explain that his powerful radio produced a strong magnetic field, which Rosinante's aerial, which was parallel to that on the car, transformed into an induced current that had been strong enough to activate its lights. I'm not sure they understood the explanation but it worked. After that encounter I bought a 'bikeman' with no wires or aerial to get me into trouble—the only problem being that in order to receive a clear signal I had to position the headset and my *head* according to the radio waves! No wonder I was asked why I looked like a figure on an Egyptian fresco: with my head facing sideways to the direction I was cycling!

I do not know much about pistols. All I knew was that this one wasn't a 9 mm since I had used one of those during my military service. I wondered what it was . . .

I stood up. While explaining why it was my pleasure to be mugged, I handed the Indian my radio set and asked:

'*Deja me ver tu pistola, me interessa.* (Let me see your pistol, I'm interested in it.)'

Never, in all the Western movies he had seen, had the Indian heard any victim ask to see the weapon. He was a little surprised and, because I was naively reaching for the gun, he pulled it away to hide it behind his back.

This was my chance. Instinctively I hurled myself at the man, knocking him to the ground. He tried to punch me, I struck back; he ran away.

I chased after him. Suddenly frightened by what I had dared to do I shouted obscenities in French, partly to scare him and partly to calm me. The Indian stopped at the stream, picked up a stone and threw it at me. I did the same back. Then he changed his tactics.

'*Amigo, amigo!*' he said. '*Me rendio. Tengo la culpa, castiga me, golpa me!* (I surrender, I'm wrong. Punish me. Hit me!)'

And he held his hands over his head.

I was dumbfounded. I didn't believe him; I was still scared and all I wanted him to do was disappear. But he was sharper than me.

'*Te gusta la coco? Si? Me voy traer te una fresca. Somos amigos ahora, no?* (Do you like coconut? Yes? I will bring you a fresh one, we're friends now, aren't we?)' he said in a whining voice. 'My pistol. I need it. You see these are my cows [there were indeed some cows] and I have to protect them against bandits [the irony seemed to escape him]. Let me have my pistol please!'

So that was it. The gun had dropped and I hadn't realised it. Was his surrender just a trick to get the pistol back? But he looked so miserable now, so vulnerable, so remorseful. And I was feeling so strong! I was so proud of having disarmed this mugger that I let him repocket his weapon and invited him for a cup of coffee near the fire.

I made him some of my best ground coffee that I had been given at the Costa Rican hacienda where I had worked as a coffee picker. As a filter I was using a sleeve from my T-shirt sewn into a cone. While the coffee was brewing I told my story to my mugger-turned-friend. I told him that Mexico was my thirty-third country after three years on the road; that I was a very poor traveller, my fortune being just 300 US dollars, and that I would have to stop when I reached the US to work again and earn more.

When the small Indian left me I felt we were firm friends. After all, bandits have morals too and it is well known that they recognize courage—and as I had beaten him I must be his equal. I was his friend . . . wasn't I?

Three hours later and twenty miles further up the mountains on my way to Mexico City, I chose another nice quiet spot for my mid-afternoon *café-au-lait*. I sat down to write up my notes about the mugging while it was fresh in my mind.

I shall always wonder how they managed to follow me without being noticed. But there they stood—the small Indian in the yellow shorts and this time accompanied by two buddies. The tall Hispanic-looking one snatched my bag and began to search it, while the big one, of mixed race, and who carried a heavy club, advised me to co-operate and do as I was told.

The Indian pushed his gun against my ribs to emphasise the point. The barrel was cold against my sunburnt skin. It made me angry.

I stood up and told them I was going to walk to the road for help and made a move towards the Indian who stood between me and the road. Taken by surprise, he moved the gun aside as I pushed past. This would be my only chance. My 300 dollars were in cash. If they were stolen I would be lost. If I could get the pistol I might win again.

I hit the Indian's arm and the gun fell to the ground. All four of us dived for it. I held it for a fraction of a second, just long enough to feel its weight, but the next moment it was kicked through the air and into a ditch behind a barbed wire fence. I rushed towards it. The three men threw themselves at me and brought me to the ground. The Indian grabbed some big stones, the big half-caste gripped his club. Their eyes told me they were ready to kill me. I was scared. I managed to fend off a few blows but suddenly the world seemed to explode; the half-caste had broken his club on my head.

In the few seconds before I passed out, the most memorable moments of my journey flashed before me . . .

Greece: My Blood on the Priest's Hands

The day I landed in Igoumenitsa, Greece, I had already been travelling for almost half a year: one month in Spain and Portugal, two and a half in Morocco, fifteen days across the north of Algeria, one month in Tunisia and ten days in southern Italy. Libya had been closed for transit to Egypt, and I had to make a detour through Sicily, Italy and Greece. In other words, five months after leaving France for a round-the-world tour, I was still in Italy, the country next door! I didn't send any postcards from there.

After Italy, Greece was like North Africa to me. People stopped to offer me drinks and food. In the bars, which were vast and numerous, customers took their time to drink their coffee and chat—in Italy, motorists had gulped their *expresso* without even bothering to sit down they were so anxious to get back to the wheel.

It was on my second day in Greece that I was offered a job. Vassili the café owner had invited me to have a second cup of coffee on the house and had put forward his proposal then.

It was Turkish coffee: so thick and sweet that it always comes with a glass of water to rinse one's mouth out. The café was quiet and Vassili seemed pleased to have somebody to chat to. He didn't speak anything but Greek but he was a very good mime.

He had noticed that hanging from my right front pannier was a mason's trowel. Was I a mason, he asked in gestures. I answered yes, a stonemason; I specialized in the restoration of old houses. I had taken my trowel with me on my journey because it was just as useful to me as a knife: in a good mason's hand, a trowel is a weapon as well as a tool. Handled skilfully it can slap faces or caress women . . . Mine was an Italian 'smoothing trowel', it had already been very efficient against Moroccan sheep-dogs and I was to use it later to dig my bed in desert sands, chop my firewood and free Rosinante from equatorial mud. Unfortunately, I was to lose it among the eucalyptus leaves of an Ecuadorian bivouac . . .

The job offered by Vassili consisted of plastering the façade of a newly

17

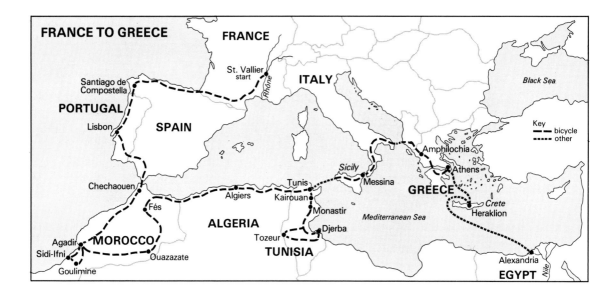

FRANCE TO GREECE

FRANCE
St. Vallier start
ITALY
Black Sea

Santiago de Compostella
PORTUGAL
Lisbon
SPAIN
Rhône

Key
— bicycle
···· other

Amphilochia
Athens
GREECE
Sicily
Messina
Crete
Heraklion

Chechaouen
Fés
Tunis
Algiers
Kairouan
Monastir
Mediterranean Sea

ALGERIA
Tozeur
Djerba
Agadir
Sidi-Ifni
MOROCCO
Ouazazate
TUNISIA
Goulimine
Alexandria
Nile
EGYPT

built house. It belonged to a police officer who he summoned to the café. Vassili 'translated': I was to be offered meals at Vassili's and the use of the empty apartment, already furnished, in the new house. On top of that, Vassili wrote, I would be paid 350 drachmas per *mera.*

Greek is a strange language. You understand nothing at first. Even 'yes' and 'no' are confusing. For 'yes', Greeks say *nay* and shake their heads; for 'no', they say *ochi* while nodding. But in occasional words you recognize most of the roots of French or English: *megalo* means large, *micro* means small, *pente* five, *nycta* night, *gala* milk, etc. So very soon you think you understand Greek . . . but you don't!

And just then, I got confused: 350 drachmas per *mera,* I decided, could only be 350 drachmas (£3.50) per hour and I accepted the job.

That very evening, after a pleasant meal of traditional tomato salad with fetta cheese, I was introduced to Vassili's niece who by good fortune spoke French! She was twenty and very good looking even though one of her eyes was half closed. But far from being unattractive it gave Maria tremendous charm. I was hypnotized and wished I had the whole night to court her. When she left I asked her in passing to confirm the terms of my employment—350 drachmas per hour, wasn't it?

Maria asked Vassili. Her uncle chuckled and Maria translated:

'Non, Vassili ne pense pas que c'est 350 drachmes de l'heure, il pense que c'est 350 drachmes par jour. (No, Vassili doesn't think it is 350 per hour, he thinks it is per day.)'

Five days later, the police officer owed his plastered walls more to Maria's

18

charm than to his money, but my work had at least attracted more work. Several farmers in the village had reserved their place in my schedule. One even offered 500 drachmas, but still per day.

Vassili was very pleased; he was paid as long as I stayed. He even seemed determined to marry me to a village girl. He didn't ask for my preferences but insisted on taking me to Sunday mass, where all the village girls would be able to see me, and I them.

He had also publicly wondered about my sex life. This was the less pleasant part of my stay here. Everybody seemed preoccupied with this side of life. A Swedish traveller, who happened to stop at the café during one of my breaks, was really upset: 'These Greeks don't have any respect for private things! They're always asking about your sex life. They totally lack education, it is still the Dark Ages around here!'

To improve my looks Vassili persuaded me to shave. He even shaved me himself! A moustache, that's okay for a man, but a beard doesn't look clean enough for a Greek girl, he explained.

Before the mass, I was introduced to the village Orthodox priest. He wore a long beard, but Vassili explained that he was not supposed to seduce any more girls, he was already married. He insisted on pointing out the difference between Orthodox and Catholic priests: *'In Gallia* [France] *papa no ficka-ficka!'* he said, roaring with laughter.

This priest spoke some English and shook my hand for a long time. He was a giant of a man, and his grip was like steel—he virtually crushed my right hand between his two.

Both my hands were in a poor state after Tunisia. After three months of African summer sun, my fair skin had given up and any cut developed into a nasty looking infection. And after a week of plastering, my right hand had suffered numerous blows. Under the pressure of the priest's grip, the wounds began to bleed.

The priest didn't notice anything but he conducted the whole mass with his hands stained with my blood. No doubt everybody thought the priest was presenting Christ's stigmata! This was my contribution to keeping this village in the 'Dark Ages'.

Vassili's café was rather primitive: just a vine arbour outside and a small cramped room inside. But it was strategically placed in a curve of the main road between Ionnina and Athens, and it was never empty.

Most of the customers were regulars. After a few evenings, I began to know them well and give them nick-names.

A neighbouring farmer was called 'One-tooth' for the obvious reason that he had only one tooth though it was emphasised by his singularly large mouth. His face was always lit by two smiles: his mouth formed one and his eyes—which were very wrinkled and seemed to reach from ear to ear—the other. One-tooth was never parted from his cap—a battered navy blue cap which gave its owner the air of a Midwestern farmer.

The 'Mafioso' was a lorry driver in his fifties. An unusual lorry driver, he wore a three-piece suit and he was fastidious about it: he adjusted his shirt collar from time to time and before he sat, he always pulled up his trouser legs to save the creases. What earned him his nickname was that he often tried to speak Italian to me. It was in fact a jumble of Italian and German words, and it impressed everybody in the café except me. But I was tactful, I always answered with another blend of Italian and French and nobody except us knew that we were both pretending . . .

The 'Devout' might not even have believed in God. But he was always fiddling with a kind of rosary. I was to discover that it was nothing religious, just a row of beads to play with and another relic of the Turkish occupation.

The 'Elegant' was a remarkable specimen of 'homo mediterraneus' with low-waisted trousers whose creases fell impeccably on fine shining boots, white shirt opened to the fourth button revealing virile, hairy chest, shirt-sleeves rolled up to the elbow (never further), a big waterproof wristwatch and an enormous signet ring. The white shirt would have been useless without its breast pocket: this is where 'homo mediterraneus' kept the instruments of his trade: a cigarette box, a lighter and . . . a comb.

I was persuaded that the Elegant was a kind of pimp since he spent whole days in the café, sipping ouzo with no visible means of support. But one early morning I was amazed to meet him in the road leading a flock of sheep and goats, and even more surprised to see he was wearing his shining boots and irreproachable trousers. Later I was informed by Vassili that that indeed was his job; while the Elegant led his flock to the pasture and back, his wife ran the farm . . .

Vassili's customers, regulars and others, were interested in only two things: politics and sex.

Politics was something new in Greece which is probably why the customers were so fanatical. As parliamentary elections approached (it was October 1981), I was party to increasingly heated arguments between the supporters of the Nea-Democratia and those of the PASOK, the Socialist Party. Only the Mafioso had any sympathy for the 'Kappa Kappa', the K.K.E., the Communist Party.

And when they had made their peace over glasses of ouzo, they turned to me. Their main pleasure was to ask me to translate into French for them, 'hot' words such as penis, tits, etc. But what made them laugh the most was to teach me the equivalent Greek words. As the women were in the kitchen, they would whisper the rude word to me, then encourage me to repeat it loudly so that the women could hear. Some of them laughed till they cried.

The problem was that, like kids, they never tired of a good joke. They would do it again, and have me do it again, for any new customer . . .

After a week, since everybody was so taken with my work and my presence in the village, I decided to ask for a rise. Figures in hand, and without Vassili's help, I managed to tell my boss that my work deserved better payment.

It is very difficult to conduct salary negotiations in a language you know only by way of linguistic roots, so I only got a 100-drachma increase. However, as if moved by sudden understanding the police officer took me to a cupboard in the apartment, showed me the bottles inside and seemed to offer them as a kind of bonus. There were ten bottles of retsina wine, a bottle of gin, another of vodka and a magnum of ouzo.

Meanwhile I was not very successful with Maria. It was not easy to meet her as women were never seen in the café (probably another Turkish legacy) and I constantly had to invent translation problems so as to be allowed into the kitchen when Maria was there.

The main problem in fact lay elsewhere—Maria was not the only attractive girl in the village. As a matter of fact, I met two others. One was the policeman's niece who arrived from Athens one Saturday and threw a party. She spoke English, which helped, and living in the capital, was much more inclined towards . . . dissipation . . . than Maria, and that helped even more.

But only on Saturdays . . .

At the first party I also met Andriana, One-tooth's second daughter. A sexual bombshell, she dared to go bra-less, which was unheard of in the Dark Ages!

On the pretext that my first layer needed to settle before I could finish the top layer of plastering, I announced that I could begin the work on One-tooth's farm the following Tuesday. The real reason of course was Andriana's lack of brassiere . . .

One-tooth paid 500 drachmas a day but didn't want me to eat in Vassili's café. I gathered that Vassili was also charging 500 drachmas a day. And I heard him telling One-tooth that in my coffee I took only the Nounou brand of canned milk. Eager to please me, One-tooth bought cans of Nounou and despite my constant efforts to explain to him that only the milk was important, and that his cow's milk would be fine, I could not get him to understand.

My job there was the rendering of the tobacco barn. Easy. My aim was to seduce Andriana. Not so easy. First, Andriana had a sister, three years older, who acted as a *duenna*. To seduce Andriana, I would have to seduce the sister first. Secondly, on a farm, in the Dark Ages, girls have to work all day along and have very little time to go behind the barn and be courted by the *Gallos*.

To cut a long story short, after three weeks in the village, I was still alone at night. So, having finished off One-tooth's job, I announced my intention to leave and continue my journey. The Devout immediately objected saying that following President Sadat's assassination, I had little chance of being admitted into Egypt, my next destination. But this was pure spite, as he wanted me to build a wall in his garden . . .

That last evening, as is traditional in stone-masonry, I organized a party around a fire of cement bags. There were the bottles of gin and vodka to finish, mandarins and chestnuts. Maria was the first to arrive, bringing her young brother and a present—a brand new French flag to replace the tattered one which flew on Rosinante's radio aerial. She sewed it herself and it would withstand the weather better, she said.

Next were Andriana and her father. One-tooth was the only one to drink alcohol. And of course, I ended up by myself near the chimney, with a bottle of wine still to finish . . .

Two days later, nearing Athens I found to my surprise that my urine was a constant dark yellow. Next day it was brown and I wrote in my diary 'viral hepatitis???'

Part One: Cairo to Cape Town

Sudan: Riding the rails in the Nubia desert.

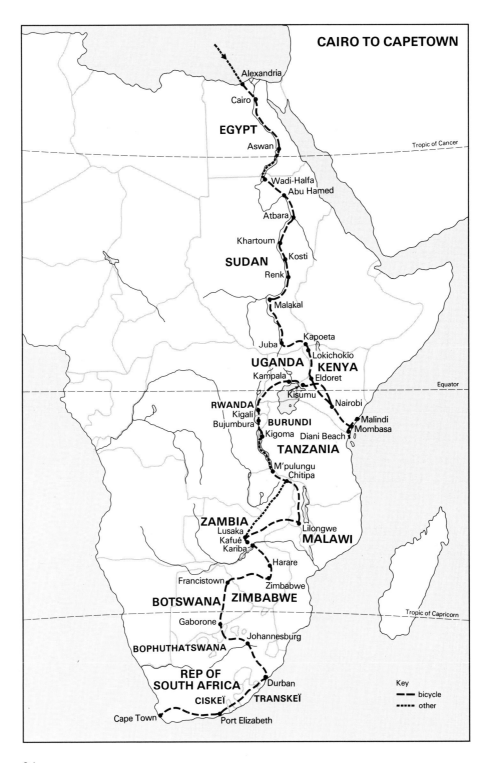

CAIRO TO CAPETOWN

Alexandria

Cairo

EGYPT

Aswan

Tropic of Cancer

Wadi-Halfa
Abu Hamed

Atbara

Khartoum

Kosti

SUDAN

Renk

Malakal

Kapoeta

Juba

Lokichokio

UGANDA **KENYA**

Kampala Eldoret

Kisumu

Equator

RWANDA Nairobi

Kigali

BURUNDI

Bujumbura Malindi

Kigoma Diani Beach Mombasa

TANZANIA

M'pulungu
Chitipa

ZAMBIA

Lusaka Lilongwe

Kafué **MALAWI**

Kariba

Harare

Francistown

Zimbabwe

BOTSWANA **ZIMBABWE**

Tropic of Capricorn

Gaborone

Johannesburg

BOPHUTHATSWANA

**REP OF
SOUTH AFRICA** Durban

CISKEÏ **TRANSKEÏ**

Key

Cape Town Port Elizabeth

– – – bicycle
••••••• other

24

Egypt: Our Bicycles are Looted

It begins as a torpor. It gets hold of your head and you become tired and lethargic. When it reaches your stomach, it begins to hurt. Not very much but enough to make you feel sick, profoundly sick. It thickens your urine but dilutes your will. And when it has you well in its grasp it gives your eyes the appearance of yellow amber.

Jaundice, viral hepatitis, that's what it was. The longest miles of my life were the three from Athens to its harbour, Piraeus. I was so sick that the smallest gesture required an enormous effort of will. I managed to catch the ferry to Crete and joined Gernod and Bobo in Heraklion's youth hostel. They were to be my chaperons. They helped me to the Danish ship which took us to Alexandria, they helped me through the Egyptian chaos to another youth hostel, in the suburbs of the town, and there I collapsed.

I met Bobo and Gernod in Athens. They were both long-distance cyclists. Bobo was British but everybody mistook him for a Japanese, as his father was a Chinese migrant in Australia. In fact, Bobo had dual nationality. That was a secret but since he intended to reach South Africa, he hoped that a second passport might help him out of trouble. His mother was French, and Bobo spoke French better than I spoke English. That made him dear to me. He advised me to read Alan Moorehead's *The White Nile* and *The Blue Nile*. They were good preparation for our common aim: to cycle up the majestic river, through the difficult Sudan.

In *The Blue Nile*, I read that the first audacious explorers to reach the source of the Nile in Ethiopia (at that time it was thought that the Blue Nile was the real one) were a French physician, an English minister and a Danish navigator.

And Gernod was Danish. Just as blond and pink as Vikings are supposed to be. His aim was also a round-the-world trip through the Sudan. So history itself was binding us together.

However there, in Alexandria Youth Hostel, we were concerned with quite different problems.

Mine was to get over my illness. I had met a doctor on holiday in Heraklion who had told me that the only cure for jaundice was rest, and the only diet was the one dictated by my desires: 'Your body knows instinctively what's good and bad for it.' I believe that. Being an incorrigible coffee drinker, like most French people, and having had the utmost difficulty in Algeria and Tunisia satisfying my need (Moorish coffee being rare and too strange for my palate), I carried with me several one-pound tins of Nescafé. But now I was not only unable to drink coffee, the mere thought of it made me nauseous. That was why I became a 'tea-totaller'—for a while at least . . .

Bobo's and Gernod's problem was riding the 'Desert Freeway' to Cairo. There are two roads between Alexandria and Cairo: the old one, through the crowded delta, which was a three-day ride, or the new direct route through the desert which meant two days riding on brand new tar.

For Bobo and Gernod, this would be their first desert. So they prepared for it very carefully. Bobo read *How to Survive in the Desert,* and Gernod had his shining fifteen-gear bicycle checked by a local bicycle dealer. To be sure of everything, they delayed their departure by a day. After all, it was a serious enterprise. Bobo had filled twelve one-quart bottles with water and Gernod two five-litre tanks, but would it be enough for two days in the desert? Would their European bodies bear rapid dehydration? Would their fair skins resist the cruel attack of an African sun? Would their senses be able to distinguish reality from mirages? These were the anxious questions they faced.

D-Day came. Bobo and Gernod got up very early and after the long preparation they shook hands with the other travellers. They looked grave. Adventure and glory were awaiting them . . .

According to the Michelin Guide statistics, it rains an average of five days a year on the Nile delta, but, on this D-day, it probably rained the equivalent of three years' worth in a single morning. Bobo and Gernod couldn't even get out of Alexandria. Traffic was clogged up by flooding and the town was a mess. Loaded down with their water reserves, the two cyclists each suffered a fall and came back sheepishly to the hostel, their equipment soaking wet. They had discovered that to survive in the desert, you had first to avoid rainy days!

I was to discover myself that to survive in the desert you had only to pick up the phone, but for the moment, a week after my companions had left, I was becoming restless, bored to death by this imposed idleness. Tired of resting, I got back on the road, slowly, three weeks after the jaundice had appeared. And I made the acquaintance of Egypt.

Imagine a road along the Nile, crowded with a never-ending flow of

Egypt: In the delta, a buffalo activates a noria.

vehicles, in every direction, obeying no rules. Along the road are two lines of people. Each line consists of twenty million people. And each of them, I mean every one of them, is shouting to you: 'Hello mister, what is your name?'

To answer 'Marlon Brando' or 'King Hussein' doesn't help . . .

One person in two is a child who, after asking your name, decides to stop you, by any means, and then to relieve your bicycle of what he reckons you don't need. There was not a single village where kids didn't try to stop me, by throwing sticks in my wheels or stoning me. It was probably a game for them, but a very unnerving experience for me. I had to force my way through all these improvised road blocks—and to do it without hurting the 'poor underprivileged kids'.

Every three miles or so, big signs said in English and French that it was forbidden for foreigners to leave the main road. I had to do so twice because there weren't enough youth hostels. Then the density of the population prevented me from finding a single spot to camp. The first night I had to suffer a humiliating search by army officers. I ended up being invited by a youngster who showed me around his family and village as though I had landed from the moon. The second night, the police drove me back to Beni Suef where I had to sleep in the police station on a bench, under the spotlights.

When I arrived at the Sohag Youth Hostel, Gernod had already been there for a couple of days. This youth hostel made a big impression on me as soon as I opened the door; it was full of lovely female Egyptian students. And my arrival seemed to be a wonderful event for them. They prepared tea and gathered around me to listen to my stories. This was a nice change from the road fights, I felt that I was going to stay a while in this hostel . . .

Half the girls were already in love with Gernod. They spoke of his blue eyes and blond hair with ecstasy. I hoped that my red hair would interest some of the other half . . .

Gernod had met a Scot who taught English at the University of Sohag. A student of his invited us all to visit the ruins of Panopolis which were newly discovered in the suburbs of Akhmim nearby. We would finish the visit with a meal offered by Ahmed, the student.

As Panopolis wasn't yet open to tourists, the inhabitants of Akhmim weren't used to seeing Westerners, so the arrival of three typical white people with blond or red hair, was like the landing of Martians in Wells' *War of the Worlds.*

Riding to Ahmed's house, we attracted about fifty kids, highly excited by our presence. There, we were joined by three other students, Ahmed's colleagues, who had attracted another fifty kids. The students were impressive too: they were Sudanese from the southern tribes, tall, very dark negroes with tribal scars on their faces, and very smartly dressed.

Very soon, there was a big crowd in front of Ahmed's house. Everybody wanted to have a look at this extraordinary congregation of three *hawadjas* on bicycles and three negroes in white suits. Ahmed was outflanked: he could not close his door, one window broke open, and we had to retreat up the stairs. Ahmed gave a few coins to an adult and asked him to block the way up. And for a brief moment we stayed together by ourselves on the terraced roof.

Only for a brief moment because, the streets being so narrow, it was easy for the crowd to approach us again by invading the neighbouring roofs. At least they could not touch us, just stare and laugh at the freaks chatting together. Our main topic of conversation was the Sudanese roads. Were there any? Where were they paved? The students gave us encouraging answers which were to prove completely inaccurate.

One hour later, the visit to the ruins was a nightmare. We got special permission from the archaeologists to enter the excavation pit, about five yards below ground level. There was an impressive statue of a pharaoh lying there. The problem was that we now had the whole town behind us. And from the bottom of the pit, it was very frightening: militiamen, policemen and guards were containing the crowd but for how long? The director of the excavation hurried over to beg us to leave; in a moment, he said, his whole work would be crushed by thousands of feet if not buried again, along with us aliens.

Pretending not to worry, Ahmed said that we were going to visit a water pipe factory just nearby where we would see craftsmen moulding, out of the Nile clay, the small furnaces for the pipes. They were kind, smiling men, and they showed us how to fire the pipe and let us have a go. But again, our visit could only be brief: the crowd was still on our tail and it meant that thousands of feet were now crushing the delicate clay furnaces which were drying in the sun.

We had to flee once more, but this time it was with great efficiency. As quickly as possible we boarded a *felucca,* a typical Nile sailing boat. And in the middle of the river we could relax, at last.

Back at Ahmed's place, we found our bicycles stripped. Fortunately we didn't have any luggage and the bikes were locked together. But everything that could be ripped off had been. I was especially sorry to lose a collection of olive stones carved into clogs, souvenirs of Morocco, and a minute tea-glass, used as a flower pot on Rosinante's handlebars, a souvenir of Tunisia.

Ahmed was aghast, and insisted on all six of us staying for the meal. The feast was served by his mother and sisters. Ahmed was proud of the quantity of food he was able to offer us, while explaining in his hesitant English that he wanted us to forget the bad things that had happened and remember only the good ones.

I have indeed forgotten all the bad things concerning Akhmim ruins and instead remember only the nice ones . . . such as the Sohag Youth Hostel female students!

Northern Sudan: A Phone Call in the Desert

Resting in Aswan from the frenzy of Egypt, I realized that I still knew very little about the Sudan: on my map, it was a blue area on my way to Cape Town, but I didn't know that of the 2000 miles I was about to pedal, only 200 were paved; I didn't know that I would be so thirsty and so sick that I would consider death as a release; I did not imagine that I would be caught in the middle of a raiding party.

Bobo and Gernod were ready, again before me. Being first to reach Cairo, they were able to apply for Sudanese visas one week before I did. So they got them one week before I did, one month later, after a memorable return trip by train, in an overcrowded but extremely cheap third class carriage (50 pence one way).

Bobo and Gernod were ready because they had gathered some information—contradictory information, except on one point: the Nubian Desert in northern Sudan is impossible for bicycles. Even motorcyclists take the train.

However, since four-wheel-drive vehicles were crossing the desert with a motoring permit obliging them to stay in convoy, we decided that 'impossible' was not in our Danish, English and French vocabulary , and began to stock up with food reserves. I made it light: two gallons of water, two pounds of sugar, four pounds of dried milk, fifteen pitta breads and a tin of processed cheese. On the black market I exchanged 45 Egyptian pounds (about £40 sterling) for 50 Sudanese pounds. That would last 20 days . . .

At Wadi Halfa, after a two-day ferry ride across Lake Nasser behind the Aswan Dam, the Sudan begins: 'the middle of nowhere', as Bobo said. We waited until the train had left and only then asked for the police station. Registration with the police is compulsory and we were afraid we might be ordered to take the train.

The policemen were embarrassed: they asked for our motoring permits. We showed them that our bicycles didn't have motors and insisted that, as there were three of us, we actually constituted a convoy. They finally agreed and we were allowed to sleep on the sand outside the station. One of the men took us 'out' to dinner. The restaurant was a small cabin serving the Egyptian *fool:* red beans.

Next morning, we left in convoy along the railway line, but after a mile, Bobo left us: he had decided to follow the Nile. This meant 1200 miles to Khartoum instead of 600 along the railway but he was at least sure to find plenty of water.

Gernod and I discovered that the space between the rails made a smooth cycle path and by noon spotted a building in the distance. A station? A mirage, already?

No, it was a really good old railway station, built in concrete by the British. We were told that such stations were built every twenty miles along the tracks, for maintenance—and only maintenance of course. They had water in rusty containers and we were able to replenish our bottles. Once out of sight, we added a few drops of iodine to sterilize it, but never in front of our hosts. They would have been offended.

Very soon the sand between the rails became softer. Gernod had thin tyres and an enormous load of food. He could not push his bike any more, except by balancing it on one rail and walking alongside. Thanks to the 'half-balloon' tyres of Rosinante, I could still pedal. But this meant that I had to wait for my companion. Every hour, I had to stop and read. I was reading the autobiography of Leon Trotsky. A very entertaining story, yes, but not in the middle of a desert . . .

The third evening, after we had dug holes in the sand to protect us from the cold winter wind, I told Gernod that I had only six pittas left and we had gone no more than seventy miles!

'I don't like the idea of cycling on my own', he said sadly, 'but you are right. I don't have enough for two, so the most reasonable thing is for you to push on at your own speed and just wait for me in Abu Hamed, where you'll be able to buy food.'

On the fourth morning, pedalling at full speed, I passed a station without stopping; I still had half a gallon of water. But in the afternoon, approaching the next station I saw the station-master running towards me, waving madly and shouting: *'Telefoon, telefoon!'*

I had to glance behind me before I believed it was really me receiving a telephone call in the middle of the desert! There was a line running from station to station. The station-master didn't speak English but the telephone did:

'Bernard? This is Gernod. My backrack broke. I found refuge in the station you passed this morning. A train will stop here in two days. So I am giving up. See you in Khartoum!'

On the seventh day, I reached Abu Hamed and the Nile. Plenty of water. I could bathe for the first time since Aswan ten days before, but on the other hand the sand was now very soft and I had to adopt the Danish solution: balancing Rosinante on one rail, I had to walk along, from sunrise to sunset, for the next twelve days.

In fact I reckoned that I could pedal for half the time, thanks to particular patches of sand which were covered with a hard crust. If I could keep the bicycle fast and straight and didn't break the crust I could gear up to my 52 x 16 gear. This sand looked like the surface of water with the waves frozen stiff. It made my tyres sing—until they ploughed through the 'ice' and then I had to 'swim' back to the rail.

In Berber, the ancient slave market, I was offered a meal for the third time that day, in a beautiful house with concrete columns finely moulded and painted in apple green. It belonged to some local dignitaries. I guessed they must be because the two men had a car, although they could not go out of the town as only the streets were paved, and outside, the sand was too soft.

I was given soap to wash my hands and I summoned up all my Arabic to contribute to the conversation until the meal came. It was enormous and multicoloured.

Normally I like salads but I was put off this one by the abundance of pepper, whose red I mistook for tomatoes. So I turned instead to the meat and a very curious dish, a slimy green soup, made from a kind of spinach. Everybody of course dipped their hands in the dishes and conscientiously kneaded the food in their hands before putting it in their mouths.

I was the last one to get up from the carpet where we had had the meal but I was not allowed to leave: the young boy who had served us, dressed in a clean safari jacket, brought another tray: a watermelon and a custard cream. After that I just could not stand up any more and the 'pepper coffee' was of great help.

I was advised to ask at the police station about somewhere to sleep. It definitely seemed to be a Sudanese custom, policemen looking after travellers' sleeping arrangements. I was welcomed at the police station by a man without a uniform and speaking perfect English. He looked at my passport, copied the details into a register and showed me where I could unroll my sleeping-bag. He recommended a stretch of concrete, where crawling insects could not reach me. I asked him how far it was to Atbara.

'Oh,' he said persuasively, 'on a lorry it is very far but with your bicycle, you will be there at half past four tomorrow. Excuse me but I am going to make some tea; if you need anything, just ask me, I know the place very well, I have been here for two years because I killed a man . . .'

He was in fact a prisoner! A little later, he came back to introduce two of his friends. All of them had killed somebody but they were as free as the air. Where could they go anyway, with the desert all around?

Just before dark they brought a policeman and posed for a family snapshot. The policeman was ill at ease, small and shy between his three healthy and smiling prisoners.

On Friday, 8th January, I unrolled my sleeping bag as usual, ten yards from the rails, at the foot of a telephone pole. Its music would lull me to sleep. But in the middle of the night I was suddenly woken by a torch shining in my face. I was far from any village and I felt very vulnerable. There should not have been anybody in the desert! With my heart pounding, I said 'Good Evening!', and as nobody answered, I repeated it in Arabic, *'Massa el kheir'* followed by a prudent *'Salaam aleïkum* (peace to you)', before I realized that there would be no answer. I was talking to . . . the train!

It was still two miles away. I could not hear it because it was travelling against the wind, but its single front light looked just like a torch.

On Sunday 10th January I reached a station by 4 pm. The railway workers offered me a *kissra*, a thick pancake made out of sorghum. They also gave me to understand that I would find shelter at the *kilo mia*, 100 kilometres from Khartoum.

It was pitch dark when I reached the *kilo mia*, where there were barracks made out of railway sleepers. I heard voices and then nothing—only the beat of my heart.

I moved away from the railway, onto the soft sand. I could barely distinguish the dark mass of the barracks and suddenly I stepped back . . . This enormous thing in front of me . . . could it be a dromedary? Then it must have a master. I shouted *'Massa el kheir'*, to reassure him. And I heard new voices, which reassured me. They came from the barracks. I headed for them making as much noise as I could, thinking of the dagger everybody carries here up the sleeve of their robe.

'Salaam ô Aleïkum!' I said.

'Aleïkum salaam,' came the reply. The fright was over. They came out to shake my hand.

'Franssawi, enta? (You're French?)'

'Aiwa, Franssawi,' I answered, wondering how they had guessed. I found out in the barracks, where I was told to settle: there was a telephone on the ground. Unused to the dark I lay on the wire and every time I moved in the night, the telephone, probably because of a loose connection, rang!

On Monday 11th, all I had left was sugar and *karkade*, a nilotic tea made out of hibiscus flowers. It infuses even in cold water and thus saves fuel. It now saved food: when I had drunk the tea, I had to eat the flowers!

33

So when around 2 pm, a military compound barred my path, I went in to ask for food. I was sent to the Colonel who agreed and I soon found myself in the midst of hundreds of soldiers, eating their food in the canteen. In *Asterix the Legionary,* I remembered, it said that the stronger the army, the worse its food. If that is the case the Sudanese army must be pretty weak: its food was delicious!

The soldiers gave me an unexpected dessert: there was a tarred road going to Khartoum, beginning three kilometres from the compound. After that I didn't leave my saddle until I reached the town I had been longing to see for twenty days. In the suburbs, a taxi driver wanted to invite me to dinner. I didn't even stop to reply so he chased me in his car and I had to waste half an hour placating him and making him understand why it was important for me to reach Khartoum before nightfall.

It was nonetheless dark when I reached the confluence of the White and the Blue Nile. I went to the Youth Hostel. Gernod was there, he had pitched his tent in the yard, and he ran to me.

Sudan: Rosinante, with her flag flying, rests beside the Nile.

Bobo arrived a week later. He hadn't been able to follow the Nile as he had planned. The sand was much too soft and after three days, he had followed our tracks, which then became my tracks alone. He could see these in the sand, and cursed his thin tyres each time he saw that I had been able to

34

pedal where he could only walk.

Ten days later, as I was entering the Youth Hostel yard, Gernod said dramatically:

'Bernard, sit down, I've got bad news!'

I thought he was joking and began to smile.

'Don't smile, Bobo's been hit by a bus, he is in the hospital.' I stopped smiling.

'How's that, hit by a bus? Here in Sudan? In Egypt OK, it could have happened hundreds of times, but here in Sudan, how come?'

The hospital looked like someone's home that had been requisitioned in a war. The corridors were congested with rows of mattresses. On each mattress there was a patient surrounded by his whole family, complete with a gas stove, electric fan and incense burner. The previous night, we were told, a lorry had crashed into a bus. Seventeen people had died on the spot and forty injured had to be accommodated here. Bobo had arrived in the middle of this panic with a compound fracture of his arm!

As soon as he saw me, he began to speak French:

'Tu sais, je suis sûr que le conducteur du car l'a fait exprès . . . (You know, I'm sure the bus driver did it on purpose)' 'When he passed us the first time,' he continued 'he cut in front and I gave him the finger, so he got his revenge. Look, it couldn't have been an accident, he hit me with his front. And twice! I though I was going to die. I was worried about my legs. I knew my arm was lost right after the first shock but I didn't want to lose my legs!'

Then he left for the operating theatre; the bones were to be set. We were asked to leave. In fact we had another task. To report to the police. Not Bobo's accident, but the loss of Gernod's bike. Taking advantage of the general panic, somebody had stolen his beautiful bicycle. Poor Gernod could not explain it clearly. He was taking care of Bobo, of course, and didn't bother about the bikes . . .

In the police station where we waited to make our report, a white woman was complaining about her husband. He beat her and she wanted to sue him. The policemen were smiling shyly, obviously very ill at ease. They probably thought this very strange: if all the women in this country came to complain each time they were beaten, there wouldn't be enough complaint forms!

I admired this woman for being so persistent among these contemptuous men. She showed her bruised arms but they didn't move. If she had been a native, they would have laughed at her, but she was European, and even though she was accusing a European diplomat, another source of trouble, they finally condescended to give her a form to be filled in by a doctor.

Gernod made his deposition through another diplomat. He was the Military Attaché at the British Embassy and knew Bobo's father. He spoke fluent Arabic and the policemen listened to him with respect.

When we went back to the hospital in the afternoon, with the mattress we had been asked to bring and which we borrowed at the Youth Hostel, male nurses were trying to wake Bobo. They pinched his earlobes and stroked his hair. Bobo didn't move. Only at the sound of my voice did he open his eyes and try to talk. Tiredness and trauma overcame him. He cried.

'Shokran, shokran. Thank you', he said, while shaking hands with us and the nurses, who looked sorry and tried to make him laugh. They called us his 'brothers'.

The British diplomat arrived with a nurse friend of his; we could take Bobo with us. We didn't need the mattress any more; the diplomat took us to his home. In his Land-Rover, I fanned Bobo with his x-ray photo. My 'brother' put his head on my shoulder and cried. I also felt like crying: a single bus, a gesture, a heated word and a dream comes crashing to the ground. Bobo still hoped that in two months' time he would be able to remount and continue his trip, but in the sadness of his words, I could tell that it was all over. Even surrounded by four pounds of plaster, a double compound fracture can be very tricky.

The diplomat's home was like something out of a movie with its luxuriant garden, purring air-conditioning, large fans hanging from ceilings, a leopard skin on the carpet, walls covered with books, an ornamental Arab rifle over the couch . . .

The diplomat himself was like a Hollywood star: Nordic blond hair, quiet authority and efficiency, long bony and elegant profile, tanned skin and a vast amount of knowledge: he talked to his boy in Dinka, a language of the South . . .

'Let's have some tea first,' he said, 'then the problems will sort themselves out. What do you prefer, China or Indian?'

It was indeed all over for Bobo. After an examination in a private clinic, it appeared that he had to be operated on again, if possible in England. He had to sell all his equipment, except the bicycle which was completely ruined and would fetch nothing, and fly back home.

I left Gernod still looking for his bicycle, and putting adverts in newspapers when I headed for the South and the famous Sudd, all by myself.

Southern Sudan: Scars instead of Bras

The Sudd is one of the largest swamps in the world. That is where both Roman and Napoleonic armies, and several British explorers, gave up looking for the source of the White Nile. In winter, though, some parts are dry and passable. I had to follow lorry tracks through the burnt savannah. It was like cycling on a washboard or over a long cattle grid—there were bumps every yard. My guidebook said: 'On the washboard, just maintain 50 mph and you won't even feel the bumps!' I bet the author never tried to reach 50 mph on a loaded bike!

The first six days were easy: I was still in Muslim territory. These were sweet and hospitable people. Every night somebody took me home and fed me *kissra,* and ultra-sweet tea. In the Sudan you live on the sugar in your tea.

The difficulties began on the seventh day. I had to push my bike over deep furrows and could not reach a village before dark. In fact, I didn't know where I was. The only map I had was a copy I had made myself from Bobo's Michelin Guide. The Nile was probably far away, meandering carelessly along, and I had only a quart of water left. Carelessly I hadn't refilled my bottles in Renk, the last village.

The most frightening thing for me was to sleep in the open African savannah. I had been told not to worry about lions: 'they don't like human meat'; not to worry about hyenas: 'they attack men only when they are in a pack'. No, according to adventure specialists, I need worry about only one thing, snakes: 'since you don't use a tent, they can be attracted by the warmth of your sleeping bag and sneak in!' So every morning when I woke up, I tried to figure out if I was still alone in my sleeping bag before daring to move. The eighth morning, I was still alone. So was my quart of water.

By 10 am I had my tenth puncture. The Sudan is well equipped with devilish thorns. They have three legs which means one point is always upright and unavoidable. Without water, I could not repair the puncture and without repairing the puncture, I could not look for water . . .

It is difficult to explain how desperate I became. So desperate in fact that I tried to escape reality by reading more of Trotsky's autobiography while finishing my dates and peanuts; it was as though I didn't want to die of thirst without knowing the end of the story, or leave my food to the ants. It was while I was doing this that a human shadow suddenly appeared across the pages.

Like all non-Muslim southerners, he didn't wear a robe or a turban and he would have been stark naked without his 'government shorts'[1]. He was carrying two spears and a shield. He didn't speak much Arabic.

Neither did I, but I did understand that there was a village only an hour's walk further on. It took me the whole afternoon to reach it, by which time I was practically on the rims of my wheels, and when I smiled in greeting my lips stuck to my teeth because my mouth was so dry. Every time I wanted to smile after that, I had to put my lips into place with my fingers, which is not very polite, even in the Sudd . . .

The next day, loaded down with water, I made good progress until the road forked. A handwritten Arabic sign pointing to the right said 'Maloot'. But there was no 'Maloot' on my home-made map. I did not have the patience to wait for a lorry which might tell me the way to Paloïch, the village I was aiming for. And since the 'Maloot' branch had recently been improved, I decided that 'Maloot' must mean 'detour' and took it at full speed.

The sun was very low when I finally reached a hut.

'Fi Paloïch? (Is this Paloïch?)', I asked the occupant.

'Mafi Paloïch, fi Maloot! (It isn't Paloïch, It's Maloot!)' he answered.

He showed me a narrow path through the tall elephant grass which he said cut back towards Paloïch. I had to sleep out again and I reached Paloïch at noon the next day, very thirsty.

According to my copied map, Paloïch was equipped with 'tourist facilities'. Either Michelin were wrong or I had copied wrongly because although there were indeed a few shops, so I could buy some food, there was absolutely no water. I had to carry on grim-faced.

The sun was again about to set when I met a man wearing a northern robe. He spoke Arabic: 'Yes, the Nile is near, follow me.' His name was Nejib Dong, and he was a Manjuluk from Sennar. He led me to a camp on the banks of the Nile, and introduced me to his companions. They were seasonal fishermen. Their catch was drying on top of some poles. A young boy was responsible for frightening animals away.

They all had tribal scars. Three of them were Shilluks, with their very peculiar scars, like a crown of peas on their foreheads. One was a Shaikyya, with impressive V-shaped scars across his cheeks. Nejib Dong had a shiny piece of metal hanging from his lower lip. I realized that it was the front of a bicycle pedal—it made him quite difficult to understand!

They fed me with sorghum pasta, mixed with Nile perch—my first 'meat' in a month, and Nejib Dong offered me his mosquito-net. I didn't want to deprive him of his valuable protection near the Nile, and took out my insect repellent.

After I explained what it was for, I had to face another problem: all the fishermen wanted to try the lotion and there was almost none left for me . . .

After nine days of 'washboard' I arrived at Malakal. Passing under the large arch that welcomes all visitors, I could not believe my eyes: the road was paved—but for just one mile to the town hall!

At Malakal, one has to cross over the Sobat, a large tributary of the Nile, by ferry. But there was an acute shortage of petrol in the Sudan: when I left Khartoum, it was taking two or three days of queueing to get a maximum of two gallons. So the Sobat ferry wasn't running and many lorries were waiting on the river bank. Some of them had been there more than a week. I crossed in a dug-out canoe for 50 piastres and did not meet another local vehicle for the next 400 miles—only foreigners with extra tanks built into their vehicles. There was a Belgian family driving from Uganda: they couldn't sleep or eat in their camper because it was occupied by a 150-gallon drum of petrol!

The Toyota roared on the dirt road and the driver, a camp leader for the French company which was digging the Jonglei Canal, lit a funny cigarette.

'C'est pas du tabac, ca? C'est de l'herbe de Juba, du Bango? (It isn't tobacco, is it? Is it Juba Grass, Bango?)'

'Non, c'est du Marocain, tu veux une tafe? (No, it's Moroccan cannabis do you want some?)', he answered.

The road was surprisingly smooth and the speedometer showed 120. On the right the African sunset, invariably spectacular, coloured the savannah red. This dirt road reminded me of what I had heard a few days before in Renk. I was drinking tea, surrounded by a small crowd. Two Belgians had come up to me because they saw Rosinante's flag (the one sewn by Maria), floating over the crowd. They were historians and began joking. 'You're not in Fashoda yet!²' they said and, agreeing that the road was really bad, they added: 'It is such a bad road that the French who are digging the Jongleï Canal are building their own road.'

'In fact, it is only the earth we take out of the canal,' explained the camp leader. 'With bulldozers and graders it is easy to build a road here, it is as flat as my hand!'

'Anyway, it is a great improvement for me, I can travel twice as fast as I could before Malakal. I was lucky to meet those Italian tourists, they put me on the right track . . .'

'Ah yes, they asked for water, and of course we refused, we are not UNICEF here. For you it's different, you're not pretending on your bike, but these bourgeois in expensive, comfortable camping cars, they don't really need us! Tomorrow we begin to move the camp from kilometre 80 to kilometre 140. We can drive you there if you like.

'No thank you, I don't want to miss anything . . . Here we are, aren't we?'

'Yes, here is the monster!' muttered the camp leader into his moustache. 'The only machine in the world capable of shovelling 60,000 cubic metres per day. They call it a 'shovel-wheel', but I call it the 'queen-bee', because all these workers around it look like busy bees. I wish you could hear it in action, it hums! Unfortunately we have run out of petrol like the rest of the country. We are negotiating to buy our petrol direct from Saudi Arabia . . .'

'What's this canal for?'

'To prevent the Nile from losing its waters in the swamp. It's going to be fifteen metres wide, six deep and longer than Suez and Panama put together when it's finished! Come and look at the front of the machine, it looks a bit like an alien's mouth!'

Two whites came up and shook our hands. They invited us for a coffee in a mobile home.

'*Alors comme ça vous voyagez à bicyclette?* (So, you're travelling by bike?)' said the first.

'*Heureusement qu'il y – a qui bossent! Si tout le monde partait à vélo sur les routes, y'aurait plus de route!* (Fortunately, there are still some who work, otherwise there wouldn't be roads to cycle on!)' said the second, showing his pettiness.

'*Fais pas trop attention à ce qu'on te dit. Les types en ont marre après un an de brousse. Et puis c'est bien connu les Français sont râleurs.* (Don't pay too much attention to what he says, the guys are tired after a year in the bush. And it's well-known, Frenchmen are grumblers!)' the camp leader said soothingly when we got back.

We passed a large water hole. Cattle and men were gathered round. Big fires had been lit.

'You see, they're happy, they understand that the canal will bring them water for their cattle all year round. They don't bother about the rest.'

'Are they Dinkas?'

'No. These are Nuers, more nomadic. Some are sorry that they will become more settled by the canal, and more controlled by the northern Government, but their living conditions will be greatly improved. By the way, how do you manage to find water? And do you have anything to purify it? Any medicine?'

'I don't think there is a better cure for disease than a day's cycling. But I put iodine in my water—when I am alone, not when I am offered it. In one village, north of Malakal, I was offered a calabash of water. It was fresh and I was so thirsty I didn't mind that it wasn't purified. In fact, it was so muddy that I couldn't see the bottom and on the surface I could see an insect. He was swimming around the edge and so I could only drink after he had passed my lips! Fortunately I was much too distracted by the women stripped to their waists to bother about the water!'

'Well here the men are stripped to their toes! We just employed a whole tribe, completely naked. We had to give them some shorts to satisfy our Muslim workers!'

Near the camp we met some old women hitch-hiking. The camp leader gave them a lift too. They were smoking something much funnier than the camp leader.

'What are they smoking?'

'Dried cow-dung . . .'

That night in the air-conditioned mobile home I ate with my brain and my stomach didn't understand. I ate omelette and chips and cheese and a lot of other things which reminded me of France. I even drank wine after months of tea, red beans and *kissra*. My digestive system couldn't remember how to handle it all and I was woken in the night by a very strange feeling.

I had to run to the toilet several times and empty myself at both ends until dehydration, I think, made me lose consciousness. On the second run to the toilet I decided to stay there. I was too scared of passing out for good, so, when at dawn I heard somebody come in, I pushed the door open.

I recognized the engineer who had made fun of me the previous afternoon. He was shaving. He had probably classified me as a real freak because, seeing me there, lying across the bowl, half naked and probably stinking, he behaved as if it was quite natural.

'*Salut, tiens t'es là?* (Hi, so you're here),' he said before reacting properly and getting the camp doctor.

I had to spend the next day in bed and only got back on the road the following morning. The camp leader promised to meet me and bring me water at the end of the day, but before I left he took me to the camp warehouse.

'Here you are, tinned food, dried fruits, medicines, you take as much as you want!'

I only took as much as I could, of course.

One month after leaving Khartoum, I was leaving Juba. The dirt road toward Kenya had been improved but my health had not. My guidebook said: 'If your faeces are only blood and mucus, you probably have amoebic dysentery and you'd better hurry to the nearest hospital.' That was exactly my problem and it hurt badly; it was as if my intestines wanted to get out, every 30 minutes. The nearest hospital was in Nairobi, about 1000 miles further on. I had no choice, I had to try to reach it.

In the meantime I took the camp leader's medicine. It was called Enterovioform and it said on the box that it was not to be taken if there was any weakness of the liver. And indeed every pill made my insides turn upside down. The first night I slept under the mango tree at Liria police station, but I often had to leave my sleeping bag to answer a false but painful need.

On the second day I reached Torit and witnessed my first witch-doctor ceremony.

Because the rainy season was late that year, all the witch-doctors in the region had gathered to placate the heavens. I counted twenty-two of them, each dressed in bright colours. Half of them were in yellow and the other half in green. When I arrived, they were scattered around a large field, doing their individual warm-up dances. The civil authorities were seated on the side of the field, on a platform with little pink cushions, under a small thatched roof. Policemen in fresh uniforms, with red berets and white batons, contained a restive crowd around the field where the witch-doctors were gesticulating.

I understood, from the tension on the faces and the shouts of encouragement, that the fate of the next sorghum crop lay in the hands of the witch-doctors. The one I presumed to be the chief wizard advanced from the grandstand with an object under his arm, the importance of which soon became apparent. It was not a crystal ball as one would expect in the West but it might have been. It was opaque and decorated with black spots and obviously elastic. The most surprising thing, to my European eyes, however, was that the witch-doctors used it with their feet. By small sensitive taps with their bare feet, they turned the sphere in every possible direction and sometimes made it do superb turns in the air.

My scepticism got quite a shock when, at the precise instant the black and white sphere was projected into one of the two wooden frames standing at each end of the field . . . the first drops of rain began to fall onto the dusty ground.

The Torit witch-doctors were highly conscientious. Shining with sweat but not satisfied by this first result, they continued to propel the sphere alternately into the wooden frames. Each time they did it, the crowd cheered and expressed its delight. Each time the rain increased.

On the platform, the officials eventually reckoned that it was enough for the sorghum. The police chief and the mayor climbed back into their Mercedes limousines and left. The policemen held onto their berets against the storm but the witch-doctors were still performing. When finally the thatched roof collapsed onto the pink cushions, the witch-doctors stopped dancing and ran to shelter at the police station. Then, their beautiful outfits now stained with mud, they congratulated one another, visibly proud to have influenced the rain gods for another year.

In the late afternoon of the next day, I lay down under a mango tree in a village, so as not to lose consciousness. A young man came up, obviously drunk, but it didn't surprise me. Every morning since Malakal, I had been offered sorghum beer instead of tea. And I was no longer a 'tea-totaller'.

'Hello, my name's Valerian,' he said in good English, 'you cannot stay here without the permission of the village chief. And as a man myself, I think that it would be better for you to sleep inside. Come with me, my brother will look after your bicycle . . .'

Dizzy and thirsty, I followed Valerian through the alleys of the large village where he frequently asked for Chief Louis. 'He is dispensing justice under the sausage tree', we were told. When we got there, I was about to faint again. I had to sit down immediately. Chief Louis wasn't there, so I was causing no offence. And I was introduced instead to the 'Chief's warrior'.

'That's the one who gives punishments after the chief's verdict,' explained Valerian. 'As a man myself, I think it is not pleasant to receive punishments, especially from this man, here, look how strong he is!'

We left again. When we passed the village water pump, I was introduced to the ladies. I shook their hands and they giggled. They were all topless of course, and I noticed the scars all over their busts. They had a decorative purpose, no doubt, but these scars were so crude, so hard, so solid, that I think they also served as brassieres . . .

'As a man myself,' said Valerian again, 'I think you are tired. Do you like sorghum beer? The white stuff as we call it. After we have paid our respects to Chief Louis, we'll go to my house and we'll drink beer. We are already friends, but after the beer, we will be brothers!'

At Chief Louis's side, when we found him, was his bodyguard, a soldier from the Dinka tribe, carrying an AK47 machine-gun. He had two magazines, the famous curved Russian magazines, tied together with a piece of bicycle tube. So, when the first magazine was empty, it was quicker to engage the second one. That was something they didn't teach me during my military service.

Valerian had already told me that Chief Louis was an important man, his brother being a representative of the tribe, the Latukas, in Khartoum. Chief Louis was also a very nice man. He took me home, along with Valerian, the bodyguard and a few others, and offered me a drink. It was a kind of brandy, very strong. And then I asked him to give me a tribal scar.

I had already decided that my best souvenir of the Sudan would be a tribal scar: it was after all, cheap and light to carry. And the Latukas had a very interesting tribal scar: their ears were cut all around like lace.

Chief Louis refused. He said that I had to do it myself, with my knife or even better a razor-blade, because that was the way to show that I was a 'real tough he-man'. Well, it was a bit late that night—perhaps I would wait and see if I was a real tough he-man the next day. 'As a he-man myself, I reckon it is painful!' Valerian added before he took me to his 'young woman's' house where I was presented to his latest child.

'He isn't christened yet. Give me a Christian name!'

'Well, why not Bernard?'

But the pronunciation was difficult, both the English version with its soft 'r' and the French with the rolled 'r'. An older son managed it quite well but Valerian asked me to pronounce Bernard again every time the conversation flagged. And the whole family repeated it, 'Bereunar, Bairrnarr, Bewenawd . . .'

It was dark, and I was lying on the clean smoothed ground between the huts. I was very weak, half dizzy, but I kept speaking. I pleased Valerian by telling him that the Dinka huts, made with elephant grass, were not as good as the Latuka huts made from coconut palms. The palms reached down to the ground all around and only habit, probably, allowed the inhabitants to find the door without crashing into the small clay wall. A sister of Valerian's was grinding peanuts. I was asked to taste the butter she was producing.

My Christian name was pronounced rhythmically by all the family when the women brought us steaming black sorghum, which we were to roll in our hands before dipping it in a meat sauce. Later, not immediately but as a direct consequence of this stay with the lace-eared Latukas, I followed the example of Nejib Dong the Manjuluk and pierced my left ear with a bicycle spoke nipple . . .

After five days of dysentery, I was so weak I had to lie down every now and then to avoid fainting. I collapsed in the police station at Kapoeta, the last village in the Sudan. This was where two Swiss missionaries found me and decided that I needed a lift across the border. I probably owe them my life, for that, and for another reason: in the long no man's land between the two countries, people suddenly appeared running towards our lorry and shouting for us to stop. One of them was pointing a machine gun at us. I dived inside, the powerful Mercedes lorry sped away and the missionaries laughed.

'They didn't shoot because they were too far away and ammo is too expensive for those poor Toposa raiders . . .'

An hour later we pulled in at the dispensary of Lokichokio, the first village in Kenya. A white nun ran up to us.

'I hope you're not bringing any more casualties! The hospital is full. Raiders attacked the village last night and stole some cattle. Four of our men died and seven are wounded . . .'

When she learned that I was travelling by bicycle, she wanted to put me off continuing and took me inside to see the most terrible wounds, like the man dying of a bullet in the belly.

But one of the Swiss ruined the effect:

'Don't panic Bernard; the Toposas wouldn't have killed you, nor taken your bike. It is useless around here. O.K. they would have taken your food and valuables, and since you don't have cigarettes to offer them, they would have beaten you pretty badly, but they wouldn't have killed you!'

---

1 Government shorts: Ashamed that Southerners lived naked, the Muslim authorities have distributed thousands of these uniform blue and white shorts.
2 Fashoda: In 1898, a 150-man French expedition, commanded by General Marchand, after crossing overland from Senegal, formed an alliance with the King of the Shilluks in Fashoda, his capital, and claimed the whole of the Sudan. But the British, under the command of General Kitchener, after General Gordon's death, were just in the process of conquering the country. Fashoda became a well-publicized diplomatic crisis, and Marchand was eventually ordered by the French Government to abandon it.

Kenya: Golden Specks on Naked Bodies

One year without sex is probably like 40 days of fasting: you don't die of it but there might be some after-effects . . . So it was time for me in this Kenyan paradise to look for some romance.

Yes, Kenya was paradise—the best example of what I mean is probably to describe the way they served tea. In southern Sudan I had to queue to pay for the sugar (sugar was the most important ingredient), then I had to queue for the tea itself, with my glass half filled with sugar. Everything was done in the street, the 'tea-shop' being two windows with bars. After half an hour of queueing, I had to drink the tea in the middle of the street, with two people hovering at my sides, waiting impatiently for the glass.

It will come as no surprise then that, when I bought my first cup of tea in Kenya, I thought I was in heaven: I was sitting down at a table, inside, and was served there with tea in a *cup,* and—I almost cried at the sight of it—a saucer! It was delicious.

In Nairobi, having cured my dysentery, repaired Rosinante, and realizing that I had spent only £630 in 11 months of travel (out of a total fortune of £1800), or less than £2 per day everything included, I decided that I deserved a little more paradise. I wanted to go down to Diani Beach on the Indian Ocean coast near Mombasa. The accounts of it among travellers in Nairobi were just as good as those I had heard about Lamu, with one difference: during the rainy season (as it was then), I had no chance of reaching Lamu by bicycle. Diani Beach looked like a shore in the *Odyssey* and I could only hope it was the Siren's shore!

All the travellers were staying at a campsite called Dan Trench Camp, behind the Trade Winds Hotel. This hotel was a four-star establishment, usually out of reach of low-budget travellers. But as Dan Trench, the campsite owner, used to be the manager of the Trade Winds, the travellers were allowed in. Every night there was a dance or a show, and by law they could not charge more for beer than anywhere else in Kenya. In front of the Trade Winds, the beach was blindingly white, consisting not of sand but of coral dust, and shaded by coconut palms; fishermen sometimes landed there in their brightly coloured pirogues. It was a paradise indeed.

Here I met up again with Ali Baba. Ali Baba was just a nickname. He was a Canadian, from Quebec, and quite a character. The first time I met him was on the ferry on Lake Nasser. He was posing as a travel veteran. He had been to India, and he told exciting stories about the Americas. Now he had been converted to Islam, and he wore a turban and traditional baggy breeches. Moreover he had a store of wonderful stories about his crossing of the Sudan where he was received by the Sheiks of the Dar Kebabich.

It was a spectacle not to be missed in the Dan Trench Camp, when Ali Baba prayed. It was a treat to see him unroll his large scarf under the mango tree and begin to sing the first Surat—especially when it was accompanied by most un-Islamic explanations:

'This is very good exercise. Look, when you prostrate yourself, your blood comes to your head, very good for the brains; and then all these ritual movements of the neck, to the right, to the left, good relaxation! There are even finger movements, and body bending to complete the exercise . . .'

He also had unexpected news for me:

'I took a lorry in the southern Sudan and guess who I met inside: Gernod the Danish cyclist! He's found his bicycle. Quite a miracle. Somebody had reported the thief to the police, and anyway he couldn't sell a shining 15-gear bicycle, worth almost a thousand dollars, in a country like the Sudan.'

The first night, having shaved my beard and straightened my moustache, Ali Baba and I invited two English girls, Lynda and Stephanie, to the Trade Winds.

The sumptuous garden was lit by green lights, the swimming pool by blue ones and the bar looked like hell, all red. The orchestra was the Palm Grass Band from Mombasa. They had just come back from a concert tour of Germany, but, according to the Tourist Elite Guide, none of the six musicians knew how to write or read music. They were nonetheless famous for their hit, heard everywhere in Kenya, *Jambo Bwana* (Hello Sir).

Ali and I agreed: red-haired Lynda was for me, brown-haired Stephanie was his. After an hour of fast rhythms came a few slow dances which found us in the arms of the girls, all according to the plan. I heard Ali Baba playing with the words ship, chip, sheep and cheap, all of which sound alike to us French speakers.

However, a few slow dances are not enough for romance and on the second day Ali Baba ruined our chances. He could be very crude when he was trying to be funny. He had found a wooden phallus which he put under his baggy breeches, and started to brag about his sexual prowess.

'Me, I have made love with a prostitute in Mombasa . . . You know, zat is very strange, she had been cut, excisée, and zat was dry and hard. No feeling, just like putting a nickel in a pin ball machine and my zizi at the ball's place . . .'

The two English girls didn't seem to appreciate his humour and went to join a group of Britons.

Around Ali Baba, the group of travellers was more cosmopolitan. Every night, the Québecois counted how many nations we represented. It was always over ten. Even the couples were international: A Belgian girl with an American, an Italian girl with an Englishman, a Dutch girl with a Frenchman. But they were not always like their national stereotypes. On the seventh night on the beach I found myself with Lief and Marianna. The Belgian girl was as brown-haired as the Italian was blonde. The breasts of the Southern European girl were white and heavy, those of the Flemish were sun-tanned and small.

As we watched the African dances put on for the Trade Winds' rich tourists, I noticed that the women were wearing bras and shorts (under their skirts), both things they don't do in real life, and commented that that was a pity. Lief and Marianna retorted vehemently that that was a male chauvinist view, and my hopes for Belgium and Italy disappeared . . .

I had never been so excited. I was dancing with a young Dutch girl: her long hair fell in unruly curls over her bright eyes which sparkled in the darkness; there was perfect harmony in our movements, and the space between our bodies was nonexistent. I was pretty sure that the French charm was working. Our lips met in a burning kiss. But then, with a contrite pout, she disengaged herself from my arms and left the dance floor. With a vanquished heart I saw her meet up with a tall bearded blond guy who, by his look, could only be staying at the hotel itself.

From my seat I watched the girl try to calm his jealousy with small kisses and then pull him on the dance floor. There I got my revenge: the tall man did not dance, he merely stood about and looked completely ridiculous. The girl looked tiny by comparison, and seemed a little embarrassed. Still, I had to go to bed by myself: Sweden, or Norway, had cheated me of Holland . . .

The next day I met Vicky on the path to the beach which went between the Trade Winds gates and those of the neighbouring property. Her first gesture was to get hold of my testicles, as if it was a form of handshake. She laughed at the ridiculous size of the thing and I lost my wits. She turned around and showed me her bottom, wiggling it. Two beautiful spherical buttocks, such as only African women have. I felt obliged to put my hand on them casually. At that, Vicky asked me to escort her that night to the Trade Winds, where she could not be admitted if not accompanied by a white.

And after all that, it was one of the two newly arrived Australians who slept with her. Next morning he shared the experience with us: according to him, it began in a very romantic way:

'I love you. Do we make business?'

He paid her 15 shillings (75 pence). He also described the mutilated organs of the Muslim woman. And Ali Baba started again on his pin ball machine story to relax the atmosphere.

In the Big Mama tea-kiosk, the one whose back wall was a cut down baobab, I saw Vicky taking her breakfast— *Chai na maziwa na mandazi* (white tea with cakes). She didn't look very satisfied with her business, even if in her hand the box of Australian cigarettes looked like a trophy. The Australian came for his *chai* too but my heart bled, they didn't seem to recognize one another . . .

Disappointed and finally bored with the evenings of dancing, I decided to leave Dan Trench Camp on the fifteenth morning of my stay.

On the evening before a whole bus-load of English teachers arrived: English girls who'd just finished school. This reversed the male-female ratio. *'A moi les petites anglaises!'* I thought as I unloaded Rosinante.

I made the acquaintance of one of these teachers. She wanted to try the local grass. It was called *bango* and had a good reputation, but this girl, like me, wasn't a smoker. She preferred to take it like tea, by infusing the leaves in sweetened milk or, better, by decoction . . . another 'tea-totaller'!

Confident that such agreement on the best way to get high might lead to other shared interests, I agreed to schedule the big brew for the fifteenth evening of my stay in this paradise.

There were four of us. Ali Baba and another English teacher had joined us around the big pot of milk where a whole handful of bango was infusing. As planned, the effect came only after an hour—enough time for me to confirm by discreet touches that, unfortunately, the girl wanted only to get high.

When the effect came, it was a shock, a delirium. I felt my heart pumping more and more violently and became afraid that it might explode. Then I felt my vital forces flow back to a body centre which was not the heart, but was somewhere on my spine, level with my kidneys. I was scared, and promised myself that if my brain came out of this madness intact, I would not expose it again to any dope.

'I feel my soul,' cried Ali Baba, 'it hangs on the walls on my inner being.

But the walls are smooth, and there's nothing below, so if my soul doesn't hold tight, it is going to fall down . . . Help my soul! Help!'

That was still in English but, very soon, we could not even speak good French. The whole camp site came to see the two stoned Frenchies. And seeing us that much *défoncés,* some of them made another brew of the same bango and six more people joined us in our trip. The drinkers of a third brew weren't spared either. It shows how strong the first brew was.

I went to bed at 6 pm and if I didn't leave on the sixteenth morning, it was only because I was still stoned. So was Ali Baba. We met at the Big Mama tea-kiosk and confided gravely in one another. He had a big project: to cross the Saudi desert on camels. He was looking for a reliable companion.

'Replace the camels with bicycles, and I am your man,' I said.

Finally on the seventeenth morning, I extracted myself from the delights of Paradise, still unsatisfied. I went to dream under the walls of Fort Jesus in Mombasa and found myself asking for a bed at Kanamai Youth Hostel, a youth hostel famous for its coconut trees. If you were careful enough to wait for dawn—because during the night you might have one land on your head—you could feed on the nuts. The only people there were two Dutch girls—not the low-budget type but regular bourgeois tourists, enjoying their annual holiday. This was my chance.

Marjon and Irena seemed to appreciate my presence as much as I desired them. When I said I was intending to stay only one night, they answered that they would work hard to persuade me to stay. So I began to carve some more clogs out of olive stones, the curious trick I learnt in North Africa.

The best way I found to touch their skin was while attaching the clogs as necklaces, bracelets or—wow—ankle bracelets. And to ask for a kiss as a reward.

When they came back from the town where they had bought *kangas,* they immediately tried to drape them around their lovely bodies. I could not stand by without helping.

Irena was red-haired with surprisingly white skin. An hour before in the showers I had admired her bare rump: it had the luminosity of china, the smoothness of marble, and I longed to touch it with my hands . . .

Marjon was brown-haired. She had blue eyes but her skin took the sun more readily than Irena's. Her breasts pushed their tips through any material and she had this delightful habit of undressing when I was present or, when she was wearing a dress, of sitting down to ensure that her legs were shown to best advantage.

Marjon was tired, so it was Irena who came with me to the beach after sunset, arm in arm. In the afternoon we had got on very well in our sexual advances while bathing and playing around in the warm water. But that night we could not go further because I was wearing a *gandourah,* an ample Moroccan robe. And in the dark, we were mistaken for two women and importuned by scores of men. We set up a rendezvous for two days later in the next youth hostel, in Malindi.

Malindi's beach wasn't as gorgeous as Diani, but its sand contained minute specks of gold. At night however, the beach did not have a good reputation. In the hostel entrance, there was a sign saying: MALINDI IS A FRIENDLY TOWN BUT NOT ALL INHABITANTS OF MALINDI ARE YOUR FRIENDS. BE VERY CAREFUL IF YOU GO ON THE BEACH AFTER DARK. BE AT LEAST FOUR PERSONS WITH AT LEAST TWO MEN.

It was not surprising therefore, when Irena dragged me there for our reunion that night that I didn't feel completely happy. Not only did I wonder if, after a year without training, I was going to be able to perform . . . but I was also scared to death. Irena was not, and not even conscious of my fear. My *gandourah* seemed to have an enormous effect on her imagination and she did all the work.

We were dressing again when we heard male voices. We ran back to the youth hostel and, despite the night watchman, we both sneaked into the girls' bathroom for a second helping. We marvelled then at the golden specks which had stuck to our skin, all over our bodies.

Weeks later, in my most intimate parts, the golden specks would still remind me of Irena. With those precious memories of her, I felt able to live another year as a celibate . . .

Uganda: Soldiers Brandishing Guns

During the prosperous days of the East Africa Community just after independence, the Ugandan shilling had the same value as the Kenyan shilling. But when I arrived at Busia to enter Uganda, I was given twenty-five for one on the black market, i.e. the real market. For the five Kenyan bank notes I had left, I was given, at a street corner, an enormous wad of Ugandan notes, mostly ten- and five-shilling denominations making up a total of 12,500 shillings. It was useless to try to squeeze them into my wallet so, without taking the time to check them, I had to stuff the wad into my bag, before pedalling to customs.

I didn't feel at all safe. I was entering Uganda only because I had to: the border between Kenya and Tanzania was closed.

The Kenyan officer cast a quick glance at my currency declaration form, which I hadn't falsified, even if I did change my money on the black market. He was much more interested in Rosinante and asked more questions about her than about official subjects. In showing off my wonderful mount I became quite dramatic and with an inopportune gesture, dropped my bag at the officer's feet. The Ugandan bank notes fell out.

'Ha ha ha!' he laughed. 'Black market, uh? Let me help you, yes you have to be crazy to go to the bank when you get ten times more money in the street!'

On the Ugandan side, the officers were more interested in the 1000 Greek drachmas I declared than the $100 in cash and the 12,500 shillings which, of course, I didn't declare and was very careful not to spill on the ground.

After the border, I felt as though I was back in Sudan. Everything was so dirty, broken and loose. Nobody wore new clothes. Most men were wearing shirts with so many holes that, if they took them off to sleep, they would never find the proper holes for head and arms . . .

Ten kilometres further, there was a marker against which I leant

Rosinante. It was dedicated to the 'gallant youths who shed their blood here at the hands of the murderous Amin's soldiers'.

In its shadow, I comfortably counted my mattress of bank notes and divided it into several small batches which I distributed in my luggage. To finish, I indulged in a cup of my favourite brew: Ivory Coast Robusta, tinned in Kenya under the name of a famous Swiss brand.

Whilst savouring it, I stood up and gave a casual glance behind the marker. The Ivory Coast Robusta suddenly lost its flavour: there, among the grass, between the marker and the trees, hundreds of bones were bleaching in the sun.

With my heart in my mouth I was looking at very human-looking skulls, thighbones and humeruses, at collarbones and shoulderblades mixed with shreds of clothing. The 'gallant youth' probably . . .

But why weren't they buried? Was it lack of time or to prevent people forgetting Idi Amin Dada?

It was not easy to find lodgings in war-devastated Kampala. Reputedly cheap hotels were asking 1400 shillings per night (£3—a fortune for a poor traveller like me). Sikh temples, a godsend for poor travellers (they lodge you for the price you think is right) are rare in Kampala and their few places were all occupied by the handful of courageous travellers who had dared stop in Kampala, which was still under martial law.

After a two-hour search, I became discouraged and stopped at a restaurant for a *amatoke na n'koko* (plantain bananas and chicken). With three cups of black-market coffee, it amounted to 40p, but I would not be hungry again until the following morning.

Facing the restaurant, a large brick building attracted my attention. On top of it four white letters gave me hope: Y for Young, M for Men, C for Christian, A for Association. Because I had stayed a while in the USA, I knew the YMCA provided accommodation. Not here. But the director took a liking to Rosinante, and some space was found for us in the cubbyhole where they kept the duplicator. It was free of charge, I was told, but there was a strict condition: I must get permission from the police station nearby.

The police officer had a strange translucent look, explained by his alcoholic breath. But he spoke excellent English, as do most Ugandans.

'My dear man, you are welcome to stay under my authority at the YMCA. I hope you are a clean man and that you will stay so. My colleague, here, and I are ready to testify, in case of an accident, that you appeared before us as an honest person. But if you hope to leave Uganda in good health you must mind your own business and leave our business to us. I am sure you understand that, my dear man, and I am happy to wish you a very good stay in Kampala.'

I understood what he meant very well indeed after 5 pm: not a single soul was left in the streets and, louder and louder as night came, there was the sound of automatic weapon fire . . .

I had never been in a radio studio. I had imagined it to be a little more comfortable, with armchairs, a window and maybe a bar in the corner. This one was definitely Spartan.

It was difficult just to get in; we had to pass several army checkpoints. I was in a country where *coups d'état* always began at the radio station . . .

Behind the consoles, there was only one technician—but a tyrannical one. He insisted on conducting the interview in his own way. He insisted that I show a route around the world on his map, which he pulled from his bible—it was a map of Palestine!

They were four journalists who interviewed me in English. It was quite a challenge for me. After an hour or so, another interviewer arrived, who was responsible for French broadcasts to Uganda's French-speaking neighbours. He had not yet been trained in Paris as planned, but he nevertheless had to interview me in French. That was quite a challenge for him!

I was now staying with two French *coopérants* who were teaching

French at the Alliance Française, the equivalent of the British Council. They were quite young as the two years of teaching in Uganda were to replace the one-year military service which I had to do. Young but privileged. They lived in a very nice large house. And as they explained, they could not take the house without the 'furniture'. They meant a cook, a 'house-boy' and a night-watchman. And they had to do nothing once they got home, no cooking, not even a cup of tea, no dishes to wash, no beds to make, no socks to wash or lawn to mow . . .

Being privileged in Kampala had some inconveniences. Many whites had recently been killed by robbers. So my two hosts had a pistol in their car and a Russian machine-gun under their bed. This was the kind of 'furniture' which didn't come with the house but which the Embassy provided! And if these young *coopérants* didn't have any domestic concerns, they did have others.

'The Embassy forbids us to leave the capital. What do they expect us to do at week-ends? Practise shooting?' exclaimed the first.

'They aren't wrong, especially now after the failure of the Paris Conference. The guerillas might decide to take French hostages. And I am not sure that our weapons are adequate. The pistol in the car, maybe, but look, if they attack the house, we'd better not answer with the machine-gun, otherwise they'll blow the house apart! We'd better sell the Kalashnikov back. I saw Durand from the security service, he said that the demand is so high, he can buy the Kalashnikov back for more than he sold it to us for!'

In Uganda, bananas are seen everywhere.

It was with some trepidation that I viewed the prospect of cycling and living in Uganda for the next 15 days on my way to Rwanda.

Road-blocks were major features of Ugandan roads. Civil servants, including soldiers and policemen, I was told, were still paid their old salaries, from more prosperous days. And now they were worth nothing, so they had to earn their living from something else. Hence the road-blocks. And to persuade people to pay, they had to scare them, and the best way to scare them, so the story went, was to kill a good percentage of them. No wonder I sweated profusely when I came across these road-blocks.

There is a distinction between police and army road-blocks. At the first, I frequently met educated men, lucid and concerned for their reputation. At these I sweated less.

At the second kind, it was another story. The first army road-blocks I came across were 12 miles before and 12 miles after Kampala. The soldiers were half drunk and wanted me to speak Luganda instead of English. At first they wanted to see all my luggage but I managed to make them laugh (fear can make one quite inventive!). Rosinante helped in that; she was so strange. After Kampala I had an advantage; I suggested that they listened to my interview on the radio. They were impressed.

At one road-block two days later, my blood ran cold. When I arrived, the soldiers had all the passengers of a *matatu* (a collective taxi) lying in a ditch and they were shouting at them, threatening them with their weapons. Some of the people were crying, begging the soldiers for mercy. Was I going to witness a mass killing?

My arrival changed everything. The soldiers forgot their victims and gathered around me. The victims rejoiced and gave thanks as though they had been given back their lives. I just hoped it was not in exchange for mine. But by now my little show with Rosinante was running well and soon I left, not only unscathed but accompanied by applause and promises to listen to the radio that night.

Two hundred yards further on, however, I had to swallow a pint of water to compensate for the sweat . . .

The radio interview which I had recorded in Kampala was only broadcast three days after I left the city. I could not listen to it but the next day, soldiers on a road-block recognized me instantly and, with visible admiration, complimented me.

'Eh mister, what a fast cyclist you are! Last night you speak on Radio Kampala and today, you are already here, 200 miles away!'

Rwanda, Burundi: Does Rosinante have a Soul?

To extend the life of my belongings was both a virtue and a necessity—especially when it came to spares for Rosinante which were extremely hard to find in Africa.

From the two inner tubes which I decided to change after 11,000 miles, I made a cushion for my saddle, straps for my luggage and a protective cover for the oldest of all my tubes, which had 58 patches . . .

My rear view mirror had been stoned in Morocco and the glass went completely when I bumped into a Polish missionary. But I kept the stem and used it for my flag—a new one I had made myself, with much more white than blue or red. White was more useful: I could write on it. I embroidered Rosinante's silhouette on one side and her motto on the other. Yes, Rosinante had a motto, Rosinante was an intellectual bicycle. The motto was *Le Vélo va loin sans violer violette,* which in her native language is an alliteration and means 'The bicycle goes far without spoiling nature'.

I had stopped taking a wheel off whenever a spoke broke a long time ago. I found that I had only to take my pliers and with two broken spokes, I could make a new one using links and hooks. The rarest of all Rosinante's spare parts, however, were the tyres. Rosinante had French standard tyres, completely unknown in English-speaking Africa. So I had to patch my old tyres and make do with pieces of string tying them up where they had holes, to prevent the inner tube from escaping. In Uganda, the situation was already serious. I no longer had punctures, I had explosions! I was contemplating changing the whole wheels. But Uganda was not the obvious place to buy imported goods, so I had to wait until Rwanda. And the day I reached Kigali, the capital, I had to use a foot of string every mile to tie up my tyres and prevent them from exploding. Four years later in Lhasa, Tibet, I met a Dutch couple. They recognized me instantly: 'Oh yes we remember you, we met at the border between Uganda and Rwanda. You had big problems with your tyres; in fact they were so worn out that you had to use *banana leaves* instead!'

Of course, it wasn't *that* bad. I was probably joking to emphasise my desperation and because in Uganda banana products are everywhere: not only on your plate but often the plate itself. So why not on Rosinante's wheels?

In Kigali, I visited every single bicycle shop reciting an English formula I wished was magic: '26 x 1½', since most merchants were English-speaking Indians expelled from Uganda. The formula didn't work. I was about to change to another formula, '26 x 1⅜' (the British standard, which would mean that I would also have to buy new wheels), when a man took me aside and, in whispered French, said that he knew where to find Rosinante's standard. I followed him to the tinplate market. This is probably the most typical and creative market in Africa, illustrating the economy of thrift: from tins every possible utensil is being made: from oil lamps and dishes, plates, forks and spoons, to small furniture and grates. My guide introduced me to an old tinplate worker who, grabbing the wheel I had brought, started off in the direction we had come from. Convinced that they only wanted my wheel, I tried not to lose him, and ran after him. Eventually, we stopped in the cloth market. The old man told me to wait with the intermediary, disappeared among the merchants and reappeared with two '26 x 1½' tyres. Meanwhile, the intermediary had explained that this parallel market (not 'blacker' than the other) could not exist on official rates. The tyres had to be smuggled all the way from Mombasa, and they cost 800 *francs rwandais* (£5) each.

I was only too happy to pay up. It was expensive but at least I could extend the life of my wheels. And in doing so, I was extending Rosinante's life as well.

Who said that Rosinante had no soul?

I didn't like Rwanda. There was something aggressive in the people's behaviour towards me. I was even laughed at because of the colour of my hair, something which had not happened since I left school. People kept saying, without any prompting from me, that what I had done was really nothing, compared with what a Rwandan did recently: he went to France and Holland on a bicycle, and *that* was really something because *he* was black. I even remembered his name, something like Faustin or Foster . . .

Burundi, the other tiny central African state, was more agreeable. Youngsters still ran after me asking for *'cigarettes patron!'* but they didn't make rude remarks about my race or hair. Anyway, the country is so small that I reached the capital, Bujumbura, after only thirty-six hours.

The night before, I slept at a Catholic mission. At breakfast, the priest said something about a Danish cyclist he had seen a week before.

I choked on my tea. 'A Danish cyclist? Blond hair and blue eyes, quiet and slow moving?'

'Yes, he said he wanted to go all the way to South Africa! He had problems with his back carrier. He had a strange Christian name, sounded like the French aniseed drink . . . Gernod if I remember.'

So, I thought, he changed his mind and didn't go to India as he had planned. It would be quite a reunion if I could make up the time.

That Sunday midday, I could only find a tin of Greek mackerel to eat in a restaurant, where everybody else was drinking Primus beer, pint after pint. I was invited to a table. One of the drinkers was drunk but indicated that there were only twelve miles before a long stretch downhill which would bring me right into Bujumbura. It should save me a lot of time, he said, so I should use the time saved to drink with him. He bought me a beer and wrote down the address of a friend of his, a sports reporter with *La Voix de la Révolution,* the national radio station. He got angry when I refused a second beer, so I had to give in, thinking that at least it would provide more bottle-tops for the collection I had started on my front mudguard.

That Sunday afternoon I got the impression that every soul living in Bujumbura was taking the fresh air on the hill because one after the other I met a Belgian family whose daughter worked for the UN in the capital and a Mercedes dealer, a German who told me that I reminded him of a Danish cyclist who came to him three days before to have his back carrier rewelded . . .

I 'fell' into Bujumbura rather than cycled into it. The drop was spectacular. The difference in altitude was close to 3000 feet and the descent was only 20 miles long. I had only a second to glance at the deep blue of Lake Tanganyika, down below, before I had to squeeze my brakes desperately. I didn't intend to reach the capital that day but I had to: my brakes weren't good enough to stop me on the descent.

In the suburbs I asked for a Catholic mission.

'Ce n'est pas un problème de place, voyez-vous . . . (It is not that we lack room, you see),' the black priest explained, 'we have several rooms to put you up in, but you see, it is strictly forbidden! The police have told us several times: it is forbidden to lodge foreigners!'

I was sorry that I had waited patiently for the end of vespers. It was dark now. I could not look for another place to sleep. What could I do?

'Well, I see only one solution,' the Burundian priest went on, 'and that is the French Embassy. Extraterritoriality, you understand. You are French, they *must* take care of you. We will drive you there, and they cannot refuse to lodge you, because of extraterritoriality, *l'extraterritorialité. Vous comprenez?'*

He pronounced the long French word as one uses a new toy: without being sure how it works but with great pride in handling it without breaking it.

I suspected that, French or not, the extrasomething of the French Embassy was not for me. But I forgot that here a white man didn't need a pass to enter anywhere, and indeed the Embassy guard allowed me in. The priest left.

The guard led me to the apartment of the only white living in the Embassy, a French teacher who was very embarrassed.

'I am only staying here temporarily. There is nobody in charge at the moment. I am not empowered to allow you to camp in the grounds, and I am pretty sure that if you do so, the guard will be fired first thing tomorrow morning.'

Sadly but without making any fuss, I remounted Rosinante, went back past the extraterritorial gates, to follow a street aimlessly, reflecting on my lack of luck. It was then I saw them: three cyclists, obviously Western bourgeois, because of their racing bikes and lack of luggage.

'Eh bien ça, c'est un vrai cycliste. (Well, this one is a *real* cyclist),' one said when I approached them.

'Graham Robinson,' said another, shaking my hand. *'Je suis américain* (I am American).'

'Claude Lecour,' said the first. *'Je suis français mais en voie de naturalisation américaine.* (I am French but about to become a naturalized American.)' It was said in a tone which indicated 'I am sick but I am taking medicine.' The third cyclist was black.

'Faustin Lusangana, *touriste africain* (African tourist). I am very glad to meet another cycle tourist,' he said warmly.

'Foster!' I exclaimed. 'But people have been telling me about you since Rwanda. What a coincidence! You are the one who's been to France by bike?'

He was. And his story was an amazing one. He had left Rwanda, his native country, many years before on a local bicycle, got into Tanzania and managed to reach Dar es Salaam. There he had asked 'What is the next country?' He was told Kenya, and went there but was stopped: not only did he not have a visa, he didn't have a passport either. He cycled home, got papers and eventually managed to fly to France. But he was refused entry: he had papers but no money. Expelled to the Sudan, he spent several years there, earning enough money to be allowed into Europe—France and finally Holland where he was given an award.

Back home he became a national hero but he had to go into exile. His tribe, the Tutsi, the aristocracy, were no longer in power in Rwanda. The other tribe, the majority Hutus, had won after a terrible massacre. The

60

same bloody feud involving the same tribes, Hutus and Tutsis, took place here in Burundi but the Tutsis won. And Faustin was now selling clothes in the smugglers' market.

He entertained me with his stories for a week, and took me to *La Voix de la Révolution,* where he had already been interviewed several times. I was staying with the American cyclist, the French one not having reached the hospitality level in his Americanization yet. I was supposed to cook typical French meals. Fortunately Graham was not choosy and was satisfied with the complex names I gave my ordinary dishes.

The day I left Bujumbura I was stopped by a white man. He was French and worked on the new road to Tanzania. He was a mechanic and he stopped me, he said, because he had heard me on the radio and it reminded him of a Danish cyclist who had come to his camp shop a week before to have his front carrier rewelded.

I didn't ask the cyclist's name. I knew only one who could break his carriers every other day . . .

Tanzania: 'Doctor Livingstone, I Presume?'

The border town between Burundi and Tanzania where I crossed was called Maganda-Manyavu. I learned this later on, because at the time I passed it without seeing it. Yes, there was a tree-trunk across the dirt road. But after Ugandan road-blocks, I needed much more than a tree-trunk to stop me!

The immigration officer had to chase after me in his Land-Rover. He caught up with me when I was drinking *goua-goua,* the local banana beer, at the top of a small pass which was, according to the officer, the geographical border.

'But I am sorry,' he continued, 'you *must* go back to Maganda to get your passport stamped. Just ask for the immigration office and wait for me, I'll be back in an hour.'

That was just the time I needed to sell my *francs bou* (Burundian francs) and buy Tanzanian shillings on the Maganda market—the black market of course, the Tanzanian shilling being in an even worse state than the Ugandan one.

The immigration office was nothing but the officer's private house, which meant three huts around a courtyard which was covered in unshelled beans. There was an enormous pile of them on which everybody had to walk. That's probably why the officer wanted me back: to help with the threshing . . .

They were beans like I had never seen: coloured beans. I mean beans of many different colours, from sherry red to jet black, through canary yellow and white spotted with brown. They were so brightly coloured that at first I mistook them for small sugar Easter eggs.

It was 8 pm when the officer came back. I had already set out my sleeping bag on his beans, encouraged to do so by his sister. He stamped my passport and, as an apology for being late, he had his wife cook a *friture* for me: very small fish from Lake Tanganyika, fried together and served with lemon, along with a pint of Primus beer.

That night, facing the stars on my bean mattress, I didn't sleep anywhere, because, according to my passport, I was out of Burundi but not yet in Tanzania!

It took me the whole of the next morning to cover the twelve miles to the Tanzanian border post. First because the dirt road had reverted to plain dirt and secondly because the fine view over Lake Tanganyika distracted me.

I came across another road block. This time, it was a locked gate which, seemingly, had not been opened since the British left. I managed to squeeze through and find a deserted building. Everything looked dirty and worn out. All around, the ground had been furrowed by the rains, so much so that three steps had been added, under the outside stairs.

I sat down to wait. I was surrounded by young children who marvelled at my bare feet. Because of the dirt, they were pitch black, and this is strange: *Muzungus* are white from top to toe, everybody knows that!

The immigration officer arrived, unlocked his office door, and as soon as he was seated, he began to read a memo, probably to show me that *he* was in charge, despite my passport and the colour of my skin under the dirt . . . It lasted half an hour, the stamping procedure included.

'Now, you sit down outside and wait for the health officer!' This time, to amuse the children, I pulled out my Swiss Army knife. It was a special one for cyclists, another marvel for the youngsters. I had to explain what every blade was for—the tyre-lever, the compass and, very difficult in a country where wine is unknown, the corkscrew . . .

I didn't have time to explain it all, the health officer had arrived. He was friendlier than his colleague. He opened my vaccination certificate and—I saw it a second before him—my damned cholera shot, done in January 1982 in Khartoum was dated January 1981! It is a common mistake, but the officer didn't see it as a mistake, he saw it as a heaven-sent chance for some entertainment.

'Oh I see, your cholera vaccination has expired. Well, Sir, I am obliged to detain you here for six days, just enough time for the disease, if you have it, to manifest itself.'

I smiled inwardly at the interesting record this would make—seven days to cross a border—then set out to demonstrate to the officer that this shot, having been entered on my certificate *after* the previous one done in Lisbon in June 1981, just could *not* have been done *before*. This took me another fifteen minutes but the officer eventually agreed with me and altered the date himself.

'Now,' he said, 'you must wait for the police officer!'

So I could not escape explaining the corkscrew to the children and I had time for many more explanations because, after the police officer, I had to wait for the customs officers. There were three of them, to whom I declared that I had no Tanzanian shillings, of course, but still five *francs bous*. At that they laughed and finally let me enter their country; it was 5 pm, East African time, and it was a new record for me: 24 hours to cross a border, but as everybody knows, records are made to be broken . . .

On 15 June 1982, I was passed by a Land-Rover filled with eight Zaïrians. They were coming from the area of Ujiji. I asked for news.

'A white cyclist has been there for two weeks,' was the reply. It made me shiver.

'A white cyclist?' I asked.

'Yes, a white cyclist.'

'How is he dressed?'

'As you are.'

'Is he old?'

'No, he is young, but he has a beard and he looks healthy.'

'Where has he come from?'

'From a country which is on the other side of Zaïre and which is called the Sudan.'

'So it is, and you said he is in Ujiji?'

'We saw him less than eight hours ago.'

'Do you think he will be there when I get there?'

I was told 'without any doubt' because he was waiting for the boat and the boat was not leaving until the next day.

So I was going to meet Gernod again, after five months of parallel travels! I hurried as much as I could on a dirt road which was more like a staircase and around noon I reached the tar road to Ujiji. A little later, I asked a child if he knew where the cycling *muzungu* was.

'I saw the bicycle, mister, under the mango tree. It is beautiful.'

What I would have given then to have a private piece of desert where, without being seen, I could go mad; bite my hands, turn a somersault, whip the trees, in a word let out the joy which overcame me. My heart was thumping wildly but I didn't let my face show any emotion, for the sake of the dignity of my race. Then taking what appeared to me the most appropriate course, I parted the crowd and headed, through two rows of curious bystanders, towards the semi-circle of Arab merchants in front of whom was standing the man with the bicycle . . .

As I was walking slowly and saw only his back, I first noticed his blond hair and his apparent tiredness. He was wearing a pair of beige shorts, a red shirt and a cap with a faded gold stripe. I would have liked to run towards him, but I was a coward in front of such a crowd. I would have liked to hug him but he was Danish and I didn't know how he would take it. So I did what cowardice and false pride suggested—I advanced with a quick step and, with a tap on his shoulder, I said:

'Gernod Mogensen, I presume?'

Tanzania: Under the 'Livingstone Tree'.

He was not Gernod. He was not Danish. He was American. And his name was Kevin. He *was* travelling around the world on a bicycle though. Another one!

He had started from Europe. At the time he thought that three years would be enough, but he spent four years in Europe alone. So now, ten years seemed a more realistic prospect.

He had arrived in Ujiji from West Africa through Zaïre, on his bicycle, which was dazzling indeed. Although it had been through the Sahara, the machine looked brand new. It had strange covers on the panniers— Kevin's idea: they protected his luggage from rain and thieves. And they were nicely printed with a gull. Jonathan Livingstone Seagull was the logo of Kevin's travels.

Meeting him at a place that seemed like the end of the world was just as important emotionally for me as meeting Gernod. We talked for hours, sitting on the ground. Yes, he said he knew Gernod, he had left a week ago by train for Dar es Salaam. Kevin had strange principles: he never paid for accommodation. He had found an empty house nearby and was staying there, waiting for the boat to leave.

I didn't have such principles and when I found cheap accommodation, I took it. That night, it was in the Community Centre of Kigoma, the major town near Ujiji. And on the morning of the 16th, in this Tanzanian wild west, which was totally unconnected by road to the rest of the country (forcing me to take the boat too), I woke up and realized that I had *mail*.

There was a letter on the ground, near the door. It read: 'Dear Bernard, we didn't want to wake you. Heard you were in town, we couldn't believe it. The boat is leaving tomorrow at 4. We're going down the lake to Zambia. We'll come to the Community Centre at 10 o'clock. See you then. Love, Stephanie and Lynda.'

My first thought was '*Crénom,* this place is fated to be the meeting place of wandering Europeans!', and my second was '*Ah oui,* I prefer this kind of Doctor Livingstone to the male kind!'

I had met the two girls again in Nairobi and at the foot of Mount Kenya, in the delightful wooden youth hostel there. I had great trouble getting to it as the road was a foot deep in mud. But once there, it was heaven. I got quite close to Stephanie. She told me about her early life and her dislike of 'cold grey English landscapes'. We were sitting in front of a wood fire, she was weaving a belt with multicoloured cotton strings. I was savouring my third Tusker beer (the one with the cap which began my collection on Rosinante's front mudguard) and found myself slowly falling in love with her.

In response to the gift of a pair of olive stone clogs, she offered me one of the ear-rings she was selling, and which she had bought in Israel. Since then my heart beat for her with every hill I descended, because then the strange ear-ring, activated by the wind, began to chant—and my heart with it.

When we had parted, at the foot of Mount Kenya, I could only give a poste restante address in Malawi in the hope of seeing her again. Fortunately, *she* played Stanley in Ujiji. And there was of course no hesitation about joining the two girls on the trip to Zambia!

'It's ten feet deep, isn't it?'

'There is a good way to find out,' said Kevin. 'If anybody had a golf ball, a completely useless golf ball, it would be great. It would reflect the spotlight so we could see it reach the bottom.'

The day before I won the 'most useless object' contest with the golf ball Kevin was referring to. Lynda had started it because ever since she left England three years before she had carried a very old doll. Completely useless. And a useless object is a luxury, when you travel with a backpack.

I had been given this golf ball by an American traveller in Athens. A very American American. I mean a cross between Ronald Reagan and Elvis Presley. He had the strange profession of 'caddie'. (It had to be explained to me that golfers were a pretty lazy lot who had servants to carry their clubs.) He affected an air of ruthlessness by sniffing with an exaggerated grimace, instead of blowing his nose. He nonetheless fell in love with Rosinante and me, and offered us this token of friendship, the shining white golf ball.

And now this other American, Kevin, was asking me to throw it into Lake Tanganyika. A very different American, Kevin. He was typified by his beard: not completely brown, not completely blond, not too thick but thick enough to be elegantly trimmed. It looked perfect and had no weakness. It was clean, without a hair longer than the others and sufficiently deep to suggest it might be hiding something.

This would be an elegant gesture. A golf ball, white and shining in all its dimples, a famous brand, flown from the US to Greece and then carried by bicycle from Greece to Tanzania, and ultimately sacrificed to the second deepest lake on earth, that had some panache, *crébleu!*

So we waited until as many people as possible could watch the event. Rowing boats and dugout canoes were milling around the steamer. In those ports where the *Liemba* stopped, there were no quays. The passengers, day or night, had to jump into the lifeboats launched by the crew or into their relatives' canoes.

'The *Liemba* is the King of Prussia's old yacht,' explained a Belgian technician. He had embarked to check on the maintenance. 'I'm talking about the time when Tanganyika was a German colony. When the *Liemba* was built in 1910, she was very modern. She had to be brought piece by piece from the coast and armed with cannons for the First World War. They scuttled her in 1918—fortunately not in the middle of the lake. The British refloated her and transformed her into this sort of freighter. After independence, they stopped using her for seven years to equip her with diesel engines but since then, she has had inexplicable steam problems. That is why I'm here. I'm supposed to perform miracles because they can't take her in for repairs, she is the only one functioning on the whole lake!'

We had our sleeping bags and bicycles lined up on the First Class deck, with the two girls standing between the two cyclists. To sit to read, I would lean against a pillar which separated Stephanie from me and when she sat too, our hair touched. The caress was almost imperceptible but it electrified me and I could not think of anything else.

A favourite topic of conversation was the comparison between Rosinante and Jonathan Livingstone. Kevin's wonder-bicycle had brakes which braked, true wheels and fifteen gears in working order. One day I

67

expressed my admiration for such a gem and Stephanie, hidden from Kevin, silently mouthed her opinion, that she preferred Rosinante because she had more character. I couldn't have been happier if she had said it about me . . .

So, when the two British girls, the Belgian technician, the Tanzanian captain and the American cyclist, not counting several pirogues, were ready to watch the show, I proceeded with the sacrifice and held up my arm to throw the golf ball.

It quickly disappeared and Kevin said that I hadn't thrown it properly, but there was much applause.

Malawi: Ten days to Cross a Border

I didn't have a Zambian visa. I should have applied for one in Nairobi, but from there Zambia looked so far that I decided to get it later. However in Kampala, Kigali and Bujumbura, there was no Zambian diplomatic representation. So I planned to test my luck and try to get a visa on the border.

Zambia began for me at the southern tip of Lake Tanganyika, after the 48-hour cruise. Kevin had left us at the last Tanzanian stop. He planned to reach Dar es Salaam where his German girlfriend was joining him. Stephanie and Lynda, as Commonwealth citizens, didn't need a visa. I had to take my chance with the two other white passengers, two Swiss expatriates who taught in Dar es Salaam. They had to enter Zambia only because it was the quickest way back but they hadn't planned it that way.

Before the negotiations with Immigration, however, we had to confront a squad of health officers. They wanted to be sure that everybody was vaccinated against cholera. And they vaccinated those who weren't, most of the locals, with the *same* needle. Very soon I heard one of the Swiss squeal: 'But I assure you this is a mistake, I was vaccinated in 1982, not in 1981. They made the mistake in Dar es Salaam because it was done in January, but look, it cannot have been in 1982 because the previous shot was from July 81, look yourself Sir! No Sir, I'm not pretending that you can't read, no Sir, but yes Sir, it is a mistake.'

The Zambian officer looked as hard to convince as the Tanzanian officer had been in my case, and I could hear the Swiss begin his explanation again, in a teacher-like tone which the approaching needle made less and less assured.

The corrected date on my vaccination certificate was overlooked and I was offered a 48-hour transit visa. That was enough for the Swiss, but not for me: I needed five days at least to cycle the 200-mile dirt road to Malawi.

'You just put your bicycle on top of a bus,' said the officer, 'I am not allowed to issue tourist visas.'

So I kept quiet and let him write 21 June as the final date. He was using a regular blue ballpoint pen so, as soon as I was alone, I changed the 1 into a 4. Easy.

On 24 June, 1982, I presented myself at the border post at Chitipa, Malawi, having just left Zambia within the time allowed.

I didn't have a Malawian visa either . . .

The reason was the same as for Zambia. But now I was more confident and asked for a transit visa to reach the capital, where I could regularize my situation. But the Chitipa immigration officer didn't have a single smile to waste.

'The situation is clear: first you are French so you need a visa. Secondly you don't have a visa, so you cannot enter Malawi. Go back to Zambia.'

I hurried back across the six miles of no man's land which separated the two border posts and presented my problem to the Zambians: was I condemned to finish my life in this no man's land?

'No Sir, there is always a solution. Let's see. We are not allowed to issue tourist visas, as you know. And a transit visa isn't of any use in your case, so we shall issue, if we may, a business visa, valid for three weeks, which will allow you to go to Lusaka, our capital, where you'll find a Malawian High Commission and can get a Malawian visa!'

Lusaka was about 700 miles to the south, and there was no way I could cycle the return trip just for a visa! But who was going to keep Rosinante in the meantime?

The immigration officer, when asked, said that he could not compromise himself with a 'non-registered vehicle'. The health officer was less strict. He was willing to look after Rosinante 'even if she isn't vaccinated against cholera', but on one condition: he wanted to try the beast first. It was like a circus. The officer needed two men to hold him while he put the toe-clips on and a complete miracle to prevent him falling off while he pedalled between the buildings.

After eight days of uncomfortable travel, by train, bus and hitchhiking, I was back at the Zambian border post, with the precious Malawian visa stored in my passport. Rosinante had been well cared for and I had presents ready for the health officer. I pedalled again the badly maintained no man's land and gave my passport to the same Malawian immigration officer. I suppose that my smile of victory didn't please him because after completing half the form, he stopped still without a smile.

'What does this mean: *auteur,* as your passport says for occupation?'

(Yes I know, I said I was a stonemason. That was the truth, but not the whole truth because I had published several booklets and my occupations being numerous I had thought that 'author' would cover all of them.)

I explained to the officer that I did write books and give lectures about my travels. This was not the truth, but mentioning religious sects, on which I had done some work, would have seemed more suspicious. I was wrong.

'So you are a sort of journalist, aren't you?'

'Oh no! I am not a journalist, not at all!' I tried to protest, suddenly worried because the officer wasn't continuing with the paperwork. 'No, look, I wrote a book, yes, but very long ago, it cannot count now, and if I was a journalist, I wouldn't be riding a bicycle, would I?'

'The problem is,' he said triumphantly, 'that a journalist needs special permission from our Ministry of Information. And because you don't have that permission, I am obliged to bar you from entering Malawi . . .'

I was refused entry, again! Refused entry in spite of my brand new visa which cost me about £25. No, I could not accept that. I demanded to speak to the officer's chief.

I had to wait for him under a NOTICE TO VISITORS which said: 'In Malawi, it is traditional for women not to appear in public in dresses that expose any part of the leg above the knee. Accordingly, there is a restriction in Malawi on the wearing in public of dresses and skirts that do not fully cover the kneecap when the wearer is standing upright. Also restricted for women are shorts and trousers in public . . .'

And to distract my mind, I tried to imagine what the same ban would be on the French border:

'As it is traditional to picture Frenchmen with a beret on their heads and a *baguette* of bread under their arm, it is accordingly required that foreigners visiting France present themselves at the borders with a beret on their head and a baguette under their arm. Also forbidden is the wearing of any tropical helmet, oriental turban or baseball cap . . .'

The immigration chief was an old man who didn't speak good English. In fact, he didn't speak English *at all*. He just pretended! He carried on a conversation which contained English words, which sounded like English, in such an assured way that at first I doubted my own comprehension. But it was soon very clear: this man was lining up words without meaning anything, except sometimes: 'We don't want publishers here,' or 'Go back to the Zambians.'

Diplomacy made me pretend not to understand English well myself, because of my nationality, so that the officer had to repeat himself without feeling offended. And progressively, it gave him the opportunity to show clemency. At one point, I dared suggest that he referred the matter to his superiors, stressing that I was not a journalist. He didn't seem to hear me but after a long while: 'OK Sir, what I blablabla keep your passport, blablabla allow you for the *night* blablabla tomorrow blablabla out of charity blablabla.'

I slept right under the office porch, at Rosinante's feet, and her company comforted me after these setbacks.

At least I was back with her, wasn't I? Without her, during the return trip to Lusaka, I was nothing. People had seen me, of course, and often pointed at me, but not with the admiring look which only the bicycle encourages.

She had suffered too, during my absence. She might have feared some infidelity, shivered in case I preferred the speed of the train, the comfort of the car, or the freedom of hitchiking. She probably wept too: her bell was hoarse, her handlebars rusted and her front tyre was flat . . .

But all that was forgotten now. I was back with Rosinante, and with her healthy rhythm, the quiet nights she imposed on me, the atmosphere free of exhaust fumes. I was back with Rosinante and I felt at home, even in this country which had rejected me. And that night I watched her carefully, rereading her contours, redefining her faults, smiling at her graces, I stopped short of caressing her: maybe *she* was not yet pacified and she might slap me back!

As I guessed, the chief kept me waiting because he wanted to phone his superior at the district capital. That should be at 8 am, the officer confided. And indeed at 8.30, I was summoned back into the chief's office.

'I blablabla this delay didn't infuriate you. *Today* we blablabla you in Malawi. *Yesterday* we couldn't blablabla but *today* is OK. Welcome in Malawi blablabla you understand we only did our duty, don't you!'

I didn't. This change of attitude was pretty strange, but I was glad of it and I did understand that my record for crossing a border had now increased to ten days!

To avoid the same difficulties in entering South Africa, which has the same laws against journalists, I would be careful and declare my occupation as 'mason.' The officer, a very British-looking white man, would ask if *auteur,* as my passport says, really means 'mason'. I would then have to pretend, as straight-faced as the Pope, that indeed, in good French, a 'mason' was an 'author—of walls'.

Zambia: A Rat's Tail in my Teeth

Re-entering Zambia after Malawi, I was careful not to ask for a tourist visa which I knew was unobtainable at the border, but applied instead for a 48-hour transit visa 'to cross to Zimbabwe'. The immigration officer was a woman this time and she smiled.

'Forty-eight hours to cycle all that distance? Come on, you're not so fast! I'll grant you a 15-day visa!'

Those unexpected fifteen days were to be filled with three major events in my journey: the most troublesome insect, the most exotic meal and the most miraculous accident . . .

The newly surfaced road from Malawi followed the border with Mozambique. This was a remote region with very few villages. That day the heat was unbearable, and on top of that, tsetse flies bit me every time I slowed down. And because the region was far from flat, on every ascent I had to sweat under the painful bites of these insects.

This was the second time that I had suffered from tsetse flies: the first was in Sudan. I welcomed it, then, with all the jubilation of a conscientious adventurer: crossing Africa without tsetse fly bites wouldn't have looked right. So, I identified the insect with enthusiastic patience, noticing the familiar scissor-like folded wings. I was glad to be bitten, it was my duty as an adventurer, and it lasted only a few hours.

But this time they were working overtime. They hadn't left me in peace since morning and now that I had to repair a puncture, they drew tears: despite my mosquito repellent and the extra clothing I had put on, they reached my skin and tortured me. I began to worry about the sleeping sickness which tsetse flies spread. To complete my task, I needed to be completely awake . . .

By 4 pm, I had reached the bridge over the Luangwa river, a tributary of the Zambezi. Since Mozambique's war of independence, it had been heavily guarded. Soldiers stopped me. An officer checked my passport, sent a man to fill my 5-litre tank at the river, sixty feet below the bridge, and adopted a very serious expression.

'Now, I have to warn you, the area is infested by lions and, last week, a local cyclist was eaten alive. If you don't believe me, you can go to Chipata morgue and ask to see his remains: by that I mean the bicycle, which the lion couldn't eat.' At that he smiled, but instantly resumed his serious mask. 'If you persist in your foolish enterprise, I shall give you good advice. In case you meet a lion, you'll have to salute it in the Chichewa[1] way: you must kneel down, clap your hands and say *"Mulibwanji"* which means "How are you?". If the lion answers *"Nilibwino"*, which means "I'm fine, thank you and you?", you're OK, but if the lion doesn't answer, then you'd better pedal very fast!'

As nobody was smiling, I did not dare to laugh and the next moment I was pedalling as fast as I could, wondering which one came first: *'Mulibwanji'* or *'Nilibwino'*.

It was twilight when I made out the huts of a village. I asked for the chief, and explained to him that I was not very keen on sleeping in the bush. He showed me to a small hut in the very middle of the village.

'Does it please you to sleep under this roof?'

I accepted promptly, and as I unrolled my sleeping-bag, the chief was already back with dinner. This was *n'sima,* the southern African staple food, pounded white maize. It looked like a big ball, and could have filled a dozen men. It has often filled my stomach and I like it, whatever comes with it. That night the 'dressing' was a pumpkin sauce.

The chief was teaching me other words of Chichewa (just in case the lion spoke first), when the women brought some more *n'sima*. With it came a plate in which, because of the dark, I could only just discern long black things.

'Now in your honour, we will have a dessert,' said the chief.

'Oh yes, and what is it?'

'It's a local delicacy. These are rats, help yourself to one!'

I couldn't believe I had heard correctly until I brought the long black thing up to my face. It was indeed a rat! Complete with skin and tail, bones and insides, head and ears and teeth; dead, yes, but complete! Were they making fun of me? Me, a rich European being fed by poor Africans, was I being made to feel ashamed?

A glance around persuaded me this was not a joke: the men were sharing the rats. Being the guest, I was the only one to have an entire animal . . .

Because I have always been a diplomat, I bit into the rat. I could clearly feel the fur on my lips and the bones betweeen my teeth. But it was good. A delicate taste. I was told the recipe: the rat is boiled for several hours and

74

dried in the sun. It gives it the taste of a dried sausage—well, of a *furry* sausage. My difficulty in fact, was to eat without looking at it, for then, it was truly enjoyable—except that is for the head which was hard to chew because of the teeth and the tail which got stuck between two of my molars. I had to dispose of that discreetly behind my back.

Anyway, this was a good recipe to take home for times of famine or plague, cheap and very simple—just catch, boil and dry . . .

Two days later, sixty miles from Lusaka, the capital of Zambia, I ran into a road-block with a huge sign saying 'STOP—TSETSE FLY CONTROL'.

All right, I thought, they're going to check my blood and tell me whether I've got sleeping sickness or not . . .

'No,' said the policeman, 'the road-block is just here to prevent the tsetse flies reaching Lusaka. You see, we put up the big sign, "STOP", which is an international word, yet there are still some tsetse flies who can't read it.' He was smiling with all his teeth. 'Years ago,' he continued, 'we tried to educate them. Everywhere we set up big signs saying "ILLITERATES, EDUCATE YOURSELVES!' We had no result with these lazy bastards. That's why I am here, with my butterfly net . . .'

There he was indeed, in the middle of the road, butterly-net at the ready, to stop the tsetse fly invasion. He laughed loudly at my puzzled look and, suddenly serious, explained.

'The truth is that tsetse flies really are lazy bastards: they don't want to fly long distances, so they stick to vehicles and hitch-hike—like this one on your bike, look!'

He was pointing to the big insect hiding under my suitcase. A twist of his hand, a flick of the butterfly-net and the would-be trespasser was caught. The policeman took it between two fingers, killed it between . . . his two front teeth . . . and declared: 'You're OK now, you may proceed, have a good day!'

In a library in Lusaka, I finally found the answer. Sleeping sickness—which is literally a 'sickness of the sleep', which means the sick person *can't* sleep and gradually falls into a torpor mistaken for sleep—is now restricted to remote areas and anyway takes 3–5 years to kill somebody. That should be enough for me to complete my round-the-world tour . . .

Much worse, oh so much worse than tsetse flies for the adventure-cyclist, is the road traffic. In southern Morocco where roads are reduced to a couple of yards of tarmac, I had had to fight for my right to use it. A bicycle is not a vehicle to most drivers. It goes with pedestrians and donkeys and is expected to leave the road when a car comes. In Africa, the internal combustion engine is the master of the tar, beyond dispute.

Zambia was no exception. Here it was even worse because its drivers are well-known drunkards. When I was climbing my first miles in Zambia, up from the shores of Lake Tanganyika, I noticed, on *every* hairpin bend, the wreck of at least one truck. That struck me so much that I asked the 'Rhodesian' who gave me shelter why it was.

'Oh,' he answered, 'they are the results of the "Zambian gear": when they're drunk, they shift into neutral to go faster downhill!'

No wonder local cyclists ride on the right hand side of the road, facing the traffic, and as soon as they spot a car in the distance, they hide in the bush! All things considered my accident had to be in Zambia if it was to happen anywhere.

The 30-mile stretch between Lusaka and Kafue carries the most traffic in the whole country. Here vehicles bound for the Victoria Falls join forces with those bound for Zimbabwe. Yet it's no wider than anywhere else.

I felt the heat of the engine against my right thigh before I jerked back with the shock. I had a glimpse of the greenish Indian-made Tata truck and then everything was yellow: it was the elephant grass in which I lay. It didn't hurt, I was just sleepy. This is how it ends, I thought, completely detached, not a bit worried, this is how it ends—in this yellow elephant grass . . .

This truck driver wasn't drunk, but nevertheless looked funny: he was pale. He was pulling me out of my sleep, out of my shock, by pulling on the bicycle spoke that I had worn in my ear since the Sudan.

'When I saw the spoke sticking out of your ear,' he explained later, 'I thought that during the accident, your head had gone through your wheel or something, and you had got the spoke through your neck! And I was afraid, you see, I didn't want to pull your whole brain out!'

My thigh hurt badly. Rosinante and her luggage were scattered around but only the suitcase was destroyed. It had absorbed most of the shock, like a big bumper, and probably saved my life.

I insisted on going to the police. The driver took me to Kafue. The traffic officer was definitely drunk and the paperwork took two long hours. That was enough time for the truck's owner to arrive. He was manager at the Kafue mills and offered to pay for all the damage.

'And it will be my pleasure', he continued, 'to drive you to the Riverside Motel where I will pay all your expenses.'

After another thought, he turned to the policeman.

'Is he alone?'

'No,' they said to my astonishment, 'his brother is waiting outside . . .'

My 'brother' turned out to be Kenny, a cyclist from Quebec who happened to pass along a moment before (no great surprise as this road was the only one open between central and southern Africa). He had been sponsored by a Zaïrian bicycle manufacturer and had to ride a strange machine with balloon tyres, rod-brakes, no gears, straight handlebars and wooden carriers. The policemen had stopped him saying that his brother had had an accident and was inside!

We did indeed have the same colour skin and the same unusual vehicle. The policemen didn't need any more evidence to assume we were brothers. What they didn't know was that even our mother tongue was the same. I eagerly greeted my 'brother' in French, explained everything to him and we were both taken to the Riverside Motel. This was a luxury for us. We had a delicious *n'sima na n'kuku* (Chicken *n'sima*) without feathers (or insides . . .) and I could even test my bruised leg on the dance floor—luckily, nothing was broken—and before we went to bed, still marvelling at our clean double room, we agreed that tomorrow it would be the Québecois's turn to be knocked off the road by a truck, so that we could get another luxury night . . .

1. The Chichewa tribe occupies most of Malawi and parts of Zambia.

Zimbabwe: Why don't you Rent a Car?

Unfortunately, Kenny's route and mine split shortly after Kafue: Kenny was heading for the Victoria Falls and I was more interested in the ruins of Great Zimbabwe. I have always been more attracted to the feats of humankind than to those of the Supreme Architect—whom I suspect of a usurped reputation. However, Kenny was to return the favour without knowing it, at the end of my stay in Zimbabwe.

But for the moment I was confronted with the difference between 'black Africa' and 'white Africa' as it has often been expressed to me, here on the Kariba dam. The two countries, Zambia and Zimbabwe, may share equally the electricity produced by this enormous scheme inaugurated by Queen Elizabeth II in 1960, but they certainly don't use it for the same purposes.

I arrived there at night, it was dark and I was guided by the numerous lights on the Zimbabwe side. There were none on the Zambian side and after having closely missed a local cyclist coming the other way—we were both following the yellow line and nearly crashed head-on—I wasn't so lucky the next time and fell into a big pothole, and broke my back rim.

I would have to spend a fortune (15 Zimbabwe dollars, almost £15!) on a new wheel in Kariba. There was one consolation: it would allow me to buy 26 x $1^3/8''$ tyres. My Rwandan tyres were already more than worn out and the only solution I had found was to sew patches of local tyres on the outside of them!

On the Zambian side a rusted road sign said that it was forbidden to stop there. I nevertheless had to sleep under it that night because the officers didn't want me near their barracks.

On the Zambian side, the road was surfaced with a rough tarmac, as rough as a grater for my poor tyres; on the Zimbabwean side, there was a smooth asphalted surface which my feet appreciated first. I had decided to 'do as the Romans do' and, after wearing out my only pair of shoes, I was now pedalling with bare feet. I just had to smooth the pedals with flattened

Coca-Cola tins . . .

On the Zambian side were dirty slums, squalor and poverty; on the Zimbabwean side a holiday resort with lawns, flowers, clean dustbins and public benches. Yes, there were lawns and flowers at road junctions; I had forgotten they could exist!

On the Zambian side were immigration officers without uniforms or ink for their stamps. On the Zimbabwean side smartly dressed and well-mannered black officers were just as strict on formalities as their Malawian counterpart.

This time, thanks to France's support for Mugabe's government, I did not need a visa, but the bicycle seemed to be a problem. The official had twice counted my travellers' cheques and, not knowing that half of them had been declared lost in Zambia for that very reason, asked:

'There is more than 2000 American dollars here, so why don't you rent a car?'

The difference between the countries took on a very different aspect when, my wheel changed, I looked for a place to sleep in the Kariba African township.

This was a very different Africa from the one I was used to: streets were tarred and nobody wore rags. Even the kids had clothes without holes! No more bare feet, not even tyre-sandals. I probably looked more 'African' than these people. But the most important difference for me was the perplexity I provoked. What is this white man coming here for, people seemed to be thinking. Until then contact with African people was very easy and I almost always encountered kindness and friendly curiosity. Here, I was met with suspicion, I had to adapt.

After a while, after I had asked if I could sleep in the school, people realized that I was not a local white and gathered around me. An army truck stopped and the officer told a member of the Youth Brigade to lead me to the school. As the head was not there, I was taken to the beer hall.

I knew very well what a beer hall was and, at that late hour, I expected to see the whole male population there, slowly getting drunk on maize beer—a kind of thick white soup which the Zambians drank in big 2-quart buckets.

It was exactly the same here except for the addition of a few women and the barbed wire fence surrounding the hall. The beer was also different, not home made but the famous Chikubu brand which I had already seen sold in cartons in Malawi. I was led to the very centre of the beer hall, between some huge barrels: somebody handed me a bucket and they began to interrogate me.

Yes, the criminal police were here. My presence was definitely suspect.

A white man asking to sleep in a black township, I slowly realized, was something difficult to believe in 'white' Africa. But my natural naive ways, along with my liking for the Chikubu beer (I gulped the two litres without flinching), persuaded the police that I could not be a South African spy.

Eventually I was invited to the home of the Youth Brigade Commander, a tiny cubicle with water and electricity, and after dinner he took me back to the beer hall for another gallon of the 'white stuff'.

'I want people to see you with me and alive, because they probably thought I was taking you to jail. And now we must learn to live together, whites and blacks. But it isn't easy. Remember that three years ago, we would both have been put in jail, I for taking you home and you for accepting . . .'

It was near Fort Victoria in southern Zimbabwe that a big car passed me and stopped. Three whites got out.

'Could you be the French cyclist who crossed Africa through Zaïre?'

More fans, I thought, who mistook the Sudan for Zaïre—not uncommon among Europeans. I said 'Yes, it is me, the famous transcontinental cyclist!'

I had become famous indeed.

I had arrived in Harare with something of a shock, because on my map it was written as Salisbury! Three years after independence, Zimbabwe had been overtaken by a fit of name changing. To change Salisbury to Harare was understandable, so was the demolition of the statues of Cecil Rhodes, but to spend millions of dollars on changing the mere spelling of local names which remind people of Rhodesia when the Rhodesians took them directly from local dialects seemed extreme (e.g. Sinoïa had become Shinoyi). Not only I felt this way but also the *Herald's* cartoonist. He showed a street scene, a mother and child on a zebra crossing. Mother: 'No Joseph, since the government new-names policy, you mustn't say RObots but ZIMbots'[1].

I was still angry and resentful after the Zambian accident when I arrived in Harare and decided to give vent to my feelings in a few well-publicized declarations.

I went to the *Herald,* the main daily newspaper, and told my story. The black reporter understood my feelings very well and put my anger into good English. The white female photographer immortalised Rosinante's right side, on which there was a sticker saying 'left-hand drive', and the next day, the caption under the photo was supposed to quote me: 'Some warped-minded people regard cyclists at the very bottom of the social ladder. But I want to prove them wrong.'

When I had found a dictionary, I realized that I had said some quite interesting things: that my round-the-world trip was aimed at proving the usefulness of bicycles, even today and especially in developing countries which are poor in energy; and at persuading the world that cyclists shouldn't be considered as pathetic washouts who couldn't afford a car. This article had tremendous repercussions. The next day, the *Herald* editorial itself was entitled 'Two-wheel sense'. It quoted me again and urged the government to follow my advice and favour the development of bicycles instead of petrol-guzzling cars.

Then the national television asked to interview me. The story about me was second in the evening news, to the astonishment of the journalist who talked to me. And I was invited to a chat-show along with an Irish conjurer. After that of course everybody recognized me in the streets and the whole thing was crowned by an *Agence France Presse* wire to the major French newspapers, speaking of a 'young cycle tourist who had overnight become the idol of Zimbabwean media'. By the time I left Harare I wasn't surprised to be stopped several times a day to give autographs, to be given money as a gesture of support, and to pose for souvenir snapshots.

So I was not surprised by these three whites near Fort Victoria. They had probably seen me on TV, too. I accepted their invitation without suspecting that they were confusing 'French' with 'Québecois'. They were missionaries running a famous high school. One of their ex-pupils was there and shook my hand. He was the Zimbabwean Minister of Education. I was impressed.

But nobody was impressed by me. During dinner the confusion was cleared up: they had mistaken me for Kenny. They were waiting for him because he was a relative of one of them, but they had never heard of me, the media-idol!

---

1. 'Robot' is the South African word for traffic-lights.

Botswana: Do Blacks and Redheads Smell?

The Kalahari Desert was close by, and I was crossing the semi-desert of sparsely populated Botswana; it was very much like the Sudan. This encouraged mystical thoughts: when I was asked, as I often was, what I lived on, I answered that God provided, which was similar to the Muslim formula: *Allah Karim,* God is generous!

And it was true that, since Harare, money had seemed to fall from the sky. In the whole of Zimbabwe, it was rare to have nights without a hot shower, or evenings without a good dinner and a TV soap opera. And it was rare to go through a day without receiving a gift, usually 2-dollar bills 'to help me along'. Always it was as a consequence of my TV fame. Even at the mission near Fort Victoria, if the missionaries didn't know me, the nun-cook and her troop of native helpers certainly did. After the meal they summoned me to the kitchen where I had to tell a few stories. They seemed so excited by my mere presence that it was a pleasure being there and I almost refused their present: they had clubbed together to give me money!

Even here in Botswana, where Zimbabwean TV and newspapers are seen, the manna continued to fall. Once I was so desperate to find an inhabited place before dark, that when I finally saw a building a mile from the road, I quickly pedalled towards it, mentally preparing a fast presentation in order to win a favourable decision as quickly as possible.

But the white man who came out of the house did it for me. 'Don't tell me,' he said, 'I have seen you on TV, I am Polish and you are French, what would you say to a good steaming bath . . . I'll have a room prepared for you . . . You can stay here as long as you please . . . Everything around, everything that is mine, treat it as if it was yours!'

I stayed two days and enjoyed two baths and five meals. When I left, the Pole gave me a 20-pula note (£12) so that I could send him postcards. *Allah Karim* indeed!

But in Botswana's deserts, I learned later, it is quite usual for money to fall from the sky, because *pula,* the monetary unit, also means 'rain' . . .

However something the heavens had forgotten so far was a human companion for my nights, but even she arrived eventually: like most Tswanas she had a light skin, but unlike Hottentots who also inhabit the country she didn't have a big behind or bust: when the straps of her dress fell, nothing escaped from the bodice: her breasts didn't need a bra. Her face was the same: thin and graceful.

I tried to look kind, she looked so frightened. She confided later that she mistook me for a 'Rhodesian mercenary come to kill her'. I asked her permission to sleep under one of the trees which surrounded her house and to use the tap which stood under the orange tree. She agreed. The orange tree was blooming. I mistook its fragrance for jasmine.

When she saw Rosinante and watched me undo my luggage, she smiled and said that, when her father came back from work, I would be allowed to sleep inside. I discovered that she was 25 and that the two children playing around were hers. Her father was a plate-layer on the Zimbabwean railway which passed nearby.

As her father was late, she fetched her aunt who ran a shop next door. The old shopkeeper, elegantly dressed and speaking perfect English, came to inspect me by the light of her torch. Probably satisfied by my innocent air, she invited me to set out my sleeping bag on the veranda of the big house.

'My daughter,' she said, 'will prepare some *bugobé*. Do you like *bugobé*?'

'Yes of course, that is what they call *n'sima* in Zambia and *sadza* in Zimbabwe! Thank you very much for your kind invitation. If you've got a moment, I'll show you my travels on my maps.'

And so, when my sleeping bag was unrolled on the veranda, I spread out all my maps on my suitcase and played my usual role, showing photographs and newspaper cuttings and especially the maps. I had noticed how fascinated Africans are by maps. There were now three women and four kids gathered around my candle, like moths to a flame. I realized suddenly that we were very close to the Tropic of Capricorn and explained my excitement: crossing a tropic isn't something you do every day. It would be the first time in my life that I would cross this one. But the women didn't share my enthusiasm.

'Yes, I know,' said the aunt. 'The "Capricorna" is near, but what's extraordinary about that? It's just a small concrete table with a copper plaque. I should think your Eiffel Tower is more impressive!'

Instead of *bugobé,* the thin beautiful woman brought me a big bowl of white rice, with bottles of South African dressings: extremely spicy tomato ketchup and mayonnaise. The other women left when I asked if I could wash after the meal.

When I came back from the shower, the young nice-looking mother was alone and reading on the veranda by the light of my candle, sitting on my sleeping bag. She showed me what she was reading: a South African clothes catalogue. Half of the models were black, no *apartheid* in marketing, it seems . . .

'In this remote place,' she complained, 'we don't have anything else to read. Don't you have a book to lend me?'

I had. Since *The Blue Nile* and *The White Nile,* I had kept swopping books with travellers: English books mostly. But now I hesitated. Should I offer her *Fair Stood the Wind for France,* the story of an English airman who married a French girl during World War II, or *The French Lieutenant's Woman,* the story of an English girl seduced and abandoned by a French sailor. Two situations which I hoped were close to ours, but with quite different endings.

I suggested the first. And I began to ask the questions which were on my mind.

'Are you married? Wait, what's your name first?'

'Theresa . . . No I am not married. My first child came when I was still at school and the second when I was working in Francistown far from my family. My father takes care of them now and the man who marries me will pay my father for that. The *lobola,* the money paid to the bride's father, is in proportion to the number of children the bride has.'

'But I guess it discourages suitors now . . . Couldn't you . . . well, have avoided having kids before you marry?'

'Oh yes, but I am allergic to the pill and the coil makes me sick.'

'And your boy-friends, couldn't they use condoms?'

'Use what?'

To make her understand I pulled out of my suitcase an envelope given to me by a Swedish traveller, which I hadn't opened yet.

'Ah I see, you mean French letters?'

'Yes, in French, we call them *capotes anglaises,* which means English overcoats!'

She laughed first and then shyly explained: 'Yes but you know, in the heat of the moment, one often forgets this kind of prophylactic accessory . . . Speaking of medicines, do you have anything for nettle rash?'

There was no anti-allergenic in my pharmacy nor any rash on her skin, as far as I could see, but ten seconds later I was carefully massaging her arms with a neutral antiseptic cream.

'No rash anywhere else?' I asked, my heart beating fast.

'Yes, on my chest but . . .' and she became flustered.

'Oh don't be shy, most of the women I meet down here are bare-breasted . . .'

'Are they?' she said, undoing the top of her dress.

84

My hands then began to anoint her small hard breasts.

'Why don't English women show their breasts?' asked Theresa after a while.

I was now rather short of breath, but I managed to summarize Desmond Morris' 'Automimetism' theory. I had read about it in the Pole's house.

'Some animals, among which man is one, reproduce their sexual excitement signals on parts of the body which are more visible than the sexual organs themselves. According to this theory women's bright red lips are just the unconscious representation of their vaginal lips swollen with blood from excitement. Thus it is a popular belief that a man with a big nose also has a big penis. Thus a woman's breasts would be the representation of her buttocks, their more or less provocative exposure would be an indication of the more or less advanced sexual excitement of their owner . . . Consequently, dear Theresa, if English women, by which I guess you mean *white* women, don't show their breasts, it's because either they have read Desmond Morris' theory, or they don't want to make love!'

Theresa followed my lecture with a very interested look, not at all troubled by my application of layer after layer of cream on her breasts.

'Desmond Morris is right,' she exclaimed 'I have got girl-friends in Francistown who put on rouge only when they want to make love with English men, and for money of course. They're called menice, d'you know why? It's because they're always asking their customers: "Me, nice? Me, nice?" They don't speak English very well you see . . . Anyway, I couldn't do their job, my belly is too fat!'

'You, fat? Come on, show me, otherwise I'll call you "Me fat"!'

She laughed again and pulled up her dress. I had completely lost my breath now and didn't have any more cream but she was in full control and pulled my hands onto her 'fat' belly. We were so close to each other that our lips couldn't miss one another.

The Swedish 'prophylactic accessories' hadn't suffered from the desert heat, and afterwards Theresa showed me her photo album which included pictures of her relatives and even her fiancé, soldiering in South Africa. She asked how we say 'father' and 'mother' in French, laughed at the translations and started every time a train stopped because her father might still come back . . . And then, suddenly: 'The English say that we blacks are smelly, do you think so?'

Since Zimbabwe, where I heard this kind of nonsense for the first time, I had made up a ready answer: 'In my country, people say that we redheads are smelly, do you think so?'

Johannesburg: 'Yes, but you are White!'

In Johannesburg, the world's gold-mining centre, I did not find a gold mine but I found the next best thing: through a South African potter I met in Lusaka (she was part of a *Botswana* exhibition at the Alliance Française) I met a German immigrant who offered me a job. I was to be paid 3.5 rands an hour (£2.80) to hang wallpaper. My workmates were black, and this was a unique way, being white, to meet blacks in South Africa. We worked ten hours a day, two of them at 25% extra pay, in the city centre, and we had two breaks: half an hour for the 9 am tea-break and almost an hour for lunch. Officially it was much less but the supervisors came only once a day and after they had been, we were practically on our own.

On the first day, I had to put things right. My workmates called me *baas* ('master' in Afrikaans), which wouldn't do. I asked them to call me Bernard so I could call them Sidwell, Sam, Jacob, George, Hamilton, Vincent or Mohamed. I tried to get them to understand that in Europe, there is no *apartheid,* at least not in the laws.

'Do you mean that in your country a black man may marry a white woman?' asked Sam, my helper, officially my 'boy'.

'Of course yes!'

'Oh . . . So I'll buy me a bicycle and follow you back there!'

Sidwell, Hamilton and Sam were Zulus. They were tall, alert, beautiful. As I was reading *Zulu Dawn*, the fantastic account of the Zulus' resistance to the British army, I asked them what they thought of their present leader, Chief Buthelezi. Their answer was unanimous:

'We recognize only one leader now, he's in jail, his name is Nelson Mandela.'

Mohamed and his brother George were fair-skinned Tswanas. Jacob was Xhosa and Vincent came from Venda. And my education was greatly improved by conversing with my colleagues. Among them, differences of language were just as great as between, say, Norwegian and Italian. So they used *fanakalo* to communicate. This is a language born in the mines to link at least twenty different tribes, including the two white 'tribes': the English and the Afrikaners. I remembered only one word of *fanakalo: Chailé:* 'end of working day'.

I was naively shocked when I discovered that Sidwell, who did the same work as me, and who was more experienced and quicker, was paid less: 3 rands an hour. 'Boys', like Sam, Hamilton or Jacob, earned only 100 rands (about £60) a week for sixty hours' work. As I remarked loudly that I earned more than them, Sam retorted:

'Yes but you, you are white!' And his tone implied that no other explanation was necessary.

But what I, a typical European brought up to the hatred of the South African system, interpreted as a scandalous injustice based on race, soon appeared to me in a different light: 'Yes but you, you are white!' means 'therefore you have more responsibilities'. This was true: as I was the only white in the team, every time there was a problem, or an unusual decision to be made, or someone had to talk to the boss, every time another company on the building site wanted to meet the wallpaper hangers, it fell to me to deal with it without any consideration for my real abilities.

And this reveals a lot about the South African system. It is entirely based on a hierarchy of races and tribes. A Zulu, for instance, would never accept orders from a Swazi. And for every task, there must be a white who thinks and a black who sweats. Thus, to dig a trench, you waste the white's abilities because he can only watch, and the same applies to a draughtsman: the black can only sweep the floor when the white sharpens the pencil!

South Africans themselves laugh at it, through popular stories like this one: 'Van Der Merwe [the stereotypical Afrikaner] went to Europe. There he saw three bricklayers building a wall. "Three hours to build that wall?" he exclaimed, "I could do it in half that time, just give me six kaffirs and you'll see![1]" '.

One evening after work, as I was walking to the bus station, the sky fell on my back: it was in fact a bearded colossus who was slapping my shoulder. He said: *'Non, c'est pas vrai, c'est pas toi!* (No, it's not true. It can't be you!)'

Yes it was me, and it was him: Kenny, the cyclist from Quebec. He had been staying at the Salvation Army, he said, for a whole month already and had just begun work the previous week in his field: Biology.

'And your bike?' he asked, 'how come you're walking?'

I explained, quite proudly, that I now had a sponsor as well, through

Belgian friends who lived here. Peugeot-RSA had agreed to change everything which didn't work on Rosinante: wheels, tyres, tubes, pedals, chainwheel, chain, derailleur, free-wheel and rear-view mirror. In short, everything except the frame and the Malawian back carrier, Rosinante's personal African souvenir: made out of forged iron, it weighed 10 pounds alone. The Peugeot people were working on it, which explained why I had to catch the bus to town. And in exchange, all they wanted was for me to wear their T-shirt, which wasn't very difficult!

And Kenny explained why he had arrived here so long before me: Zimbabwe refused him entry because he didn't have enough travellers' cheques. Thus he couldn't call on his relative's mission. Worse, to enter South Africa, he had to pay a 600-rand deposit. Now he planned to work for at least a year, before resuming his ride around Africa. Two days later, he moved to the youth hostel where I was already staying and for two entire months our two bicycles, the Peugeot-sponsored and the Zaïrian-built, took a lot of room there, but only between 7 pm and 6 am . . .

I left my job on 3 December 1982, and on exactly the same day Mr Oppenheimer finished his work. We were working for the same company, Anglo-American. But we didn't have the same function: I was hanging wallpaper in the new office building, he was the big boss, the president of the huge company. The newspapers said that Mr Oppenheimer had spent his whole life working for his company, the most important in the whole of Africa, and twenty-five years in the president's chair. I think my bottom would have hurt long before.

I told my supervisor three days before and on the last day he brought my pay. I shook hands with my Zulu, Xhosa, Venda and Tswana colleagues and left by the service stairs, as usual, because Rosinante was waiting for me in the basement.

Mr Oppenheimer's departure was on another scale: he had told the newspapers, radio and TV months in advance and today the police barred entry to the street in front of the Anglo-American building. Hundreds of company employees were standing there and the president made a speech. But he didn't shake hands with anybody . . .

Visiting South African farms, I was reminded of the time years before when I was cycling in northern Europe, asking to sleep in barns. Here, most farmers were Afrikaners and many of them had French family names like Dutoit, Duplessis, Joubert, Leroux or Labouchagne. But they pronounced them very differently from the original. Anyway they all had the same reaction when I began to speak English. At first they pretended not to understand until I made it clear that I was a foreigner. They still hadn't forgotten the Boer War . . .

But then their kindness knew no bounds . . .

On Christmas Eve, I passed Port Shepstone, on the Indian Ocean south of Durban, around 5 pm and began to look for a farm. Unfortunately this was a Zulu area and it was full of miserable corrugated iron huts and drunk people; I could not ask them to give me shelter. I was almost ready to sleep beside the road and feast on a quart of water when a large building appeared. Surrounded by tropical trees, and with a swimming pool in front, this could only be a white South African farm! The man listened to me and hesitated a few seconds.

'You want to sleep in one of the barns', he said. 'Well, of course . . . I can't refuse you that . . . But I just wonder if I can think of a better place . . . Come on, on Christmas Eve, you can't stay outside, come in!'

The family was playing cards: the wife, three children and two grandparents. The cards were instantly forgotten and I was asked thousands of questions, such as how I escaped the terrorists, bandits and dissidents who inhabit black African states. I also had to reassure them about my ear-ring. No I was not one of those punks who destroy everything in Great Britain. My adornments had their uses. The ear-ring to wake me up after accidents and the ankle bracelet made out of Rosinante's old chain served also as a rosary or an abacus. When they laughed heartily, I asked if I could have a shower . . .

They switched off the TV when I came back and grandpa opened his Bible. He read a passage in Afrikaans. Then the children, surprisingly quiet and still, sang a Christmas song. All was naivety and innocence, perfect peace of mind.

At 8 pm the distribution of presents began. I was ill at ease, I felt like an intruder, I didn't know where to hide. I could not imagine that their generosity could include me, the cycling punk, in their family festivities. They hadn't known me for more than an hour yet there was a parcel with my name on it. It brought tears to my eyes when I unwrapped it. It was a small South African flag and a New Testament in Afrikaans. Naivety and innocence, perfect peace of mind.

I got my pliers and my electric wire. Since Johannesburg, I no longer made olive stone clogs, my new handicraft was wire bicycles. I even sold some of them in the youth hostel. But of course it was for free that I now began to make seven copper-wire bicycles, one for each member of this Afrikaner family, during the *braai,* the South African barbecue.

The civilities over, we could talk politics. It always started with the same question: 'So! Tell us now, what do you think of South Africa?'

'Well . . .'

'You probably expected us to go hunting the blacks with automatic rifles, didn't you?' said the grandfather.

'If we are disliked overseas,' said the father, 'it is because of our attitude to blacks, but you yourself have seen black African states, you've seen they are incapable of progress. Their brains aren't like ours. They're like kids, very kind but without any ambition. All they want in life is to buy enough maize to feed their family and enough beer to get drunk once a day . . . Take some more *sosaties* and mealie meal if you like!'

This was an opportunity for me to change the subject. I was tired of arguing against primitive and naive prejudices.

'Ah yes, you call it "mealie meal". Did you know it has a different name in each country, from *posho* in Tanzania to *bugobé* in Botswana . . . and even *polenta* in French Savoy! But you're the first white I have seen eating it.'

'And look how I like it better,' added the father with pride.

And before my incredulous eyes, he plunged his bare hand into the steaming cereal and made a small ball of it in his palm, before he put it into his mouth, with that very special movement of his thumb—the very same movement I had seen made by dozens of Tutsis, Shonas and Matabeles. One thing you can't deny, I thought, is that Afrikaners are true Africans, and are to be compared with other Africans, not with Europeans as their skin colour misleadingly makes us do. They are to be judged by Africans too, not by Europeans or Americans, and by African standards . . .

'What is regrettable in South Africa,' admitted the father, 'is the law on *apartheid*. It attracts attention to something which doesn't deserve it. In every country there is a natural segregation. There are people you invite home and others you don't, just because you don't share the same culture. You respect each other, but well, you don't enjoy life in the same ways. If I invited one of my workers for a *braad*, he wouldn't be at ease, we wouldn't have anything to say. Same thing if he invited me to his hut to drink maize beer. But I agree, our laws must be changed, so . . . we will be allowed to play rugby with the French. Tell me, don't you think it's too severe, boycotting our rugby players?'

---

1. 'Kaffir' is the pejorative word for blacks used by white South Africans. Curiously, the word is an Arabic word meaning 'infidel.' Therefore one could say that white Afrikaners' ancestors (mostly Dutch, French and Germans) were themselves called 'kaffirs' by the Saracens . . .

Transkeï: 'You'll be Freed at Daybreak!'

The place was Mount Ayliff. This was my first night in Transkeï, one of the several single-tribe new countries created by South Africa in place of its old 'bantustans'. They are not recognized by the UN. I can't understand why. The UN recognizes other African states created by colonial powers just as tiny and dependent on international aid as Transkeï is on South Africa.

I didn't see any large farms, so I reverted to my old habit and went to the police station. After presenting myself and showing my passport, I asked permission to sleep in the police compound. It seemed to induce a lot of suspicion:

'Where you come from?'

'From France.'

'You took a plane to Johannesburg then!'

'No, I pedalled.'

'Come on! Don't make fun of me. France is overseas as everyone knows. So obviously you had to take a boat or a plane, stop talking nonsense!'

I had never had such a bad reception in Africa and I said so. But it was probably out of sheer weariness that the officer said 'OK you sleep on the bench behind the counter, put your bicycle against the wall . . .' I had not stretched out for more than half an hour when the police station was filled with a crowd of people. I assumed they were prisoners because their guards looked really nasty. I counted 53 prisoners and 12 guards. I had to sit up to allow the last to use my bench. I questioned the one nearest.

'They were fighting, some of them got badly injured, they were drunk, we are going to judge them.'

'Here? Without an attorney, all together?'

More amused than scandalized, I stood up to enjoy the show. The police chief behind his desk was startled when he saw my face. He turned to his subordinates and soon I was faced by two tough-looking guards.

'Excuse us, Sir, but the officer who allowed you to stay was not entitled to do so. You must go now or . . . be prepared to sleep in a cell . . .'

'All right, I'll take the cell!'

'Well . . . then we must be sure of you. Do you have any papers?'

I frowned. I had already shown my papers. And I came here voluntarily, why treat me like a criminal? So instead of pulling out my passport, I simply answered that yes, I did have papers.

'Where?'

'Here!'

I pointed to my breast pocket, and when the policeman said, 'May I see them, Sir?' he had become an enemy. The passport was not enough, he wanted to search my whole bicycle.

'What is in there?'

'My tools and spare parts.'

'Let me see!'

The whole pannier was emptied on the ground and we passed on to the second one, filled with books and exercise books. On top of them were my reels of electric wire. I laughed.

'Here you are. You'll probably think I'm a terrorist!'

'What do you know about terrorists?' He retorted without showing any sense of humour. 'You pretend to be a tourist, all right, but why on a bicycle? What are you trying to do? You're white and whites can afford cars. Why don't you? What is your mission?'

There were now three of them reading my notebooks and my mail, asking me to translate from the French. And then they passed to the front panniers. There I had a small solid-fuel heater. I bought it from an Australian ex-soldier. It looked military.

'What is that?'

'It's written on the box . . .'

'Open it!'

The policemen stood back. Could it be a bomb? Or a weapon? There was a great temptation to fight back at this humiliation, so I opened the heater suddenly under the nose of the nearest cop. No devil escaped but the man pulled out his gun. He was red with anger.

'You'll be freed at 4 o'clock,' I was told after the second turn of the key in the lock. The cell was spacious, as spacious as the commander's cubicle in Kariba. There was one room, with wooden benches and another one without a ceiling just near the door. Between the two were the toilets.

I slowly realized the mistake I had made, agreeing to be jailed: they kept all my belongings and papers. Probably they wanted to lay hands on my camera, my radio and my . . . solid-fuel heater. What was to stop them

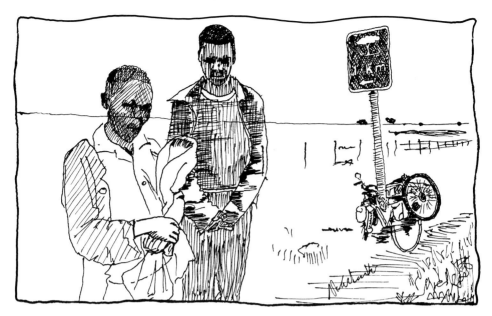
Transkei: 'Aren't you afraid of us?'

killing me during the night and pretending I had never been there? Or they could forget me in this stinking hole. Who would ever ask for me there?

To cut a long story short, instead of sleeping, I waited for sunrise or slaughter. Insects crawled on my face, mosquitoes bit me and the ground where I lay smelled of urine.

At 4 am, the sun made its appearance—but the key in the lock did not. At 4.30, I began to get nervous. At 5, I climbed onto the entrance door to reach the ceiling bars and test them. In fact they looked fragile; if I had been allowed to keep my Swiss Army knife, its hacksaw would have got rid of them. And it was probably the sound of my repeated blows on the bars which brought the policemen at 5.30.

In a lay-by two hours later, I was repairing another puncture. (South African rubber is bad: tyres don't last more than 1200 miles and tubes have spontaneous punctures. I had bought two tubes between France and Johannesburg and three since then.) Young Transkeïans gathered around me.

'Do you carry a fire-arm?' one of them asked.

'No, for what purpose?'

'Aren't you afraid of us?'

His disappointed look made me laugh. The oldest remarked: 'Yes, you're right, if you come from Napoleon's country you can't be afraid!'

I didn't try to disabuse him but remembered that in my cell the previous night, I certainly hadn't been very Napoleonic . . .

Cape Town: Learning Chinese in a Double Bed

On this Valentine's Day morning, I asked her how her buttocks were. She had burned them the day before on a nudist beach, the only one in South Africa, Sandy Bay. She asked after mine, which had burned at the same time.

On this Valentine's Day morning, we stretched lazily on her bed, alongside the wide window which overlooked Hout Bay. The sea reflected the cobalt blue of the February sky, and the Atlantic waves were rolling at the foot of Chapman's Peak.

We were eating breakfast, coffee just as good as in Italy and croissants just as good as in France, when she handed me a parcel. It was a big chocolate heart wrapped in red paper. Valentine's Day! I let her believe that Valentine's Day is an English tradition, not a French one, because I had simply forgotten about it . . .

With the heart came a card. It showed two cats tenderly embracing, and inside, in her peculiar handwriting, it said, 'To Bernard from Debbie, do you want to be my Valentine?'

Our meeting had been a series of lucky chances. I had stayed two nights in Camp Bay's youth hostel, an old hunting pavilion whose windows looked out on one of the many fabulous bays in the peninsula and which was always lit by gorgeous sunsets. I had decided on the Sunday to push my worthy steed to the end of the land, the Cape of Good Hope itself, 12 miles further. I wanted to take a snapshot of Rosinante, under which I could write: 'Here ended Rosinante's trans-African road. On this rock, she couldn't avoid it any more: she had to learn to swim, if she wanted to continue her round-the-world project'.

And then it rained. I took shelter under a pine tree to prepare coffee. A Mercedes stopped and the driver asked if it was me whose arrival at the tip of Africa had been reported in the *Argus,* the local daily newspaper. I said yes and he gave me his address and telephone number in case I needed anything. It was the twelfth address in Cape Town that I had collected in this way. No other town had been so hospitable.

I was still under my pine tree when another car stopped, for the same reason, and this time I accepted the offer instantly. For the car was a small Fiat *bakkie* driven by two adorable blonde women, mother and daughter looking like two sisters. Their house, they said, was on the Wynberg road, and I was welcome for tea. It wasn't on the Cape of Good Hope road but their house was called Spes Bona, Latin for 'Good Hope'. The two women would have made my day just with their company, but they also had tea and crusty cakes to make me forget the rain.

When I left I decided to continue on the Wynberg road to stay at the Muizenberg Youth Hostel, which meant a pass to climb called Constantia Nek. At the top, coloured people were selling grapes. They called me and gave me several clusters for free. They had recognized me from the *Argus*. They had this very peculiar smile, quite frightening, as they had pulled out their front teeth. It seems to be the 'tribal scar' of the coloured people in the Cape Province. But they showed so much interest and were so kind to me that I stayed a long while at the top of Constantia Nek. And later, Debbie told me that we owed our meeting to these coloured hawkers, because she had passed by and seen me. She couldn't stop, though, as she was in a hurry. When she passed a second time in her beetle car, I was still there, and she stopped. She came up to me while I was answering questions in a small crowd. She gave me her address in case I needed a good dinner. I noticed her beautiful legs under her short dress, her radiant smile and her peculiar writing: she wrote 'a' like the Greek α and 'e' like the Greek ε. I was already enchanted.

The evening I came 'for dinner', she was wearing a white dress slit to the thigh, something to feed my fantasies for a whole week. Two days later she invited me to a friend's house. She had another striking minidress and stayed so close to me that I stored up sensations enough to provide for months of solitude. And when she invited me to a French restaurant, her light blouse sported an inscription in Chinese. Never in my life had I been so interested in Chinese ideograms. And late that evening, she taught me Chinese on her wide bed which, at night, looked as though it was suspended over Hout Bay. It was also lit by the lighthouse on Chapman's Peak every ten seconds, just as though to give a rhythm . . .

On the wall in front of her bed she had souvenirs from Namibia: Bushmen's bows and arrows, regular-sized ones and miniature ones.

'These are for seducing women! Yes, during ritual dances, men must shoot their small arrows at the women they fancy. They have to aim at their buttocks. The arrows aren't sharp of course, and the woman shows her assent by shooting back!'

On the same wall were Zulu adornments too, because Debbie, although of English descent, was born in Natal. And because she got close to witch-doctors there, she did magic. It was her psychic power, she said, which held me long enough on Constantia Nek for her to return and meet me.

She was pretty good at Tarot cards, but also read my palm and referred to a big book she called *Tai Chin* . . . My Valentine was a witch and I loved it. Every time I woke up and felt her small tender body against mine, I felt good, I felt like a man, I mean like a human . . .

She had two black cats, one slept near the phone, the other between our legs. On Valentine's Day morning the telephone rang and the black cat didn't answer. It was one of the ship's officers Debbie shared the house with, the radio officer.

'Look through your window!' he said. 'Do you see the big white ship in the bay, no she's not the Bey of Tunis yacht, she is mine! And I'm calling you from there . . . We had to take on board some scientists for our mission to Antarctica, and they're so precious that we wanted to save them the trouble of driving to town, we'll just send a launch to their house. And I couldn't resist the pleasure of waking you up, you lazy Valentine!'

The next day, I arrived with a bouquet of red roses. I put it on her bed with my souvenir card, the one with Rosinante's motto on, and it said, 'OK, I'll be your Valentine, when do I continue, tonight?'

In the mornings she went to work and I went to the yacht club in search of a captain sailing for South America who would be prepared to take me along as a hand. I was not willing to pay 900 rands to fly, and Rosinante was not yet very good at breast-stroke. In the afternoons, she took me to the summit of Table Mountain to eat wild figs or to Wreck Beach to walk on strange jellyfish she called 'bluebottles'. They were inflated with air and burst with a funny noise. On Sundays, she took me to Fransch Hoek (the 'French Corner') to make love on the bank of a lonely stream, or to Seal Island to take photos of her.

Oh yes, this happiness was worth hundreds of deserts, thousands of punctures, years of solitude. But sometimes I became depressed and I would tell her, 'It is too good, I'll have to pay for it some day!'

She would answer, 'No, you've already paid for it, now I am your reward!'

One Sunday the cards were bad for me. I didn't believe them, everything was so good: I had just found an Australian captain who would take me to Brazil. I had to pay 12 dollars a day for my food but the one-month cruise across the southern Atlantic still cost much less than an uninteresting seven-hour flight. I sent my passport to the Brazilian Embassy in Pretoria, along with a letter from the captain. Everything was fine . . .

Except for the Devil Card, the Death Card and the Bad Luck card . . .

Morocco: Rosinante gets accustomed to the desert, 1981.

Egypt: Rosinante visits Gizeh; note the flag flying on the aerial, 1981.

Only the Jack of Diamonds showed hope.

On Monday bad news began to come in. First from the bank, where I had saved my paper-hanging money: I was not allowed, they said, to convert my rands into American dollars. And any South Africans who agreed to do it for me would be asked to show their passport and plane ticket. That was the Devil Card.

French expatriates working on the Koeberg nuclear plant were willing to help me. They had invited me to give a lecture at their primary school and the teacher gave me a cheque for 8500 convertible francs in exchange for my 1400 rands in cash. But their South African bank needed three weeks in order to be able to give me the corresponding sum in . . . rands. That was the Bad Luck card.

In the meantime the French Consulate, the only one so far which had received me with any enthusiasm and which was now helping me to get a Brazilian visa, telephoned with more bad news. Because I was not resident in South Africa, the Brazilian Embassy had to send my file to Brasilia! The first telex would cost *me* about 30 dollars and the visa would not be back before the boat left. This was the Death Card, and I cancelled the visa application. Holding back my tears, I returned for the last time to the Royal Cape Yacht Club to tell the Australian Captain. Adieu cruise and Brazil!

I had another address to try, a friend of the French school teacher: a travel agent who had a brilliant idea. He would sell me a ticket to Argentina at a 25% reduction. First because, after checking in his books, he discovered that French people entering Argentina did not need visas, and secondly because he would pretend that I was a sailor joining his ship in Buenos Aires. South African law would then entitle me to the discount. . . . The travel agent even managed to find, in one of his reference books, the name of a real cargo ship that I was supposed to join. That would be 675 rands instead of 900, and would mean less to change into dollars.

'But then,' he said, 'there's a problem. A sailor coming aboard with a bicycle would look strange. You had better hide it; what about a big box?'

So poor Rosinante had to sweat and lose her excess fat to fit into the box and fall within the weight allowance. And I still had 700 rands to sell. Happily the Jack of Diamonds entered the scene at this very moment.

He was riding a bicycle loaded with two enormous panniers made out of Tanzanian maize sacks sewn together and fitted with zips. The bicycle also had a 'bow'. It was a witch-doctor's rod pointing forward from the front rack and decorated with small African flags. All African except the first, a white cross on a red background. He had left a message for me at the Consulate: 'Would you like a chat? I arrived last Thursday and I am staying in Retreat with the secretary of the Bike Power Association. She told me you were in Cape Town. I thought you were in India! . . . Gernod.'

Having missed him in Ujiji, I had given up hope of seeing him again. I had heard about him in Zambia but since then, no news. And here we met up again just before leaving Africa. He was flying back to Denmark, it was all over for him and that was my opportunity. He had changed his remaining dollars, quite a lot of them. And because he had conscientiously kept the receipts, he was allowed to change 300 rands back into dollars.

The remaining rands were sold to several other Capetonian friends and Debbie drove us, Rosinante in the boot, on 27 February, to the airport. I could not pass through immigration: Argentina had just changed its laws and in retaliation for French restrictions on immigration, now required a visa. The Tarot cards hadn't predicted this one . . .

Debbie was glad to keep me another week, time enough to get the visa from the appropriate Consulate, fortunately in Cape Town itself. That very week there was an 'African Concert' in town with Steve Kekana and J. Clegg, the 'white Zulu', and it would have been a pity to miss that.

These women have walked 12 miles to get their water.

The major road of North Sudan.

Sandals made out of tyres.

The tyres are tied up to stop the tubes getting out.

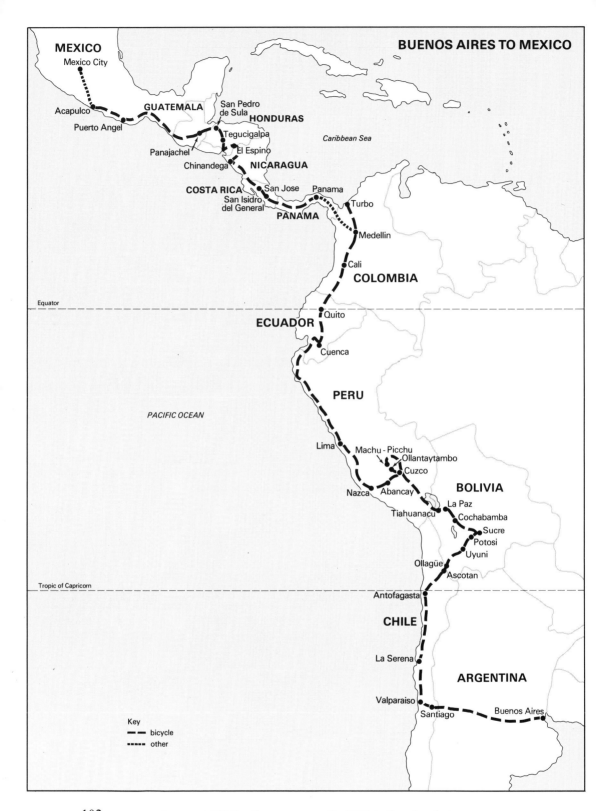

BUENOS AIRES TO MEXICO

MEXICO
Mexico City
Acapulco
Puerto Angel
GUATEMALA
San Pedro de Sula
HONDURAS
Tegucigalpa
El Espino
Panajachel
Chinandega
NICARAGUA
COSTA RICA
San Jose
Panama
San Isidro del General
PANAMA
Turbo
Medellin
Cali
COLOMBIA
Caribbean Sea

Equator

Quito
ECUADOR
Cuenca
PERU
PACIFIC OCEAN
Lima
Machu - Picchu
Ollantaytambo
Cuzco
Nazca
Abancay
BOLIVIA
La Paz
Tiahuanacu
Cochabamba
Sucre
Potosi
Uyuni
Ollagüe
Ascotan

Tropic of Capricorn

Antofagasta
CHILE
La Serena
ARGENTINA
Valparaiso
Santiago
Buenos Aires

Key
— — bicycle
····· other

(see page 151 for the map across the USA to Los Angeles)

Part Two:
Buenos Aires to Los Angeles

On the Uyuni salt flat bicycle track, 1983.

Facing page: Riding in Ollantaytambo, Peru, 1983 (photo: R. Puill).

Peru: Riding over 12,000ft of altitude (photo: R. Puill).

Chile: 'You will Freeze, Señor!'

In Valparaiso, Chile, Rosinante introduced me to the Pacific Ocean: nothing but water, rather dirty, with unspectacular waves, nothing but an ordinary sand beach, without a single nymph, in this the tail end of summer. Nothing but a flat horizon, congested with grey clouds. If I had been brought here blindfold, I would have said, 'What? This is the Pacific Ocean? Come on! You're making fun of me!'

But I was sure, it was even written on my map, it was spelled out PA-CI-FIC O-CEAN!

And it had taken me almost thirty years to reach it. The Pacific Ocean, it was something on my planisphere-lamp, a dream name which went with Tahitians and Antipodes, an inaccessible thing, on the other side of Japan or California, and now it was here, at my feet, ten yards from Rosinante. I wanted to take a picture of it, put it in my pocket, take it away and show it to my friends: 'Look, this is the Pacific Ocean and I saw it. I went there, and it was *there!* I went there on a bicycle, after a two-year trip, and it had waited for me!'

The ocean and the desert and the mountains. Chile is a corridor: going north you cannot lose yourself, just keep the ocean on your left and the mountains on your right, and you'll cross the driest desert on earth.

It really begins after La Serena, capital of the Fourth Region. 'The desert that flourishes', say the tourist pamphlets, because as soon as it rains, seeds which have been waiting for so long hurry to grow, bloom, and produce new seeds, because it might be their only opportunity in a century . . .

From now on, I would sleep all my nights under the unveiled stars, between rocks at the bottoms of river beds formed in the Tertiary era, facing the Southern Cross, twenty yards, no more, from the Via Panamerica, where long vans cruised imperturbably . . .

Desert doesn't smell. Or it smells of rotten corpses, but that is rare. So when a car or a lorry passed me, I was sensitive to the faintest odour which escaped from it. Sometimes a complete world engulfed me for five seconds.

Apart from the smell of warm gum and exhaust fumes, there was always tobacco and the indescribable smell of somebody's home. With the long distance buses which crossed the desert so fast, it was the smell of a public place, an atmosphere of a café, with the coffee, the wine and the warm bread. Smells, and noises, too. I could almost hear them, over a background noise of stirring spoons, whistling percolators and clinking billiard balls, possibly talking about having seen me.

'Un turista, en bicicleta, si! Pura bicicleta, que sacrificio! Mira, el tiene un turban, como un arabe! (A tourist, on a bicycle, yes, a push bicycle, it must be difficult! Look, he wears a turban, like an arab!)'

And I would let myself be carried away, far from the desert: if a lorry full of sheep passed, I was transported to Provence; a lorry full of grapes and my back ached from the picking; a lorry full of oranges and it was Christmas.

In this desert, where the going was easy (the road was tarred), I had to fight the kilometre-posts. There were thousands of them, and I had to reduce their numbers and show no mercy. One by one (half by half sometimes, when the wind was against me), with tightened jaw and closing my eyes under the sweat; or in rows of ten, as though I had a machine gun when the wind was on my side. I would mow them down in dozens, singing in the silence of their death.

Whether killing the kilometre-posts one by one or slaughtering one company after another, every night I lined up their corpses, in black figures in my diary, by the light of my camp fire, adding them to the vanquished battalions of the previous days. And slowly the monotonous never-ending desert began to come to an end . . .

'You're not forgetting, I hope, that you're going to have to cross the *Cordillera* in the middle of winter,' the mining engineer was lecturing me. He pronounced *cordillera* as if each letter was a capital. He seemed convinced that I was running into trouble, but didn't dare call me insane.

'Oh, it's only autumn,' his wife corrected him.

'Yes, that means the beginning of winter. You see, every year we have to go into the high sierras between here and Bolivia to rescue people like you, who've lost their way or whose engine has broken down.'

I remarked that I was safe from the last problem at least and said that I would always keep the railway in sight to avoid getting lost. It seemed to reassure him for a while. I must admit he couldn't have been confident of my mental health when he found me. I had prepared my camp on the terrace of an abandoned house here in Chuquicamata, the world's highest

Peru: On the north coast I needed my mosquito net every night, 1983.

Fire transforms old buns into croissants; note the collapsible lid on the mug, 1983.

Peru: The front rim didn't stand up to the unpuncturable tube.

Peru: The endless desert on the north coast north of Lima, 1983.

Ecuador: The Nescafé box was the price requested by the model.

Colombia: In Medellin's café (photo: R. Puill).

open pit mine, at 9000 feet. I had left the Panamericana two days before, after staying a couple of days in Antofagasta near the Tropic of Capricorn. I was tired of the desert, I was heading for the Andes.

The engineer was convinced that sleeping outside at that altitude meant freezing to death. I was not; I had prepared enough wood to keep a fire going from the first frost to the first rays of the sun. But the engineer, who only believed in the heat of his electric radiators, took me home and now he was worried. To let me leave for the high desert, without a radiator or an engine, troubled his conscience.

I didn't sleep well, it was too hot and I was accustomed by then to sleeping in the cold outside, but I was a good guest at the formidable breakfast the engineer's wife had cooked for me. It looked like a British breakfast, except for the typically Chilean avocado butter . . .

The tar stopped in the town and the engineer had to show me the start of the dirt road. It was on the other side of the mine and in the early morning I had to mingle with its monstrous lorries and excavators. The road followed a pipeline but was very sandy, and I only managed to cover 30 miles, enough though to reach a military post. Its Lieutenant, delighted at such a diversion, invited me to his table and had his men serve us. I tried not to disappoint him and chatted all evening about football and the Foreign Legion. The Lieutenant dreamed of joining it and, to prepare himself, he wanted to know the *Marseillaise* by heart. I taught it to him.

The next day, the storm-force wind prevented me even walking: leaning against Rosinante, I lost my balance and found myself under my mount every time the wind dropped or there was a stronger gust than usual. So I had plenty of time to stare at the landscape, one of the most striking I had ever seen.

At the foot of San Pedro volcano, a kind of glacial valley was blocked by a lava flow. Right in the middle, there was a secondary volcano mouth, so perfectly conical, monochromatic and smooth that it looked like a model. The railway and the dirt road skirted around it, each on a different side. As far as I could see, it contained no humans or even animals. And at dusk, I was still twenty miles away from the next *estacion* indicated on my map by a simple name: Ascotan. I decided to continue in the dark.

Around 8 pm, in the pitch black, a car passed me. It was a Land-Rover and I could read the word *Carabineros* on its side. It didn't stop at first but after a hundred yards it turned back, as if as an afterthought. ('Did you see what I saw? Mirages don't happen at night so it has to be a cyclist!') One policeman got out.

'*Buenas noches señor, a donde va?*' (Good evening Sir, where are you going?)'

'*A Bolivia, pero en Ascotan primero.*'

110

'Diga me, no es Chileno usted? ('Tell me, you aren't Chilean, are you?)'

The fact that I was European seemed to pacify the carabineros. Such a crazy thing would be suspicious in a local, but not in a tourist. They took great care however to frighten me, saying that it was going to be very cold in a moment. And since they were from Ascotan, they offered me a lift. *'Sin que,'* they concluded, *'le va congelar, señor!* (Otherwise you'll freeze, Sir.)'

I politely declined but I kept my eyes on their lights for a long time until they disappeared.

Around 9 pm, I had already put on every piece of clothing I owned. I was glad I was walking as it kept my feet warm. Around 10 pm I decided to make some more strong coffee to keep me awake, but I could not open my bottles, the water had frozen. I had to content myself with dry fig-and-nut cakes I had stocked up with in Antofagasta. And while chewing it I had to dance on the road because when I sat down, I could feel the black deadly cold creeping from the ground along my spine.

Around 11 pm, past a bend, the side of the road suddenly looked unusually white. Puzzled, I poked it with my bare hand. It was more than two years since I had touched it but I recognized it instantly: snow. It chilled me. I felt very tired and wondered if it would really be risky to sleep beside the road, with my nylon sleeping bag and my space blanket. And then I remembered the *carabineros;* they were probably waiting for me, keeping a jug of coffee on the stove, ready. It warmed me to think of it, so I carried on.

I was half asleep when, around 2 am, the *carabineros'* Land-Rover blinded me again with its lights. Poor *carabineros,* I thought, they have come back to check if I'm still alive!

'Faltan solamente quatro kilometros hasta la estacion! Carga la bicicleta, vamos ayundar le . . . (There are only four kilometres left to the station, load your bike, we're going to help you.)'

Only four kilometres! I couldn't give up now! So I declined their invitation again. But when I finally reached the barracks, the *carabineros* were asleep and I was welcomed only by angry dogs. Trowel in hand, I had to retreat into the first hut in sight and stay there, shivering under my space blanket, unable to sleep, until daybreak.

By the open door, I could read a large signpost which said in tall white letters: *PASO DE ASCOTAN: 3976 metros sobre el nivel del mar* (Ascotan Pass, 13,045 feet above sea level).

Which meant that I had walked through the night to take refuge at the highest point, and thus the coldest, on my route!

On the other side of the Ascotan pass, there was another awesome

Above: Rosinante on the Mississippi river, March 1985.

Far left: Françoise on Réjean's side-by-side tandem, August 1985.

Left: The beer cap collection on Rosinante's mudguard is building up nicely in Georgia, USA.

landscape. A sea of salt, a dead sea, the *Salar de Ascotan,* very quiet, white, ochre or yellow between the black lava rocks.

Imagine a lake whose waves have congealed, and whose foam is drawing motionless circles from the centre of the banks: icy white in the middle and then ochre, yellow and finally iron red on the sandless beaches.

That day I didn't leave the trail, not by an inch, not even for lunch: signposts forbade it, indicating that the whole area was mined; probably since the Pacific War, at the turn of the century, which saw Chile easily defeat Peru and Bolivia. The *Salar* was nonetheless gorgeous and on the flat salt crust I could reach fantastic speeds—until, unfortunately, the west wind returned and prevented me from reaching Ollagüe before nightfall.

Bolivia: Rosinante is almost Rejected

'Here in Chile, mayors are appointed by the Government. I am therefore a personal employee of Pinochet,' said the Mayor of Ollagüe without showing whether he liked this arrangement or not. 'Listen to what I have written: *Señor Gustavo Diaz Guzmann, Te pidio una favor personal: da alojamiento esta noche a este viajante frances en tu escuela. Mañana sigue su viaje hasta Bolivia. Ernesto Moalla, Alcade de Ollagüe*. With this letter you should get a warm bed. Enjoy it while you are still in a civilized country.'

He was speaking French, so I had to make no effort to understand. And it was so hot in his kitchen, where his wife presented me with tea and cakes, it was such a nice respite after the fight against the freezing wind, that I had to tell myself 'Don't fall asleep, don't! You're not in a bed yet, even if it feels better than last night's bed.'

The 36 hours without sleep made my eyelids heavy, but I still had to wait for the Alcade's lesson. He was about the same age as me and over his desk had a framed degree in geography.

'You see this map,' he said, 'you're here, past the two small salt lakes, the Ascotan and the Ollagüe. Next will be the *Salar* of Uyuni. And compared with it, the two first ones are just ponds!'

Only once had a border been so obvious, and that was between Zambia and Zimbabwe. Here, on the edge of the *Salar de Uyuni,* the Chilean dirt road stopped abruptly and nothing except lorry tracks continued into Bolivia.

It was 9 am, and I had no problem getting out of Chile: the customs officer was behind his desk in the overheated office. But on the Bolivian side the office was empty, dusty and cold. The altitude was still about 12,000 feet. I found the living quarters at the back—shabby cabins which were not heated either, as far as I could judge when somebody answered my calls. The official had only his uniform trousers on and obviously didn't appreciate being woken up. I apologized, saying that as a cyclist, I could not afford to lose time. He ordered me angrily to wait for him in the front office.

114

I had to wait a full hour. But it was a lucky delay: it allowed me to copy, by hand, the big road map stuck behind the dusty desk, in front of Simon Bolivar's portrait. This copy would enable me to cross the entire country without getting lost. No wonder, really, as most of the time I would be following the one dirt road, or else the one railway line. One of Bolivia's two capitals, Sucre, was the only capital in my round-the-world tour where all the roads leading to it were untarred.

Presently two Bolivian officials entered the office and asked me to stand up. I had a visa, obtained free, which was rare, in Santiago de Chile; I could not be smuggling drugs into a country which exports them, so did not see why the formalities should last long. The two officials did.

'*Donde está la placa de tu bicicleta? De que marca es?* (Where is your bicycle number plate? What make is it?)'

And without waiting for my explanation (Rosinante is Rosinante, and doesn't care to be branded!) they began the search. And soon they found number plates. Yes, two Chilean car plates. In Chile, you buy one per year, and it carries the name of your province. Nice souvenirs. Confiscated!

When I insisted on keeping them, the two officials got cross, then became quite happy: the watchdogs had found a bone to chew on. They had to report me to their officer, they said, the case was serious: 'attempting to import official foreign documents'. Their officer was a young lieutenant. He was still in bed with his girlfriend. He invited me to enter and left his subordinates outside. What a lieutenant! Caucasian, moustached, elegant and well mannered, he had nothing in common with his men. They were short Indians with very dark skins and thick hair. He had a superior air when speaking to them and his *Castillano*[1] sounded much better than theirs. I was amazed at such a difference and my preference went to the Chilean army. In the past three days before, two private soldiers had sat down next to their officer to listen to my stories. They could have been brothers, spoke the same language and the difference in rank didn't seem to matter off duty. Here, they wouldn't urinate against the same wall!

Handing my passport back but keeping the number plates, the Bolivian Lieutenant said that, if I didn't get lost in the *salar,* I might meet *un padre francés* in the village of San Juan. A missionary? As in Africa I succumbed to a primitive affinity for fellow men who resembled me and hurried on the salt lake, in the direction of San Juan.

The salt shone just like snow. And to protect my eyes I had to squint. I was therefore developing the muscles of my cheekbones and I would probably soon have them as prominent as the locals! On the other hand, I had fortunately put shoes back on because of the cold, otherwise I would have tanned the soles of my feet . . .

115

There was still the problem of the left side of my moustache: since Santiago I had had a west wind and it had succeeded in bending the left side of my moustache so that I could not eat without chewing it. To prevent that I had had to attach it by a string to the spoke-nipple earring which I wore in my left ear.

And now I was worried: was he going to recognize his fellow man, this missionary, if I came to him with prominent cheekbones and the left side of my moustache attached to the spoke in my left ear lobe?

Instead of the bearded old missionary I was expecting, there were young female Belgian nurses and they did recognize me. They let me stay there, fed me and got my money changed. I should do it now, they said, before the sale of Bolivia's annual crop of coca. Because then the dollar rate would fall.

And to get out of the *salar,* I had to stick to the railway line, which wasn't as easy as in the Sudan. Bridges were tricky: I had to keep Rosinante balanced on the rail while I jumped from one sleeper to another. This required a lot of concentration and once in the middle of a bridge, deeply absorbed in my task, I was brutally shaken out of my concentration by a blaring horn. Coming against the wind so that I hadn't heard it before, a train was about to cross the same bridge, and there wasn't room for both of us . . .

I panicked, Rosinante fell between two sleepers and got stuck there. I hesitated between jumping or trying to save Rosinante first. But then I realized that the train wasn't moving any more. It had stopped at the edge of the bridge. In Bolivia, I was to learn that trains are often one or two days late, so this one could afford to stop and let me get myself out of trouble. The driver was smiling as if he had played a good trick on me . . .

Potosi was thus one of the few towns that I arrived at by rail! I had just been passed by a tank wagon bringing precious water to the drought-stricken town. And if the railway station was crowded on my arrival, it was because of the tank wagon. Women were queueing up to get water. What irony when *potosi* means a 'mountain of riches' in Spanish! Potosi was once the major town of Spanish South America, because of its silver mines.

Now the silver is finished and the mines are extracting tin. I got a hotel room for the equivalent of one dollar and next door I went to the movies for ten cents. Now I was ready to spend at least 25 cents for a meal. I chose the Sumack Orko.

This was the restaurant recommended by my French guidebook and I hoped to meet some of my compatriots there. I was a bit early and I found I was the only customer. So, while waiting for the *quenoa* soup, I chatted with the waitress. As soon as I mentioned Rosinante, she exclaimed:

116

'*Uno mas! Ayer ya dos franceses in bicicleta estaban aqui!* (One more! Two French cyclists dined here yesterday!)'

'Two French cyclists? With their bicycles, here in Potosi?'

'Yes, a couple, him with dark hair and a beard. The wife blond and blue-eyed.'

I was instantly reminded of Raymond and Charlotte and while the waitress promised to tell them where I was if they came back, memories flowed back: first Charlotte telling on South African radio how in Malawi she was first told to wear a dress. But as on a man's bicycle it was more revealing than trousers, she had obliged by wearing trousers under her skirt. 'And I was hot, and I was hot', I could still hear Charlotte say with her delicious French accent.

I had met them in Pretoria. They were from Brittany and had cycled down Africa, beginning at the Algerian Sahara. They had reached Johannesburg on the very day I was leaving it. On the day before, I had read an article about two other French cyclists also heading for Cape Town. And on my way through Natal, Transkeï and the southern Cape Province, I kept finding articles about these two, Yves and François, preceding me by two or three days, no more. And invariably people mistook me for one of them and said:

'Don't tell me, I read about you in the newspapers, but tell me, where's your buddy?'

If I knew about them, they didn't know about me and took a week off to rest in the Karoo, so I arrived first in Cape Town and I remember a TV journalist on the phone saying, 'Oh yes, you interest me, a French cyclist coming into town after having cycled through the whole of Africa, that doesn't happen every day.'

Not every day indeed, but every other day as the other four rode into Cape Town in the following week. And the journalist cancelled his interview . . .

As I stayed two months in Cape Town, I lost contact with the others, who wanted at all costs to be in Rio de Janeiro for the Carnival. Raymond and Charlotte were planning to go to Tierra del Fuego first, Yves and François to visit Brazil. So I had no hope of meeting up with them. And certainly not here, in the Sumack Orko, Potosi, Bolivia. If they came back . . .

The next morning I visited nearly all the *alojamientos* in Potosi: no French cyclists. In the afternoon, I visited the tin mines. This was the tourists' duty in Potosi: I befriended a couple of Australians for whom I translated the guide's commentary. And they saw my emotion when at the end of the visit I found Raymond's name in the visitors' book. I told them the story and they said yes, in their hotel, there were two French cyclists.

We all celebrated at the Sumack Orko and vowed not to lose contact again. But instead of cycling together we preferred to stay completely independent and meet up only at major stops.

We therefore stayed in the same *alojamiento* in La Paz, three weeks later. From there the major tourist requirement was the excursion to Chacaltaya, the highest ski resort in the world, at 18,400 feet. It was a ski resort with hardly any snow in winter because their winter was the dry season. As Charlotte wasn't keen on this kind of trip, I took her bicycle. Like Raymond's bike, it was a custom-made machine, with 15 gears, and a bottom bracket of 28 x 28, enough to climb trees! Rosinante had 48 teeth on her only chain wheel, and that meant I had to walk up most of the passes. Until then I had pretended it was necessary, 'to rest my bottom, warm up my feet and facilitate my digestion'. And it didn't shock the locals: when we came into town, we had to climb a 25% gradient. Like everyone else, I stopped and pushed my bike. Raymond and Charlotte geared down and pedalled up. The whole street froze. And I burst out laughing at the surprised looks of the onlookers: in a country where only men rode bicycles, the sight of Charlotte, pedalling a loaded bicycle up a gradient difficult even for cars, looked like magic.

And now on Charlotte's bicycle I discovered that I was losing a lot of time with Rosinante. She was splendid, Rosinante, very good at swinging her hips, rolling her rump, in short attracting attention. But speak of efficient work and she is gone!

With Charlotte's bicycle I discovered that it was quite easy to cycle up 6000 feet of dirt, mud and snow road. With the lack of oxygen I even felt quite exhilarated. While other tourists suffered from *soroche,* altitude sickness, and had to drink an infusion of coca leaves, I experienced such elation that I climbed barefoot up the last 900 feet to the top.

A journalist was there, and asked us to visit him. Two days later the three of us were smiling in *El Diario*. Rosinante was in front, still trim and fresh looking, still spectacular, but in my heart almost rejected for the comfort and ease of the 28 x 28 . . .

[1]*Castillano:* The Spanish of Castile spoken in South America.

Peru: Machu Picchu—The Magical Village

'Oooooooooooooooooiiiiiii,' the child shouted at the tourist bus.

'*Qué quieres decir?* (What do you mean?),' I asked.

'*Significa hasta luego en Inglès* (Means good-bye in English),' he explained with a contemptuous look before he disappeared down a hidden trail to cut through the bush and meet the same bus at the next hairpin bend, 50 yards down the slope.

'Gooooooooooood Byyyyyyyyyyyyyyyyyyye,' he shouted again before another jump into the bush, another bend, and so on until he reached the foot of the mountain, as swift as a goat, lightfooted in his tyre-sandals.

The tourist route to Machu Picchu climbed a quarter-mile high semi-cliff in thirteen tight hairpins. The *treno de los turistas* arrived from Cuzco at 11 am and a string of buses carried everybody up. From 3 pm it went the other way round. Accordingly, the visitors who paid the highest price (24,000 soles, about £12) had only between 3 and 4 hours to visit the Sacred City. On the other hand, they did enjoy this affectionate good-bye. For each tourist bus had its young Peruvian jumping from hairpin to hairpin and of course waiting for a tip at the railway station.

This kid had shown his shortcut to me, and I tried to keep up with him; not to say good-bye to tourists—at least not to all tourists. I wanted to kiss only one of them good-bye, Vanda, my Brazilian *coup de foudre*. My feet were burning in their tyre sandals but I was determined to run after the train if necessary, to get another kiss from Vanda . . .

It was in Tiahuanacu, on Lake Titicaca, that I found myself in Egypt again. I mean that I found myself again the object of the frenzied tourist trade. Lake Titicaca and the Peruvian plateau toward Cuzco and Machu Picchu offer as much in the way of historical ruins and tourist entertainment as the Nile Valley. In Tiahuanacu, just after La Paz on Rosinante's itinerary, are the most imposing ruins of the Aymara civilization—which preceded the Inca settlement by almost a thousand

119

years. And it was in Tiahuanacu that I was again called 'mistair' as if all palefaces were born between the English Channel and Hadrian's Wall. It was in Tiahuanacu that I was again taken for a mug and a sucker ('Eh mistair, do you want authentic statues, collection coins?').

The archaeological site, when I arrived, was filled with Indians, who had entered free, but I had to pay. This was a commemorative day for the Aymara culture, I was told. The Secretary of State for Culture was here in person. He sported a Phrygian cap but, on top of a three-piece suit, it looked like a disguise. And why didn't he make his speech in Aymara? He would have been understood by everybody except a few tourists. It was probably because his secretary, European-looking down to her varnished fingernails and too clean to be mistaken for a tourist, would have been unable to take notes. No, definitely no, I thought, South Africa doesn't have a monopoly on *apartheid* . . .

As I didn't want to disturb the speech (all the Indians had turned toward me), I went to pay my tribute to the Gods of Tourism. I had to justify my ticket, so I went to see a 'Door of the Sun', a 'semi-underground temple' and a 'statue with folded arms'. Edifying!

When I came back, my duty done, everybody, Secretary of State to the fore, was beginning to parade back to the village two miles away, where they would probably get drunk to celebrate. As I was going there too, I joined them, and soon found myself parading, mounted on Rosinante, behind the *charengo*[1] players. They were wearing their traditional ponchos on top of warm anoraks. And before them a terrific guy was dancing like a condor. At least like the condor I saw in the Cochabamba zoo. His aquiline profile added to the resemblance, as did his long bony arms. He was wearing a dark European suit and a kind of local trilby, but he was the most authentic of them all.

Behind me the *zahampona*[2] players came, all clad in ocelot fur. But when I say 'behind me', I should say 'behind my admirers'. Rosinante and her beer-cap collection, my multicoloured cycling trousers, my red hair, and my brocaded panniers were much more appealing to the locals than the elements of a culture which made up their daily life.

When we reached the village, the Secretary of State stood and applauded me as I arrived. Enjoying the game, I waved reflecting that I could probably be as good a Secretary of State as this one . . .

In Cuzco, I met up with Raymond and Charlotte and we decided to try to get to Machu-Picchu by bike. Officially it was impossible as the only way to the foot of the cliff was the railway. But Rosinante taught the two bicycles from Brittany how to ride a rail and after two days of drama (high bridges, tunnels, frequent trains), we reached Aguacalientes. From there, I walked back a few miles to join the Inca Trail just before it reaches Machu-Picchu by the Inti Punku, supposed to be the best place to discover the Sacred City. I went before dawn, before the tourists arrived. Another advantage was that I missed all the ticket offices and therefore was able to enter Machu-Picchu free.

On my way down *Huayna Picchu*,[3] which dominates its elder brother, around noon, I met Vanda. She was resting on a rock and asked in English if the top was still far. I began to reply that it would be a pity for two Latin people to speak an Anglo-Saxon language. I thought she was Chilean or Argentinian. Her eyes were the black of dreaming nights, the black of the labyrinths in which one gets lost, the black where the fires of Hell are lit . . .

But when she spoke Spanish with a nasal twang and gentle hisses I realized she was from Brazil. Was she still far from the summit? Good heavens yes!

'Then I will go down with you. Give me your hand!'

A little further down she picked a tiny flower and tried to insert it into the wallet I had hanging from my neck. I had to pull up my shirt, and she touched my chest. I shivered.

'Have you seen the prison quarter?'

She hadn't seen anything. She was visiting without any plan, without any previous knowledge. I had both. So I could set out on a cultured courtship.

'May I be your personal guide?'

'I would be delighted, but first we must take a photo!'

She asked another tourist to take the snapshot and with the freedom this simple act always seems to give, we embraced each other in front of the lens, extremely close together even though we had met only ten minutes before and each spoke Spanish with a different accent.

'I am a mason you know, a specialist in carved stone, look at the main entrance door as it . . .'

'You want a sweet?'

'Thank you, it's good, look at these stones, this is what we call a Greek Apparel.'

'What? I can't understand you, put the sweet under your tongue!'

'How do I do that? Show me how you do it!'

And she laughed as she spoke, with warmth and frankness, in the same way as she called out to people she didn't know. I was lecturing her about the stones, while her replies were on totally different subjects but it didn't matter, the important thing was to talk to each other, smile at each other, look at each other, and sometimes, touch each other.

'In the history of masonry, one can notice a surprising evolution in the basic material: always from the biggest to the smallest. From the menhir and the obelisk to the brick and finally to the tiny components of concrete, down through the huge Egyptian or Inca blocks and the Romans' rubble stones. One can even notice nowadays an inversion of this tendency, as if the mason, finding nothing smaller than the grain of sand, felt the need to go further, even it it meant backward. Thus he has created the Siporex to make rubble stones bigger and bigger, thus he has created constrained concrete and already he is building again with monoliths.'

But Vanda had requisitioned one of her compatriots to take another photo of us, lying side by side, hand in hand on the funeral stone which looked like a ship, in the Observatory.

'When you know this rule of masonry, you can classify the masonry of each civilization according to the size of its basic material. Thus Tiahuanacu and its fencing wall straightened by monolithic poles is more primitive, for the mason, than Machu-Picchu. And the mason, while admiring the amount of work needed to adjust the incredible "twelve-angle" stone in Hatu Rumiyoc street in Cuzco, never forgets that Roman masons were building semicircular vaults where Incas, two thousand years later, could only place monolithic lintels.'

'Look,' answered Vanda, 'Machu-Picchu is magic! Do you remember, down from the prison quarter it looked grey and now from here, it is green!'

She was so excited that I was reluctant to destroy her illusion by explaining that as Machu-Picchu was built on terraces, from the low levels only the retaining walls were visible from below, and they were stone grey, while from the top only the grass terraces were visible, hence the green.

Going down the 'fountain street', she took my hand again. I was dirty from the long day's walking, my feet were bleeding in my tyre sandals and the dirt made them as black as Vanda's boots.

'Aren't you embarrassed that everybody will stare at us because of my bare feet and my turban?'

'Why, is it not the custom in your country, to go barefoot and to wear a turban?'

I desired her more and more, but she soon had to leave by the tourist train. She gave me her address at the last site of interest.

This was something we couldn't miss, the *intihuatana,* the 'stone which catches the sun'. It was the altar in the Inca religion. This was the only surviving one because it had only been discovered this century. In other places, Catholic priests had destroyed them in order to convert the Indians more easily.

From the window of her bus, she blew me kisses. She even stood up to watch me through the window, and I ran down the hill behind the child who shouted good-bye at the bends.

122

When I reached the station, the train whistle was blowing, my feet were hurting and the shoulder strap of my bag was cutting my shoulder, but the fire on my lips was more urgent and could be extinguished only by her fresh mouth. I found her window, climbed up to it and reached for her.

We went for a friendly kiss first, one on the left cheek, one on the right cheek, our lips were hesitant; then the kiss on the mouth, and our lips forgot themselves. It lasted an eternity but, alas, it had to end; I don't know whether it was after a minute or after an hour. But I can remember very clearly the texture of her tongue, and her teeth, the inside of her upper lip, her sweet breath on my chin.

But the train was moving, I had to get off before the first tunnel. That was it, a single kiss for a whole lifetime, a single kiss for a unique meeting . . .

'The vicuna's wool is the finest in the world. It explains why there are so many poachers,' said the guard, handing us a tuft of hair. 'Isn't it beautiful?'

Oh yes it was beautiful! For two days we had been pedalling over 12,000 feet above sea level on this forlorn, windy, bare plateau, and every now and then we had seen vicunas in their winter fur: fawn coloured and short on top, long and beige under the torso and belly. It was a long time before we were able to see them in the distance. We usually spotted one silhouetted against the sky on a mountain crest, and then, examining the area around it, we could make out the whole pack.

Every morning we were woken by their cries. They sounded as if they were laughing, and were a happy start to the day.

'So', asked Charlotte, 'your job is to protect them?'

'Yes, there are three of us taking it in turns. The Germans taught us how to take care of the vicunas . . . and they're also financing the reserve.'

We were waiting for the water to boil. The guards had agreed to heat our water on their petrol stove. Between Pampamarca and Yauriviri, on the dirt road between Cuzco and Nazca, it was high desert, and there was not a twig to burn to heat our ritual coffee and tea.

'In the Sahara,' Raymond told us, 'I didn't feel alone when I had lit my wood fire. With the pieces of wood dropped by lorries, I kept myself entertained in the evenings, between the sand and the stars. A wood fire actually is much warmer than a Camping-Gaz stove or even a Primus. They both produce a cold blue flame while a wood fire displays a whole palette of reds and yellows . . . And it speaks, a wood fire, it cracks, it bursts, it whistles, it blows! It even dances, a surprising choreography and one can answer it, dance with it, by feeding it fuel and blowing on the embers . . .

'And a wood fire has to be created, to be born like a child: to inseminate the kindling with a spark is a pleasure but to deliver a healthy fire is no easy business. The wood may be wet. One may have to protect the newborn against sudden gusts of wind and above all, take care it does not starve.'

When I had met Raymond and Charlotte in Africa, they had told me that, at every stop along the road, they lit a fire, to boil water for their tea as well as for cooking their rice. This impressed me. At that time I was convinced that I would take hours to heat a pint of water and I was, in any case, well used to cold coffee. Encouraged by their example, however, I tried it at the top of my first Andean pass, between Argentina and Chile, to fight the cold. And I fed it, my first baby fire, with dried cow dung.

Eucalyptus fires became my favourites because they smelled good and produced the brightest light. So did the roots I dug on the Bolivian *altiplano*. When I was following the railway track there, I also built fires with splinters from the sleepers. It was the only available wood and it burned easily. But the tar it was soaked with gave a terrible taste to my coffee. Then, after Machu-Picchu, I invented something.

I took the bottoms from two tuna-fish tins—our staple food—and bolted them together so that they could cover my mug and still be collapsible. I christened my invention simply the 'collapsible lid' . . . Henceforth, I could make all sorts of fires: bright vine-shoot fires, spitting crate fires, sweet-smelling fir tree fires, bamboo fires to get started, maize-cob fires to last; I could use anything to heat my coffee. And after Raymond and Charlotte had joined me, we made up to four fires a day.

And it performs miracles, a wood fire, when it has grown. It is not ungrateful, it rewards you well. It transforms old buns into crispy croissants, it makes milk eternal and eggs unbreakable. It heats your coffee, makes maize flourish and it even . . . cooks your food!

'How do you go about extinguishing your fire?' Raymond asked once.
'I let it die out . . .'
'Yes? Because I always piss on it to complete the ceremony, and it is very efficient . . .'
'I would do the same,' added Charlotte, 'but I am afraid of burning myself . . .'

Charlotte, to me, looked as Norman as Raymond was Breton. Raymond had blue eyes but it took me months before I realized it. His other qualities were like his eyes, they were not obvious but nonetheless they were there, in great numbers. Charlotte had large blue eyes in which one could read instantly if she was happy or not. She was incapable of hypocrisy. It was a great pleasure to travel in their company.

And we were careful not to spoil it. I didn't want to make the same mistake I had made with Gernod, with too close a tie. With Raymond and Charlotte, I tried only to meet up with them at major stages, or as was often possible, for coffee breaks. And because they were so much faster than me, I left Cuzco one day before them. The game was to see how many days the Brittany Superbikes would need to catch up with Rosinante.

The third day, I had to walk up the Abra Saccallacasa. And because I wanted to play the game to the end, I let myself be caught by nightfall near the summit. I slept there, at more than 13,000 feet, in freezing rain, only protected by my nylon sleeping bag and a space blanket. My mistake, however, was to leave this fragile but efficient protection before sunrise. Even though the nights were very cold, it quickly warmed up under the tropical skies, as soon as the sun was shining. Because I did not wait, my hands were so cold that I couldn't feel the pain any more. I could feel nothing in either little finger and that scared me. I hastily looked for twigs and fuel. And the fire performed another miracle, not through its heat, but by the movements it forced me to make to try to light it . . .

My two companions caught up with me after a four-day chase, following the 'redhead's' trail by the remains of my fires.

And here we were, sharing tea and coffee with the vicuna guards. We thanked them and returned to our labour.

1. *Charengo:* Sort of banjo whose resonance chamber is made out of a tatu shell.
2. *Zahampona:* Reed panpipes.
3. *Huayna Picchu:* Young Mountain; *Machu Picchu:* Old Mountain.

Ecuador: 'Let us Struggle for Ourselves!'

At night I often had the same dream: I was back at home and friends were asking: 'How come you're here? Aren't you cycling around the world?' And, rather embarrassed, I had to explain that I had taken a holiday and that of course, I would be back on the road as soon as possible . . .

This dream I resolved to make real for Christmas 1983, in three months' time. Actually, I didn't have the money to reach the USA and work there as I had planned. So I was thinking instead of reaching French Guiana from Ecuador, by way of Amazon boats, along the Equator.

That was a dream too: first because I probably wouldn't be allowed into French Guiana considering the ridiculous amount of money I had left and secondly because from Quito, Ecuador's capital, one cannot leave the country through Amazonia. It would mean crossing a vast area occupied by Peru in 1942 but still claimed by Ecuador. So I had to find money here and now.

In this matter, Kevin was my model. When I met him in Ujiji he was earning money by writing articles for magazines and giving lectures with some slides he was carrying. So in Johannesburg, I asked my family to send me duplicates of the slides I had sent them for processing along the way. And I began to give slide shows on the spot, in Johannesburg, at two schools I had contacted through the *Alliance Française*. One was a French school, no problem, but the second was an Afrikaans school, and I had to translate my commentary, not into Afrikaans, but at least into English.

During my stay in Cape Town, this English commentary was often used and got better, but once in South America, unable to manage subtitles, I had to work on a dubbed version. I used it first in Santiago de Chile and the second time was to be in Quito. Again the *Alliance Française* agreed to support my plan and to announce it, it got my portrait published in the capital's six daily newspapers. For my part I got interviews on Radio Quito and on TV. The show brought in no more than 20 dollars, the entrance fee being only 50 cents, but I was then invited to spend a few days

126

with an Indian family, rich breeders and exporters of chickens.

In this family, everybody was proud to belong to the *indigenas*. The mother had visited the United States wearing her traditional Indian dress, while her husband went there to teach how to pluck chickens. They insisted on making me carry with me a good store of what the South American Indian, according to them, always uses when travelling: *raspadura y harina de cebada* (a brown sugar loaf and barley flour). What impressed me anyway was that they were the very first South American family to invite me to stay at their home, in all the seven months I had been travelling there.

The second day of my stay was their eldest son's birthday. Among the guests, I was surprised to see five American missionaries of the Gospel Church. The afternoon began like a summer camp. Everyone had a piece of paper clipped to his back and, by asking the others questions, he had to guess what was written on it. Afterwards the father distributed champagne and an enormous amount of chicken and potatoes . . .

There was even a small orchestra of musician friends. Among them was the mother's brother, a social worker in charge of rural development. Everybody spoke Spanish but he insisted on singing, at least, in Quechoa, the indigenous language. And he took me aside, making no effort to hide his dislike of the missionaries. He had developed a very interesting theory.

'Clearly for me, the developing countries' main problem is self-confidence. Each day in my work I am faced with *indigenas* who don't have the least confidence in themselves because they don't believe in their racial qualities and powers. I am sure that we won't get anywhere until we become proud of our culture, proud of our race, proud of our mother-tongue which isn't *Castillano* of course, proud of our physical attributes. Very important, the physical attributes: the hierarchy between races will last as long as the standard for a man with a capital M is the blond-haired, blue-eyed, 6-foot movie star.

'Imagine an *indigena* who admires John Wayne because he has been taught to admire John Wayne and who discovers every morning in his mirror that he is the exact opposite of John Wayne: short, dark skinned, black haired and black eyed. Do you know that to say 'the spice of the life', we, down here, say *'el norte de la vida* (the north of the life)!' Why? Simply because everybody knows that to the north there is Colombia, our big sister, and also Mexico, ah, that's a respectable country, Mexico! But mainly because it is next to the original heaven on earth—the United States of America. There, you understand, everybody looks like John Wayne!

'And it is obvious to me that all UN projects, Protestant missions, health aid, and all this well-orchestrated charity business only reinforces this image. At the start of the invasion, when whites were ruthless *conquistadores,* cynical adventurers and greedy priests, we had a chance, but now it's terrible: now the *gringos* are coming to help us, they are saints, they are supermen, there is no chance of us equalling them! I have heard of a Peruvian tribe where *indigenas* began to worship the UNICEF emblem. For them it was far superior to the Sun God or Jesus Christ because the blue flag with the golden laurels was parachuting in food tins. Really, my belief is that if you want to help us, you have to let us struggle for ourselves, even if we must die in the process, instead of providing jobs for your excess doctors, engineers and charity professionals. Let us struggle for ourselves!'

Twenty dollars and some chicken legs, it wouldn't last me long . . . But it was also in Quito that I met up with Raymond again. Alone.

After Machu Picchu we had got together in Lima, the end of the road for Charlotte. She had to go back to work in France, her sabbatical year was over. I had left Lima a week ahead of Raymond but again, Raymond's bicycle was more efficient than Rosinante. He told me that he was looking for a companion to cross the Darien Gap with. If I accepted, he would lend me enough money to keep me going to Central America . . .

The Darien Gap is the missing link which prevents the Panamerican Highway being *really* Panamerican. Its local name is just the opposite of the English one. *El Tapon del Darien,* the Darien cork! It consists of a deep swamp on the Colombian side, followed by a thick jungle on the Panamanian side. According to our information, it was possible to cross it on foot during the dry season. There was even a guidebook which told you precisely how. We had found it in a Quito English library. It was called *Backpacking in Central America.* The problem for us was to follow its advice backwards, from Colombia to Panama—it described the route in the opposite direction. It also told the story of a British military expedition which crossed the Darien Gap in 1972 with cars, but six of their men drowned! Obviously Raymond and I could not accept such a percentage loss!

We had also heard about three cyclists who had crossed it with their bikes attached on their backs. The story says that after the crossing two of them became monks because they believed they owed their lives only to a miracle.[1]

Raymond and I had survived the desert heat and mountain cold, why not too the jungle humidity. I accepted his crazy proposition (it would be right in the middle of the rainy season) and we agreed to meet again in Medellin, Colombia.

1. See Appendix viii.

Darien Gap: Two Bloody Trails on the Floor

'Last year, a team of students went there to study plants, three died in a single week. Cerebral malaria! They were taking only the regular Nivaquine and over there you need a special kind of quinine, made in Germany, have you got some?'

'Six months ago, a plane crashed there. The forest closed over the wreckage. The army searched for it, they found five other wrecks, but not the one they were looking for! I hope you have a good compass!'

As I hadn't got any special quinine or a compass and as all the information we had received since entering Colombia painted a very dark picture of the situation, I decided that, in case anyone found Rosinante's wreckage someday, I would have to start a diary.

Wednesday, 19 October, 1983
Arrival in Turbo, on the Caribbean Sea. This was our last South American stage. Theoretically we won't be able to mount our bikes again before Central America. The tar felt good, we came across it only 30 miles back after 200 miles of difficult muddy dirt road from Medellin. Last night we slept in a small school beside the road. On the blackboard there was a lesson about the French Revolution. The teacher treated us with a kindness we classified as African and which, added to the previous examples of solicitude in this country, undoubtedly makes Colombia the most hospitable country in South America . . .

At the entrance to the town, we were stopped twice for drinks. We had to taste the *claro,* a fresh maize beer. The whites all wore a kind of game bag which is traditional in Antioquia province and they were teasing a black man.

'If you've been to Africa,' they said, 'tell us if it's true they're all like him over there? Because we imported him from there—in a cage!'

In town, all the cheap hotels are *bordellos,* so we had to make it clear that we wanted to sleep. We were then given the price 'until tomorrow' instead of by the hour. We chose the Residencia Libia. The girls are shy and don't even offer their services. Rains have flooded the block but the Residencia is built on piles. If we had lines, we would probably be able to fish through the floor of our room. The only luxury is an electric fan which we set at full speed to clear the air of its sewer smells.

Thursday, 20 October

Raymond spent three minutes standing on the *chalupa's* deck, trying to piss. He couldn't. Anguish? Call it excitement or apprehension, I share it entirely. If I tried to piss, I'm sure I wouldn't be able to . . .

We didn't stay long with the Residencia ladies. Yesterday Raymond came back with very precise information. He had been trying to exchange a pair of velvet trousers for a pair of shoes. Of course, nobody wanted trousers like that in such a climate and he had to buy a pair of tennis shoes. But it enabled him to meet a Peruvian who had crossed the Darien four times for smuggling purposes. This smuggler drew a map which fits the *Backpacking* guide and complements it on several points. He even spoke of a French company working in Puerto America, at the start of the smuggling trail. Raymond even found a *chalupa* owner, ready to take us up the Atrato river all the way to Cacarica.

So this morning we went to change some dollars in a shop. The black market there was less advantageous than the official one, because there was no bank in Turbo . . . Afterwards we went to the police to get our exit stamps. There aren't any border posts in the jungle.

Our appointment was at 10 am at the maize weighing place and by noon we were inside the *chalupa,* with our bicycles and panniers, under the command of its silent captain, a black man with overgrown muscles. Only when we were out of port, did he tell us, pretending to have misunderstood, that he wasn't going all the way to Cacarica but only to Puerto America and that it would cost us another 200 pesos to go a bit further, which meant a total of 2000 pesos (£20) we had to pay as soon as he filled up his tanks with petrol. That dampened our enthusiasm but the important thing was to dive in, we're sure to find a way to swim . . .

The *chalupa* took in water. The captain asked us to bale, having run his boat aground among the reeds. He was busy now filling in the spaces between the planks with pieces of green bananas! A little later, as another breach opened in the front, he handed me his machete. The instruction was brief but efficient: I was not long filling the cracks. Green plantain banana seemed designed for the job.

Around 5 pm, we stopped in Sautata, a military post controlling traffic on the *rio*. We weren't made welcome. A soldier began to search my panniers. It was maddening. In order to get rid of the suitcase, I had had to squeeze all my belongings into the panniers and this bully was spilling everything on the flooded *chalupa* floor. But I stayed calm, I remembered the lesson.

It was days ago, long before Turbo, and the umpteenth search by the military. They were behaving as if the French Connection was using cyclists. And I lost my temper. I began throwing the contents of my panniers at the corporal's face. And as they continued taking absolutely everything out of my luggage, I demanded to speak to their officer and tried to get public opinion on my side, calling out to passers-by: *'Mira como pacifico turistas estan tratado en este pais.* (Look how peaceful tourists are treated in this country.)'

The passers-by looked at me with incredulous fear and quickened their pace but the corporal, after having looked at my slides one by one, sent a man to get a lieutenant: *'Diga le que son aqui turistas bravos!* (Tell him we've got some nasty tourists here.') The Lieutenant was conciliatory, and so was I—I didn't have any choice—and we got out of trouble only an hour late . . .

It explains why I now performed miracles to stay calm. Fortunately Raymond had the good sense to pull out the *El Diario* article with the photo of Charlotte and the two of us. The officer stopped the search. If we were famous, we could not be suspect, could we?

The night was well advanced when we got to the mouth of the Rio Cacarica. This is the small village of cabins named Puerto America or may be Traversia, we haven't found out which yet. It was a strange sight, from the *chalupa* in the middle of the river, to watch the people. They were sitting down, in short trousers and stripped to the waist. And they were whipping their sides and legs with towels, as a cow would do with its tail. Mosquitoes! Swarms of them attacked us when we came ashore and we couldn't rest before we had our mosquito nets set up. The grocery shop owner made us pay 100 pesos each for the right to sleep in his extension.

Friday 21 October

'Mugs are rare, they have to be fleeced promptly,' Raymond reflected and it is a good summary of the day.

First it appeared that our captain had played with words. It was easy to do and not necessarily dishonest: for him Cacarica meant the *Rio* Cacarica, not the village. To get us there this morning from Puerto America—where of course nobody had ever heard of a French company—somebody asked for 5000 pesos.

So we hastened back to the *chalupa* for the extension already agreed. The scenery alone was worth the 400 pesos extra. We stopped in the middle of a small village on piles, in the middle of the swamp. The inhabitants were having their breakfasts, the men ready in their canoes with their chain saws or their fishing nets. The welcome was so cold that we didn't dare to take pictures, but we took it all in. Further on, the channel narrowed, the *chalupa* got stuck in the reeds and the engine stalled. The captain had to use the *palanqua* (pole) to get us out. We got to a clearing where the captain attached the *chalupa* to a tree and asked for the 400 pesos as agreed.

'The *trocha* (trail) for Cacarica begins here?'

'Er . . . no, but you can see yourself the *chalupa* can't go any further. You must wait for the people who'll bring my cargo and negotiate a ride with them to Cacarica . . .'

Soon we heard singing. And dug-out canoes appeared between the trees, loaded with sacks of maize and plantain bananas. Two hundred pesos more, and an unforgettable journey through the undergrowth, up a small stream, wondering at every curve if the canoes would get past and if the bicycles jutting out would get entangled in the branches, completed the morning.

The two canoeists said they'd drop us in Peranchito where there was a man who knew twelve different trails to Panama. And he would guide us at least to Cacarica . . . Damned Cacarica! How much are we going to have to spend just to reach it? And it is only the beginning of the trail! . . .

We were expecting a village but Peranchito is only one house. We were hungry, we hadn't eaten since last night so we asked if there was any food for sale. We were told there wasn't. So we asked if we could leave at once for Cacarica. An unvoiced concern made us reluctant to drag things out, dependent as we were on other people.

Señor Ramon, the guide, listened to us with respect and remarked that the trail was very muddy, that he hadn't used it for a long time and that there might be a lot of new obstacles across it. When we insisted, he adopted another tactic.

'My wife is going to cook a good dinner', he said, 'after that you'll get a good night's sleep and tomorrow morning we'll leave early.'

'And you'll buy me some salt,' added his wife, 'because a home without salt isn't a decent home!'

We had to make do with Peranchito then. The house is a wooden cabin on piles and only one room has walls. The kitchen is outside but as if enclosed under a dome of vegetation. There is a calabash tree growing matter-of-factly, between the kitchen and the stream along which we came, from which the drinking water is drawn, in which the dishes are washed, which serves as a toilet and on which a canoe passes now and then. To one side of the house, lemon trees and cocoa trees, to the other papaya trees. Further behind, banana trees, one or two mango trees and clearings for growing maize.

'Nobody's ever hungry here,' said Señor Ramon proudly. 'What would you like with your rice, cassava or plantain banana?

We chose cassava, and he gave his machete to one of his sons: 'Go to the north of the maize patch. I saw beautiful ones there.'

Waiting for the meal, we ate papayas, bathed in the stream and showed our photos to the family. It was a large family of blacks and when they saw black Africans in our scrap books, there was no doubt in their minds: 'Look, Colombians!'

As Raymond is a vet, Señor Ramon wanted to know why his sow wouldn't put on weight.

'There could be many reasons,' Raymond answered. 'I must examine the animal.'

I discovered then that my companion has undiscovered talent.

'Hold it firmly!' he ordered, and, carefully out of reach of its mouth, he put out an arm, pulled back one of the sow's eyelids and declared that the animal suffered from parasites.

'Come on! Don't tell me you've seen parasites in its eyes,' I joked in French.

'No, but it has pale eyes, a sign of anaemia. And in such an environment, I can bet this anaemia is due to parasites.'

Just as much at ease as in his native Brittany, Raymond dictated to Señor Ramon the name of the medicine he would have to buy in Turbo to make his sow more productive.

When night fell, so did the rain and the terrible horseflies which had bitten us all day long were replaced by the even more terrible *sancudos*, the local mosquitoes. Everybody took a towel and began to whip their sides. It was too hot to put shirts or trousers on.

'Oh, I would give a fortune for a freezing drizzle coming straight from the sea!' sighed Raymond.

Saturday 22 October

I watched the *sancudo* fill up with my blood and I didn't have the strength to slap it. In fact I didn't even feel it, it could well have been somebody else's blood.

When, in play rather than from necessity, I crushed it on my skin, I wondered if my sweat would wash away the bloodstain. If not the sweat, it would be the mud or the sludge . . .

Very often the mud reached our ankles and sucked our shoes down. Raymond went back to retrieve his new tennis shoes which were once white. I gave up going back and abandoned my pair of Bolivian tyre sandals, I was too far behind Raymond and Señor Ramon. Where the

In the Darien Gap, the sludge came up to our waists.

mud didn't reach our ankles, the sludge covered our calves. And it often hid thorns and sharp-edged leaves which I had to take out of my bare feet.

Five hours. Five hours of walking, sometimes balancing on tree trunks, Rosinante's bar cutting into my shoulder. Five hours in the equatorial heat with mosquitoes as ferocious in the day as at night. Five hours of wondering if I shouldn't keep only the minimum and abandon Rosinante in the mud . . . But Señor Ramon was there to encourage us. It was lucky we had him. Without him, we would have hesitated ten times between two trails, we would have lost ourselves ten times in a swamp or in a cluster of rotting tree trunks. He wore a pair of new trousers and a pair of gum-boots and I wondered how he managed to stay clean. He carried a rifle in one hand and his machete in the other. Quite often he had to cut through the bush but still he was much faster than us.

Now and then, we found him smoking a cigarette while he waited for us. He even had time to roll it himself. He always had encouraging words for us: 'Difficult, uh? But you are true *veracos*. Courage! Further on, it gets wider and drier, it will be easier. And it is only a short distance to Cacarica!'

Further on it was not drier nor easier, and the short distance lasted several more hours, but the small lies of Señor Ramon probably saved Rosinante from being abandoned to the mud.

In Cacarica, also called Vijao, we began to understand how misunderstandings had arisen. It seems that village names depend on where you come from. All villages situated on the Rio Cacarica are called Cacarica when your route is at right angles to the river. But when you follow the river, they have different names!

In Cacarica-Vijao, we created a big commotion. The children who gathered around us had never seen a bicycle in their lives. As Rosinante was obviously too much for me to carry, I let it be known that she was for sale. At once a buyer stepped out of the crowd—a white man wearing a cowboy hat. He showed pockets full of banknotes. The others called him *bazookata*. Bazooka is a residue from the distillation of cocaine, we had been told in Medellin, but it is used in Colombia instead of the drug, as it is much cheaper. The good stuff is for export only, like the coffee.

I wanted 4000 pesos for Rosinante. By instinct, the *bazookata* bargained and offered 3000. I hesitated. One doesn't betray a companion of ten years in a few minutes! To show his goodwill and to prove that he had plenty of money, the *bazookata* paid a man to get his wife to cook us a meal. In fact everybody looked drunk and it was difficult to be sure of anybody's intentions. *Aguardiente,* the local 'fire-water' was offered around and we were the only ones who were surprised by the price paid for our meal: 500 pesos for a miserable plate of rice, two plantain bananas and a few fish-bones. In the hut where we ate, I left two trails of blood: my feet were open wounds. I had given up extracting the thorns and the heat suppressed the pain. I'll worry about them tomorrow . . .

During the meal we asked about the next stage.

'Do you have papers or are you illegal?' we were asked. 'You're straight? Then it will be only 150 dollars to guide you to Paya, the first Indian village.'

Sunday 23 October

Oh the awful feeling of being pinned down! The hateful feeling of having lost all independence, of having abandoned one's precious freedom of movement. We are pinned down between Panama and Colombia. On our own, we won't get further than the village limits. And if we have to pay a guide, it will cost us a thousand dollars. So we began to ask how much it would be to get back to Turbo.

Last night, we were told 800 pesos per person. But this morning the rate was doubled. The haggling is incredible: first the bicycles were too heavy, the canoes too narrow, extra *muchachos* must be paid to get us to the *chalupa,* the petrol is too expensive, the river too long . . . The *bazookata* still wanted Rosinante and I was tempted. After all, £30 is twice what I paid for her ten years ago. But my glance fell on the beer-cap collection (increased yesterday by two new specimens). I could not sell that!

The children understood our state of helplessness and they suggested we give them both bicycles for free . . . Raymond, whose bicycle cost £300 got angry and the *chalupa* captain agreed to take us back to Turbo, with the bicycles, for 2500 pesos. This was Rosinante's second narrow escape. She was almost abandoned in the mud and almost sold for £30 . . .

Central America: The Only Mammalian Plant on Earth

Back in Turbo we could still have tried to get to Panama by small coaster, but the bicycles would have taken the space of three passengers. And as we already had plane tickets from Medellin to Panama—absolutely compulsory in order to get our Colombian visas—we bussed back to Medellin. At the airport the bicycles got a very different welcome: people applauded them and they weren't even weighed. So we didn't pay any extra for them.

In Panama Raymond lent me 500 dollars and rode out as fast as he could. He wanted to reach Mexico City and fly home for Christmas, he was missing Charlotte . . . And although I rode out much more slowly, I started off in Central America with an accident.

I had been passed by all sorts of vehicles, in three years on the road. I had been passed by half-tracks and by tricycles, by four-wheel drives and even by trains. I had been passed by machines in all sorts of condition: in Peru by old rusty American limousines, in Ecuador by brand new local Andinos and Condors, in Zimbabwe by mine-proof armoured cars looking like pagodas, in Burundi by bicycles made entirely out of wood, in Egypt by huge carts pulled by tiny donkeys, in Argentina by horsemen sporting berets and in Chile by Citroën 2CVs.

But I had never, until now, been passed by a somersaulting Volkswagen Beetle.

It landed upside down ten yards in front of me and I dropped Rosinante on the roadside in order to help. I was expecting to see blood but the driver was very much alive, kicking around in his desperate attempts to get out. The car was crushed, all the doors were blocked. I made him repeat that he was fine and then pulled him through the front window just as though I was pulling a foot out of a tight boot. A small crowd had gathered, and the driver explained.

'There was a *señor* on his bicycle you see, and I was preparing to pass him when this other madman came full speed from behind. He scared me and, trying not to hit the *señor* on his bicycle, I lost control. But *gracias a*

137

Dios, I have nothing broken, not even a scratch!'

The Beetle, on the other hand, was a write-off. It was losing its oil, and the engine began to smoke when somebody switched it on. The top and sides were smashed in, all the windows were broken. And newcomers to the scene, seeing the crashed car and Rosinante lying beside it but in perfect condition, came to the conclusion that it was an accident between a car and a bicycle.

'Tell me,' they said to me, 'you've got a really strong bike here, what make is it? I'd like to buy the same!'

To reach San José, the capital of Costa Rica, I had to pass La Loma de la Muerte, the 'hill of death', a pass culminating at 9840 feet. It happened to be the death, indeed, of my back wheel because it was squeezed for too long in my front fork.

The back wheel, in the front fork?

Yes, it must be remembered that I had 'spontaneous punctures' in South Africa. As a result I bought a new local invention at Cape Town: the 'unpuncturable' inner tube, which was full of rubber. At first, on the Argentinian and Chilean tar, it had been a nice respite: no punctures at all. But on the rocky trails of Bolivia and Peru it provided poor suspension and the front wheel broke down. I abandoned it in the desert of northern Peru. It might still be there, as it was when Raymond passed there eight days after me.

I replaced it with the wheel bought in Kariba and kept as a spare, fixed to the Malawian back carrier. But it still had a free wheel on and I had to force the assembly into the front fork. It was probably too tight and now the bearings had ground into the cups and I was about to lose them. So I walked.

I had plenty of time and my new radio headset to enjoy it. In Costa Rica, as all over the Americas, radio stations broadcast more commercials than music but that suited me: when I knew the commercials by heart, it meant that I was speaking the language better. And today, around 2 pm a commercial claimed all my attention. It was praising the luxury and charm of a restaurant situated, it said, at Kilometre 131 on the Panamericana. And I was just reaching Kilometre 130.

Of course this was not the kind of restaurant I usually patronized but when I entered it barefoot in my dirty shorts, nobody called the police. I ordered coffee. Fifteen minutes later, the owner and his two sons were sitting at my table, reading my scrapbook and asking questions.

'Are you hungry? Would you like to try a local chicken dish? On the house naturally . . .'

When I left, with my stomach so full that I would need no food for the next two days, I promised myself I would listen even more carefully to the radio commercials. And the first one I heard said: 'Soon the coffee picking season will begin. For lack of hands, Costa Rica may lose several million dollars this year. Costa Rican students! Take advantage of the special holidays given by the Ministry of Education and give a hand to the pickers of our golden grain. Bean by bean, get some fun while earning your pocket money!'

For a coffee-lover like me the invitation could not be refused. As soon as I arrived in San José I changed the cups of the back wheel (forty spokes to set in the correct order, quite a brain-teaser!), and left in search of a *hacienda cafetalera* who would employ and lodge me. And the very first night I found myself in a wooden cabin at the foot of Volcano Poas, among dozens of coffee pickers, impatiently awaiting my first encounter with the coffee-bush. My bed was nothing but a couple of planks and I had to cook my rice on a wood fire.

'Didn't you bring a woman with you?' the supervisor asked. 'Who is going to cook for you?'

At 4 am the radio sets began to wake up everybody in the cabins. I heard Radio Mil from the right, Radio Juvenil from the left, Omega Estereo from behind and Radio Universal from the bed next to mine. We were close enough to San José to receive all its stations. Somebody offered me a mug of boiling black and very sweet coffee and led me to the picking area.

I was given two rows of coffee-bushes without much instruction, told that I was allowed to pick only the red and yellow beans, not the green ones. And before long I was lagging behind. But everybody was very kind to me. The *encargados,* the supervisors, came to chat to me. They were easily recognizable by the machetes they wore at their belts. They used them only now and then to chop a banana tree which obstructed the way or to peel an orange. Banana and orange trees were in fact strategically distributed among the coffee bushes to provide food and drink. Once I even saw an *encargado* use his machete to clean his nails, but only *encargados* carried machetes . . .

When they came to chat, one at a time, they helped me pick. Their speed was amazing, but they were not allowed to pick. Their job was to check, when a *calle* (aisle) was finished, that not a single bean was left on the ground. One of them told me that on his day off he went picking and made more money than he did supervising.

We were paid according to the quantity we picked. The previous night I had had to pay 150 colones (the country's currency) for a basket made out of creepers and called a *cañasto*. It was tied to my waist and it took me about two hours to fill it. At the end of the day, its contents were measured by the *encargados* and I was paid 30 colones (about one dollar). The best pickers, as far as I could judge, could pick up to fifteen *cañastos,* but the majority never made more than 8 dollars a day. And my first day's work didn't even cover the cost of the *cañasto!*

But at the end of that first day, several other pickers offered me coffee or *frijoles-sanguiche* (black bean sandwich) in sympathy. A *gringo* coming to pick coffee for a living, you don't see that every day!

This first day also taught me a lot about the coffee-bean itself. It has a reddish skin, a lightly sugared flesh and a stone, whose two halves are dried and roasted. This is the only part we get in Europe. Like a cherry, the coffee bean can be green, half ripe or bright red, hence the saying 'Coffee is a cherry of which we eat only the stone.'

The next day I realized why, each time a Tico (Costa Rican) said the words *cojer el café* (pick coffee), he made the motion of milking a cow. It was because, when a branch is covered with red or yellow beans, one doesn't have to pick them individually and can 'milk' the whole branch directly into the *cañasto*. This explained another saying: 'The coffee bush is the only mammalian plant on Earth.'

On the third day, the bachelors were summoned and had to move to new quarters—a vast shed where carpenters were still working on the furniture: five beds of planks of which, they proudly told me, one had been specially designed for my height (I was unusually tall for that part of the world), three *forneros,* and hollow tables filled with dirt on which we could make a fire and cook. The advantage of these new lodgings was the sanitary equipment: toilets with running water and, an unheard of luxury, cold showers.

The disadvantage came from the same equipment: they had been put in by the carpenters too and leaked enough water to maintain a permanent swamp under the beds . . .

I had four companions: a young *moreno* whom the others called 'negro' when they wanted to be unkind to him, another youngster, half crazy, who slept stripped to his waist under his bed, in the water, and two forty-year-olds, a tall slim one and another called *El Gordo,* the Big One.

The slim one was suffering from being separated from his family and drowned his homesickness in the beer served in the *cantina* across the street. When he came back, he took his guitar and played the night away. *El Gordo* could also *tocar la guitara* but made up for the absence of his family in another way.

One evening, the slim one stopped me at the shed door. '*Stop, no paso, El Gordo está aqui con una mujer* (Don't go in, the Big One is inside with a woman)' he said with a strange smile. When we were finally allowed in, El

Gordo shone with pride and generously invited me to follow him. The lady was a poor mother who worked at the *cantina*. *'Te la regalo* (I give her to you)' he said and when I refused, he wouldn't let her leave without having her wash his clothes. It was an attitude which was hardly surprising when one knew that a man there was called a *macho* if one wanted to please him.

The *moreno* earned no more than me and spent half of it in the *cantina* every night, elegantly dressed and heavily perfumed. The other three collected over ten cañastos per day, they could get drunk every night and still save some money.

On the other hand, eating only rice, *frijoles,* coffee and milk, I could only save enough money for my Nicaraguan visa ($11) and some more film ($3). But this experience had a surprising effect on my 'cafeinomania': I stopped using instant Nescafé and started doing as everybody else did there, I boiled the ground coffee in water and used a cloth filter to separate the liquid from the solid.

And because ground coffee was so cheap (20p per pound!) I began to behave like the cowboys in western movies: I extinguished my fires, along my route, with the remains of my coffee-pot . . .

It was dusk on my 940th day of travelling. On the Pacific Ocean beach in the Santa Rosa National Park, on the border with Nicaragua, I was watching the huge sea turtles coming in to lay their eggs. They were slow and clumsy. It looked as if they wished they could escape a task which cost them so much. They dug holes in the sand and went into labour. There were a lot of mosquitoes and, longing for my mosquito-net, I headed for the park campsite.

The trail was difficult, and I had to push Rosinante. And suddenly a violent pain went through my right foot. I pointed my torch at it and saw a scorpion, defiantly facing me. It was a big coloured one and it died instantly, not because my blood had poisoned it—it would have died of that eventually as a result of all the diseases I suffered in Africa, but not instantly. It died because I wanted to show it to a doctor to receive the proper antidote, and I killed it with a blow of my torch.

The campsite was several miles away, and when I reached it, feeling quite well but tired, I went to sleep. The next morning I was still alive and the wardens told me that big scorpions are not lethal, only small ones.

The Nicaraguan visa was the most difficult and expensive in Central America. I had to pay for it in US banknotes only, provide two photographs and fill in an amazing form: I had to specify the Christian names of my parents and . . . the colour of my skin.

It was the very first time I had been asked for this detail, even South

Africa hadn't asked. So I was careful to be precise and accurate, and after a lot of thought wrote *'Rosa con pecas* (Pink with freckles)' . . .

To be white and freckled in Latin America always has the same result, you are mistaken for an American, a *gringo*. But here in Nicaragua, things had changed radically. I was mistaken for somebody else.

I wanted to leave the country by its flatter road, through the southern town of Chinandega. But I was stopped there by a military roadblock. Due to the tension with Honduras, this border crossing had been closed, contrary to what I had been told in Managua. And the only border crossing was on the northern road, in the mountains. I had a seven-day visa and it was now the sixth day. So I decided to take a small trail and cut directly through the mountains. This trail was roughly parallel to the border with Honduras and of course was filled with troops. What surprised me was that nobody checked my papers, despite my pink skin, until the eighth day, in the village just before the border crossing, where I understood why I hadn't been stopped before.

A militiaman shyly asked for my passport. Embarrassed next at the obvious illegality of my situation, he took me to the village, ordered some women to serve me a meal while somebody else called superior authorities to find out what to do with me. The militiaman, watching over me, explained: 'We noticed you yesterday but because of your pink skin and red hair, we mistook you for a Russian soldier on leave. I know Russian soldiers very well, my officer was one when I was trained. And he was like you, *rosa con pecas!'*

By phone I was ordered to present myself at the next police station to regularize my position. The officer wanted me to pay another ten American dollars for a 48-hour visa extension. But when I told him I earned my money by picking coffee in Costa Rica, he let me go.

On the border at El Espino, the two enemies were facing each other, like two pawns on a chessboard. The Honduran soldier sported a Texan hat and the Nicaraguan a Vietcong cap. Both carried gleaming rifles. The Russian rifle looked like a toy, with its curved magazine, the American one black and long, looked more serious with its square magazine.

The American pawn was freshly shaved, had a moustache and swung his shoulders; the Russian pawn gave himself intellectual airs, with his long hair, unbuttoned uniform and multicoloured strings on his rifle barrel.

The two pawns were facing each other. They were enemies but, deprived of their uniforms, of their guns, of their hats, they were brothers. Fate placed them on two different sides and coloured them in two different colours. One had to obey the white king and the other the black king. Both kings were pink with freckles, if I had got it right, but the two pawns, at a sign from their kings, were ready to kill each other, for a mere question of colour . . .

The rest of Central America was nothing but a struggle to cross borders without paying too much money. The countries are so tiny that, even on a bicycle, one can cross each of them in a couple of days. And things function as though the authorities, unhappy to see tourists stay so short a time and spend so little money, try to make up the difference at the borders.

To enter these tiny Central American states, I had to buy a visa first. But that was not all. At the border I had to buy an official stamp for the official entry form, to pay for the decontamination of Rosinante's tyres (against banana diseases apparently), to pay for the registration of Rosinante in a vehicle register and finally, a very special tax because that very day was a national holiday and the officers weren't supposed to work . . .

What made me angry was that the same taxes were also applied at the other end as exit taxes. But there I steadfastly refused to pay and after detaining me an hour or two the officers let me go. And by New Year 1984 I was in Guatemala.

Night caught me by surprise in the middle of nowhere with only a pint of water left. I set up my mosquito net under a bridge, divided my water in two, kept one half for breakfast and went to sleep. I was woken by a noise. What was it? It was horses in the field next to the road. But what time was it? I put the radio on and discovered it was just after midnight. Everybody was rejoicing, I heard laughing and feasting—on the radio of course. But to join the world in celebration, from under my bridge in this dry semi-desert in Guatemala, I allowed myself the best champagne of my life: two mouthfuls of fresh water . . .

Mexico Sequel: 'You are the First to Escape Alive'

Twenty-eight days later, having enjoyed the touristic delights of Lake Atitlan, those of Zippolyte beach and the more expensive ones of Acapulco, the small Indian and his gun were a reminder of the harshness of life. And the blow delivered by his mixed-race friend reinforced the lesson.

Half dizzy, I chose to retreat. I ran to the road and tried to stop a car for assistance. I had to kneel down on the tar to get a few cars to slow down. But as soon as they realized it was a mugging, they sped away. I had no alternative but to launch a counter-attack. It was not courage. It was just despair. Just then my earthly possessions were reduced to a pair of shorts. If I didn't react I was virtually dead. I had a chance, I thought, to snatch Rosinante out of my attacker's hands. And it was inside her saddle tube that I had hidden the 300 dollars in cash. I had to go for that.

Adopting their choice of weapon, I gathered stones in my arms and ran back to the battlefield. The small Indian was entangled in the barbed wire, looking for his gun, a perfect target for my stones. I heard the soft sound of the projectiles on his naked chest. He cried out in pain and fright, he begged again but this time I didn't fall into the trap. I didn't aim for his head however, and anyway my return was not for revenge. My aim was dear old Rosinante whom the half-caste was trying to take away along a small trail where the tall white had disappeared with my bag. Rosinante didn't like being kidnapped and she showed it. She was not a good bicycle for the Mexican. She was much too heavy and uncontrollable with her numerous panniers. He barely managed to drag her along the ground.

It was true that, whichever way you looked at her, Rosinante was not the average bicycle. She had no licence plate, not even a manufacturer's number stamped on her frame. I built her myself, practically, and she didn't show any trademark. Rosinante was a free spirit, she didn't accept any master but me. However there were borders where I was suspected of smuggling her!

144

In some countries indeed a western bicycle, no matter how special, can be sold for a good price and customs officers noted her in my passport when I came in, to ensure that I took her out. Thus the Tunisian customs wrote: *'Vu à l'entrée, vélo usagé* (Seen on entry, used bicycle)' and very honestly, two months later: *'Vu à la sortie, vélo très usagé* (Seen on exit, very used bicycle)'.

The Sudanese customs officers wanted a brand name. It happened that Rosinante was decorated with anti-nuclear stickers saying *Nucléaire Energie Suicide* (Nuclear energy is suicide) so the officers noted in my passport 'With Nuclear Bicycle' . . .

In Kenya I changed the stickers for those of a famous religious sect, the Krishna Devotees, and just as diligently the Bolivian officers noted *'bicicleta de marca Hare Krishna'* . . .

To enter Mexico I had to fill in a form and put a cross by the small drawing representing my means of transportation. There was a car, a bus, a plane, a boat and a motorcycle, nothing else and it was with pride that I drew a small bicycle and put a cross by it. I didn't know I would have to leave Mexico without Rosinante . . .

For the moment anyway, she was back with me. The big half-caste had dropped her to run away and I ran with her towards the road. The Indian was out of the ditch without his pistol and tried to stop me by throwing stones, or rather boulders. One of them loosened the *cañasto*. I didn't care, I just had to clench my jaws under the raining stones and make it to the road. I jumped on Rosinante as soon as I reached the tar and started downhill.

Half an hour later I reach Tierra Colorada. My head was swollen and hurt badly. I could not move my eyes too quickly, otherwise I got dizzy. And my torso was covered with blood from a number of small cuts. I no longer had a pink skin but a red one! I asked where the police station was.

'*Estaba una pistola como este?* (It was a pistol like this one?)' He showed me an automatic pistol.

'*No.*'

'*Como este?*' Showing a 9mm . . .

'*No, mas pequeño!* (no, smaller!)' I wished they had a catalogue.

Tierra Colorada was a town of 8000 inhabitants, as a notice stated at the edge of town, and the policemen seemed to have taken my story very seriously: they were preparing a manhunt. Two cars and five men armed to the teeth. It lasted more than an hour.

We began at the place itself. I still hoped they had abandoned what was useless to them: my maps, guidebooks, spare-parts and bicycle tools, and essential to me: my notebooks, diary and address book. But we only found the empty *cañasto*. The bandits had taken away my food, my clothes, my turban and even, I could hardly believe it, the rice I had cooked at noon and stored in a plastic milk bag for dinner. I thought I was the only one on earth who could eat it . . .

We continued to the nearby village where a woman stopped us to tell us about the three armed men. My story was confirmed but the manhunt became an iguana hunt. Mexicans, like all Central Americans, love the meat of the big lizard. It is easy to kill as well: too confident in its camouflage, being the same colour as the rocks, it stands still when it feels danger. However the policemen in my car wasted two magazines without killing a single animal.

Back at the police station, I had the disagreeable feeling of having escaped the wolves only to take refuge in the jackals' den. When I said I was going to take a bus to Mexico City, the policemen pressed me to leave them the useless parts of my luggage, such as my Swiss Army knife, my torch lamp or my radio headset for instance.

The *licenciado* who came that night to type my deposition was less greedy, though not less disagreeable. He was a young *conscientisado*. Looking at my South American visas he asked how I had found the 'oppressed' people of Chile. I would have liked to answer 'In a much better state than the liberated people of Nicaragua,' but I'd had enough fighting for one day. I told him what he wanted to hear and he assured me that I would be allowed to sleep in his office.

'You are very lucky,' he added. 'You must understand that this state is the poorest in the United States of Mexico and that the proximity of Acapulco and its luxury is a permanent provocation to violence. For a good number of people down here, violence is the only way out of misery. And *you* are still alive, don't complain!'

'You are the third to be attacked this month in the same place, but you are the first one to escape alive. One man died from a bullet in his belly, small calibre, it probably took him quite a long time to die . . . The second one lost his head, I mean literally, from several machete blows . . . So you see, you should be happy to have lost only a few dollars, your cooking utensils and a Sudanese turban! As a matter of fact, if I was in your situation, I would probably take advantage of it and go back home to kiss my mother while I was still alive!'

This was exactly what I decided to do. But it was impossible to fly from Mexico to France for 300 dollars, so I decided to try from New York. But without Rosinante whom I left in the left-luggage room of the Hotel Monte Carlo in Mexico City. I took a bus, and as I had had a permanent American visa since South Africa, I expected no trouble on the border.

I was forgetting the bicycle-smuggling problem and the cross in front of

146

the bicycle drawing on my Mexican entry form. As soon as he saw it, the officer took me out of the bus.

'*Señor, habiamo inspectado el bus, no hay una sola bicicleta . . . Donde está la suya?* (Sir, we have searched the bus, there is not a single bicycle, where is yours?)'

He suspected me of having sold it of course and neither my nervous explanations about the attack and my love for Rosinante whom I could not abandon but was obliged to leave for a while, nor my newspaper cuttings persuaded him to the contrary. However he probably pitied me and gave in.

'*Bueno, largate! Pero acorda te que esta la ultima vez que "olvidas" una bicicleta en Mexico!* (All right, clear off! But remember it is the last time that you "forget" a bicycle in Mexico!)'

Renewing one's links with the rich western civilization after three years in the Third World doesn't happen without some shock.

The first was in Laredo when I changed from the Mexican bus to the Greyhound. The difference in comfort was striking—at last I had some room for my legs—but what impressed me more was the ban on smoking. What a relief!

The second occasion was in New York City where I did not expect so much efficiency. I got out at the Port Authority Bus Terminal after a three-day ride, which was more tiring than a three-day bicycle ride, and didn't know what to do next. I had vaguely heard about a new company that had replaced the Laker Sky Train and was offering flights to London for 150 dollars. Even travel agents in Mexico City could not give me more precise information. The only other thing I knew for sure was that if it was more expensive, I was stuck there.

There was an information booth, a typical rich country's luxury and somebody was inside—a severe-looking black man who listened to my rusty English and eventually answered in *French!*

'*Ascenseur B, Troisième étage. Autocar numéro 305 pour Newark, cela coûte trois dollars, il vous arrêtera en face de la compagnie que vous cherchez, cela s'appelle People Express.* (Elevator B, Third floor, Bus 305 to Newark, it costs $3, it will take you right to the company you're looking for, which is called People Express.)'

It was already 5 pm but by 7 pm I was on the departing plane bound for Gatwick. I still didn't have my ticket. When I arrived at the counter, the smiling hostesses told me they just had one last seat, asked to see if I had any money, told me I would have to pay on the plane separately for my luggage and my meals and ushered me through customs.

That was where I had more trouble, a result of all this efficiency. When I passed through the metal-detector door, it rang. The policeman in charge was a policewoman.

'D'you have any metal object?'

'Yes I think so, my Swiss Army knife.'

'Give it to me and go back through the door.'

It rang again.

'What else do you have?'

'Let me think . . . Of course, the Swiss Army knife chain!'

'Give it to me . . . and go through the door again.'

I went through and the door rang! Before the woman exploded, I remembered.

'I had forgotten but I also have a bicycle chain around my ankle . . .

'A *what?*'

'A bicycle chain, you know, as an ankle bracelet, look, it is a souvenir from Africa.'

'OK, get it off and quickly, you're holding everybody up!'

'Hum, sorry, but I need a chain-link remover, do you have one? . . . Well a hammer and an anvil will do!'

She didn't have an anvil so she called a policeman who body-searched me . . .

At Gatwick I bought a train ticket for Paris. On the ferry I bought French banknotes. I had completely forgotten what they were like, I didn't remember them as being so big. On the Paris Metro, I was startled to hear people speak French. And I had to restrain myself from going up to them and re-enacting the Doctor Livingstone-I-presume piece. For three years, each time I heard passers-by talking French it was an exceptional event and I now had to think of it as normal again.

What I had to think of as normal too was getting up every morning to go to work. My strong desire to get back to Rosinante helped and ten months later I had saved about £3000 and was ready to get back on the road. Everybody warned me: 'There's no way you'll find your bike! One year in a cheap Mexican hotel, how much do you want to bet it has been sold?'

So I was pretty anxious when, on 5 February 1985, I entered the Monte Carlo Hotel in Mexico City. But I needn't have worried, the receptionist was the same man who had stored Rosinante. Travellers had nicknamed him *Como-no* because, being extremely obsequious, he answered all requests with 'Como no? (why not, of course!)' I asked about Rosinante.

'*Pero como no! Claro que esta aqui . . . Viene!*'

He took me to the left luggage room. Rosinante was in exactly the same place and in the same condition as when I had left her a year before. Except for her flat tyres.

'*Si, ha llorado mucho!* (yes, she wept a lot!)' said *Como-no*.

And as if she were my bride, I took Rosinante in my arms and carried her to my room.

Southern USA: Faking a French Accent

When I entered the USA via Texas in March 1985, my English had suffered from a two-year stay in Latin countries. So when in a snack-bar, I asked for a hot chocolate (and, as in French, put an accent on every syllable of 'cho-co-la-te'), I was served . . . a hot chicken leg!

In the next bar, in Austin, I was even given a public lesson.

'Where you from?' asked the barmaid.

'I am from France,' I said, with a broad 'a'.

'No sir, you're not from France; in the States, you're from Fraince and in Texas, you are from Frayance.'

The lesson wasn't enough because in Arkansas, fifteen days later, I still had a problem with my accent. That night as usual, I asked several farmers if I could sleep in their barns and kept getting frightened refusals. A lady finally explained:

'You won't find anything around here. You see, people are scared. Four years ago, we had race rats and now everybody is afraid of strangers . . .'

'Hum, what do you mean by "race rats"? Racehorses I know, but race rats . . .?'

'No, no, race rats you know, when you've got the whites on one side and the blacks on the other and they are fighting . . .'

She meant 'race riots' of course. She explained about the bridge, one mile further on, which was the boundary between the white and the black communities.

'I suggest you sleep under it because obviously, if you ain't found anything on this side, you won't on the other.'

Fifteen days later, on Bourbon Street, in the French Quarter, New Orleans ('N'Awleens' as they say), I had another communication problem: I was riding Rosinante.

'This is a *walking promenade!*' shouted a policeman from his car.

I dismounted and walked away.

'Wait a minute,' shouted the cop again, getting out of his car and

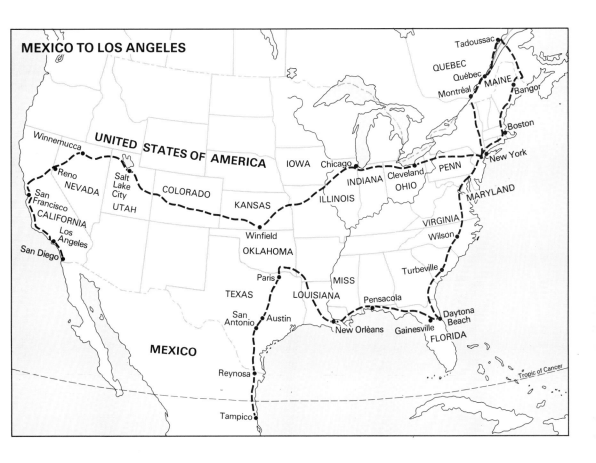

grabbing at my bike. 'What is that?'

'That is a knife blade which I found along the road and stuck into my handlebars, just in case . . .'

'And this, you found it on the road too?'

This time, he pulled out of my handlebar bag, a tear-gas cartridge. I carried this just in case I had the same problem as in Acapulco the previous year.

The policeman looked vicious and decided to bother me. He began to spray the front of Rosinante, probably thinking it was a spray paint. Unfortunately the wind was against him and the cloud of tear-gas hit him right in the face. He suddenly realized, called his partner to watch over me and ran into a restaurant to wash his face.

When he came back, he had bulging eyes and a running nose.

'I-den-ti-fi-ca-tion' he shouted with renewed anger.

I handed him my passport.

'What other weapons do you have? You been in jail before? No? Well,

151

there's a first time for everything . . .'

The two policemen were now searching Rosinante. She had put on weight. I had to explain the extra seat for hitch-hikers, the Moroccan sheepskin and the Bolivian llama fur. They poked inside my Peruvian flower pot, looking for another kind of pot, and laughed at my kerb feelers. I began to relax. But along came a big guy with a Stetson, bulging eyes and a running nose.

'Hey, who sprayed this shit around here? People are crying a block away!'

'It's him,' I said, pointing to the cop. And very soon I regretted having spoken. The policemen threatened me with six months' prison for carrying illegal weapons. This was bad news: I had already paid for three nights at the youth hostel. I pulled out my scrapbook, explained about my trip, pleaded for mercy and was finally told to disappear.

'Do you keep my . . . things?'

'God damn you, *they are against the law'* shouted the cop again, but I was far away by the time he finished his sentence . . .

So far, apart from Arkansas and the suburbs of Dallas, I had never had problems finding a place to sleep in barns. In Texas, I was often invited inside the houses or, if left in the barn, a TV set was brought out so that I could be comfortable.

Louisiana was rougher (no more TV sets in the barns) and Florida was really difficult. One night, I asked at half a dozen farms and the answers were all an angry 'no way!'. So I settled down outside a fence, near the entrance to a ranch but miles away from the house itself. I had washed myself in a pint of water and unrolled my sleeping bag when the farmer arrived in his car. He stopped.

As politely as possible, I asked his permission to sleep there, unable to imagine being refused.

'No way! Get outta here!'

'I'm sorry but look, this is a bicycle, and now that it's dark, I have no chance of finding another spot . . .'

'Get the fuck outta here or I call the Sheriff!'

I could see his big neck becoming red.

'I'm not even on your property, I'm outside!'

The farmer didn't answer and sped away. Five minutes later, the flashing lights of the Sheriff's car lit up, the night. He manoeuvred it to point his headlights at me and before he got out, he switched on a powerful spotlight. I was already up, with my hands above my head.

But the Sheriff was a young man and he was sorry for me.

'This farmer is a Redneck OK, but he is right, you are on his property, even outside the fence. Come and put your bike in my trunk, I'll drive you to a nicer place.'

The boot of the car was too small for Rosinante and I had to find the place for myself. It was a wonderful roadside park. I slept on a soft lawn and the next morning I was tempted to thank the redneck farmer: on his property I had had to fend off clouds of mosquitoes and here, I hadn't heard a single one.

Anyway, I learned a lesson and the next night, instead of asking farmers, I asked the police. By chance I passed a big sign saying 'LAW ENFORCEMENT TRAINING CENTER'; The officer in charge paged through my scrapbook and obviously took a liking to Rosinante.

'Be my guest, choose any place you like to camp and tomorrow morning, go to the cafeteria and tell the cook that Jim, that's me, said you ought to have a good breakfast before you hit the road. Oh, something else . . . This is a school here you know and there's going to be classes going on until 11 pm. I hope you don't mind?'

Of course I didn't mind—but I didn't know that the classes consisted of practical exercises like how to stop a speeding car, with real cars, all sirens going, speeding up and down the camp roads.

One night in South Carolina, it was obviously going to rain and I couldn't see any police camp. So I stopped at a farm. A young blonde woman came out, her two kids ran to touch Rosinante. I began my usual speech but when I saw the terrorized look in the woman's eyes, as she ordered her kids back, I knew that I didn't have a chance. Two farms later, I was advised to ask at the fire department of the next town, Turbeville.

There, I was sent to the Pastor who sent me to a second pastor who sent me to the city police. There at last I was offered a deal by an officer: 'The town churches are willing to pay for your accommodation but in return, tomorrow you'll have to do five hours of community work; how does that sound to you?'

The night being cold and rainy, it could only sound good. It worked out even better because the motel I was sent to was cabled into the Playboy channel and I thanked the community churches for introducing me to pornography.

Next morning I had to pick up papers and rubbish around the Post Office, under the officer's vigilant eye. And I ended up cleaning up the garden of a third pastor's house. Three different churches in Turbeville— that certainly explained why they could afford the Playboy channel . . . This last pastor gave me five dollars and using his cook's illness as a pretext didn't keep me for lunch and let me go just after noon.

I was leaving the town when a car passed me and stopped. The terrorized young blonde woman of the day before got out and handed me another five-dollar bill. She also gave me a hint about improving my accent.

'You must understand, I am a Christian and I want to be charitable but yesterday, when you explained, with a perfect *Southern* accent, that you were a *Frenchman*, I just couldn't believe you!'

From now on, I would have to take lessons from Inspector Clouzot and fake a French accent every time I spoke to farm people.

Meanwhile, I had met several American cyclists. And I was impressed. The American cyclist, I discovered, usually rode a brand new sophisticated bicycle, with a 'fully inflated' frame . . . (Well, that's exactly what an aluminium frame looks like, inflated . . .).

The American cyclist also wore a helmet, as if he was still fighting in Vietnam, and, to my delight, the American cyclist was often a . . . female cyclist. This was something I recognized from the width of the haunches—easy to see because the American cyclist, male or female, wore very tight coloured chamois. Last but not least, I found that the American cyclist was a very hospitable person, whatever the sex . . .

In New Orleans I stayed a couple of nights in the apartment of one of them (the large-hipped variety), who offered me shelter just because I was a cyclist. She was a subscriber to *Bicycle USA*, a huge cycling organization which I visited in the suburbs of Baltimore. There I was made an honorary member, given a card and a *Hospitality Homes Directory*, listing 1500 American cyclists willing to accommodate their fellow travellers.

I was impressed again: the hospitality of American cyclists was even organized in directories!

In Washington I made a very useful acquisition. I felt like spending some money after a five-hour job at the French Embassy. A guard was away, and I was paid 35 dollars to take his place, as much money as I earned in three *weeks* of coffee-picking in Costa Rica. So I bought maps of the ECBT (East Coast Bicycle Trail). It allowed me, together with the directory, to cross the frightening east coast megalopolis by small quiet roads, to stay with delightful cycling families and enter New York City on Rosinante, still alive.

Here I had an old friend. He lived in Clinton Tower. He had been a dancer and an opera singer. He spoke French as well as Russian and opened his door quoting:

"Alors jouis de ce sort vanté, ô chien, mais je ne voudrais pas d'un royaume s'il doit m'en coûter la liberté." (. . . "Then enjoy this celebrated fate, oh dog, but I do not want a kingdom if it costs me my freedom." [Aesop's Fable of the Dog and the Wolf] Bernard, you are the wolf, aren't you?'

Quebec: The 'Frenchness' of Canadian French

Along with the *Bicycle USA* membership I also received a list of all the member clubs. So my first task in the Big Apple was to write to them, suggesting a slide show about my round-the-world tour. Their answers would decide my way westwards.

To finance the mailing, I organized a show in the Café Comedy on 58th Street, whose owner was French. Publicity was not easy: newspapers, which had been very fond of me in small towns, were blasé here. The only interview I got was published after the show. So I changed Rosinante into a sandwich-bicycle and paraded her around Central Park with boards announcing the show. On the day before I realized I had made a terrible mistake: instead of '58th Street', I had written '28th Street'.

On 27th June, there were probably a lot of bicycle fans looking for Café Comedy in 28th Street; but there were only a dozen in the café itself. They were generous, however: they left ten-dollar notes and Bernard, the café owner, asked me for another show the following Sunday. But this time, *he* would take care of the publicity. The two shows brought in 120 dollars, enough to pay for stamps for my mailing and for printing 500 postcards that I intended to sell at the end of future slide shows.

That same Sunday, Françoise, my new girl-friend, arrived from France and I started teaching her about the American landscape.

'No, this is not a garbage chute, this is an American letter-box; these are not bird cages but air-conditioners sticking out of windows; these are not gangsters but New York policemen, not an imitation Montparnasse Tower but the World Trade Center, not a photocopying machine, even if it does have a sign saying 75 cents per copy, but an automatic newspaper stand.'

When she was ready we started on a 2000-mile summer cycle tour through New England and 'New France'. This was a first for Françoise, and I feared it might also be a last.

We wanted to leave New York on 3 July. We were living on the 33rd floor of a Manhattan tower and on 3 July, the three lifts broke down. So we left on 4 July. The streets were quiet and that was fortunate: Françoise had to tame a new bicycle given to me by a French sponsor and of course, built to my measurements. At the campsite where we stopped, near Peekskill, the night was very much alive with fireworks. Françoise couldn't sleep at all.

The next night I chose an isolated wood where we pitched our brand new tent. There were only whispers and the noises of nature to accompany our sleep. But even that was too much for Françoise and, woken by the smallest noise, she didn't sleep much.

The third night, using my fake French accent, I got permission to camp near a house, on a flat lawn. The young owners invited us to drinks and hot dogs. Everything looked fine—except the rain, which lasted the whole night and soaked Françoise's sleeping bag . . . Some kind of break was necessary, I decided, otherwise she was going to leave me for the next camper driver . . . so we stopped and sunbathed on the shores of Lake George.

The first French Canadian we met was riding a bicycle; he read my 'FRANCE' sign and said something to me in French. But, not understanding a word he said and still being on the American side of the border, I answered in my best American English:

'What did you say?'

Baffled, he reverted to English.

'Hum, I am sorry but I thought you were French, because of the sign on your bike.'

'I *am* French,' I insisted, still unaware of his nationality.

'Hey, what kind of Frenchman are you, not even speaking French?'

'I *do* speak French, just try me!'

This confusion could have lasted a long time, because French French is as far from Canadian French as British English is from American English. And just as close, of course.

In some instances, Canadian French is 'Frencher' than French French. In Quebec, a stop sign is an *arrêt* sign, and an interview is an *entrevue,* whereas the French use the English words. But in other instances, Canadian French looks like 'frenchized' American. The funniest example of this is the word *préservatifs* used to translate preservatives (in food products); the French French is *conservateurs* because in France, *préservatifs* means . . . condoms!

Our stay in Quebec was made memorable by two animals: the biggest, the whales we saw in the St Lawrence estuary, and the smallest: mosquitoes. I have met many kinds of mosquitos: those that are resistant to mosquito repellent, those that are indifferent to electronic gadgets, those that bite even in bright daylight, but until then I had never met mosquitoes that passed through mosquito nets. In Canada, they did.

These were minute mosquitoes called *brûlots:* they leave a tiny drop of blood where they bite and adore human scalps. Every morning, when I combed my hair with my fingers, I ended up with bloody hands. As it was another source of sleepless nights for Françoise, she confided the problem to Brother Jean-Paul who let us camp beside the lake of his monastery.

'I'll bring you a miracle product which will protect you against these *maudites bibites,'* he promised. 'It is called Noxzema.'

It took us several days before we realized that Brother Jean-Paul had given us his shaving cream. But it worked wonders against the *brûlots* and Françoise kept using it. Every night however, the smell made it seem as though I was holding, tight in my arms, the freshly shaved body of a Benedictine monk.

In New England, the welcome was overwhelming. A typical answer when we asked to pitch our tent was 'Be our guests, any place you want, and please come inside for a shower and join us for dinner!'

In Hopeville Pond, Connecticut, we stopped at a campsite for a change, and stayed five nights—for the simple reason it was full of New Englanders and they kept inviting us to dinner. That is how we discovered a couple of weird American culinary customs and this is how we explained them back home: 'The first one is called *som'ore.* You take a, wait for it, *marsh-mal-low*, which is a kind of white fluffy sweet, and you leave it in a wood fire until it is completely black. Then, you stick it between two pieces of chocolate and two large biscuits . . .'

'The second is called corn on the cob. It looks pretty simple and healthy at first because it is basically a maize cob, yes the same as we give to pigs and chickens, but boiled in water and carefully dipped in butter. The trouble is that it comes with whole chickens, ham, hot dogs, pastries and gallons of beer, all things without which Americans are afraid they'll starve. And this is probably why, after they have put on weight, they drink de-caffeinated coffee sweetened with a non-sugar sweetener and whitened with a non-dairy creamer . . .'

This kind of diet was definitely not for us when we had to buy it. So far we had managed on five dollars each per day all-inclusive and that meant looking for the cheapest food in the cheapest supermarkets.

Cheapest of all were certainly the big loaves of white bread. Often we found special offers: three or four loaves for a dollar! This bread tasted and felt like cotton. But I found that if we pressed it, it tasted much better, almost like pastry, and four pressed loaves were much easier to store in bicycle panniers than four fluffy loaves. Consequently, after shopping I always proceeded to press my bread. If done efficiently, this meant walking on the loaves steadily, until they were as flat as a saucer. Now, to Americans, careful not to deform their loaves—otherwise they wouldn't fit into their toasters—I seemed like a madman and once in Maine, they summoned a police officer who came to ask if I was OK . . .

Back in New York, Françoise was supposed to take old Rosinante home because I was going to continue on the new one given me by Peugeot. Unfortunately, the (French) airline refused to have such a monster on board. Rosinante *was* a monster, an international weirdo. She was also the ongoing museum of my travels.

The front wheel was from South Africa, the back one from Zimbabwe. The left brake was from Argentina, the right one from Zambia. The front carrier was Mexican and the back one, forged in iron, weighed ten pounds and was my special souvenir of Malawi. The pump was from Panama and my front mudguard was covered by my beer-cap collection. I bolted one on every time I got drunk, once per country and once per American state.

In Texas I had bought a new pair of toe-clips, hoping to add an American element to Rosinante, but the only toe-clips that I found were 'Made in France'.

Anyway, I now had to abandon all these souvenirs in New York. First, I tried to sell my poor companion. I was laughed at. Then, I tried to have her stolen and left her alone in front of the Clinton Post Office. Two hours later, Rosinante was still there. Even bicycle thieves weren't interested in a twelve year old bicycle which had been halfway around the world . . . so I took it to the Downhill Spokers, a friendly bicycle shop and persuaded the owner that Rosinante would make a wonderful decoration for his window.

The shop was on Madison Avenue, so please, if one day you happen to see her tell Rosinante that I shall never forget her . . .

Back from Canada, I found about twenty answers to my mailing. Eighteen were positive and decided my route westward: one club in Ohio, three in Illinois, one in Kansas, the only club in Utah, and eight in California. I had to refuse two invitations in Washington State and two others in Alaska as they were too far out of my way.

And I had seven days to reach Cleveland, my first appointment.

Across the USA: 'Do you Mind if I call the Press?'

Before starting on my road to the west, I examined a number of maps and planned and examined different routes. It had started as far back as Egypt. In the Sohag Youth Hostel, there was a map of the USA on the wall, with an invitation to join the Bicentennial Bike Ride across the country in 1976. And I copied the route in red in my pocket atlas. But in Manhattan I preferred to use the Exxon maps, which were rather more detailed . . .

I savoured the names of towns like Platte and Cimarron and finally developed a liking for a red line, Route No. 6, which linked Cape Cod with Ely in Nevada before plunging on to Los Angeles. I just had to stick to the 6, I thought, and the 6 would carry me to California. To get to the 6 from New York, I first had to reach the Bear Mountains. Full of dreams about my lectures in Chicago, Salt Lake City and San Francisco, I took Broadway from Clinton all the way to the last street in the Bronx and there I took Route No. 9A to Yonkers. In the centre of Yonkers I took the No. 9 itself to the northern suburbs on the east bank of the Hudson. It began to rain cats and dogs when I arrived there, on the Bear Mountains bridge. It was mountainous indeed: Route No. 6 crossed the bridge, went around a circle and disappeared into the unknown. Not only was there no traffic but it was raining even harder. I ran under some pines for shelter, but it didn't help. I began to cry and to swear and to hit my face for being such an imbecile . . .

I was now riding Rosinante II and she was very very heavy. But I looked the part now: Rosinante II had eighteen gears, three brakes and a computer. Yes, a 'sports computer' which told me how fast I was going, how far I rode per day, and my maximum speed in the day—in miles as well as kilometres! On Rosinante I was a clown; on Rosinante II I was still a clown, but I could at least pretend to be a serious cyclist . . .

One has to be a serious cyclist to cross Pennsylvania from east to west on Route No. 6 because the mountain ranges run from north to south. To keep up with my schedule I even had to refuse invitations. But I didn't refuse presents. I was given a magnum of white wine, which I kept in my bottles.

I kept to Route No. 6 until Scranton. There I used an address from the *Hospitality Directory*. Dick and Ann let me use their swimming pool and explained why Pennsylvania's motto is 'Keystone State'. I had always believed it referred to a real stone, something like a natural stone arch for instance. I never imagined it was due to the geographical position of the state itself in the middle of the original thirteen colonies. Dick worked in the Traffic Department, so I was happy to follow the route he drew on the official state map. It comprised only a few miles of Route No. 6. Too bad for Jack Kerouac, they were my last.

Three days later, the counter showed 65 miles, and I needed to get some water. I stopped in a very small village. In fact it was only a mobile home near a church. When I rang, an old lady came out and, after she had filled up my bottle, she asked: 'Are you hungry? Would you like some hot food? We have just had some Mexican food, would you like some?'

I didn't refuse of course. And when I had shown them my press cuttings, things got busy.

'What would you like to drink? Beer or a mixed drink? We're having rum and cola . . . Do you mind if I call the press?'

I didn't mind of course. An interview would give me time to enjoy the meal. The husband was retired from the US Air Force. Now he worked for Penzoil. He was drunk too, but he showed it less than his wife.

'Two years ago, we had another strange visit, you know. A man who was crossing the country with two horses. But what *you* are doing is much more interesting!'

'. . . Don't you think it is interesting?' echoed the lady on the phone, talking to a journalist, and then, in my direction: 'How long are you going to stay here?'

'Well, as a matter of fact, I was going to ask your permission to pitch my tent behind your mobile home.'

'Perfect! He will sleep at our home,' she said to the phone. 'You will have to come before dark, we like to go to bed early.'

'Oh not tonight,' the husband cut in, 'tonight it's the championship finals: the Washington Redskins against the Dallas Cowboys, tonight I'm staying awake!'

The husband left for a moment, and the lady gave me a twenty-dollar bill.

'Don't tell my husband, this is *my* present, to help you along . . . What about another rumcoke?'

When the photographer-reporter came, he was probably the only one who could see clearly—thanks to a special enormous lens which absorbed all the available light. He took an original photo of a typical Frenchman sipping white wine from his bicycle bottle . . .

It was 7 pm when he left and it was only 5 am when the *Bradford Era* dropped into the letter box with my portrait on the front page. But reading the article I wondered if in the end the reporter wasn't just as drunk as we were: all through the text he called me Bender instead of Bernard, simply because the address I had given him to send a cutting was care of the Benders, Vicky and Allen, who had invited me to Cleveland . . .

I got there just in time for their club reunion. They were the Lake Erie Wheelmen and I told them the Adventures of Rosinante. For the next ten days I was in clover at Vicky and Allen's house. They took me to all the town's attractions and its restaurants. They took great care that my wine glass was never empty and I used the time to write down the early days of Rosinante II.

Vicky called the newspapers and organized two other lectures. I was introduced to Cathy from the *Plain Dealer*. She wrote a very sensible story about Rosinante and took me out to see Molière's *Tartuffe*. I didn't know it could be translated and still be enjoyed. She took me to see her newspaper's offices and showed me the computer she used for writing her reports, and I found that more fascinating than any museum or monument.

And when I left Cleveland, it was with 300 dollars more in my pocket and I was accompanied by 1800 cyclists: the competitors in the tour of the south shore of Lake Erie, among whom of course were Vicky, Allen and Cathy. The finish was 100 miles further on in Toledo, on my way West, and the winners, i.e. every competitor who hadn't given up, received a baseball cap and a golden tassle. Why a tassle? Because it stood for Tour Around the South Shore of Lake Erie!

In Toledo I stayed in a very special youth hostel: it was the basement of an old couple's house, bicycle fanatics who gave their guests pancakes each morning. I arrived on Sunday, planning to stay for one night and I did not leave until Thursday. I stayed the first day for the ritual press interview and to answer questions in a French class at the nearby high school. The news found its way to the local *Alliance Française* and I ended up having to answer questions in ten different classes. And there too people were generous. The most surprising gift though was the postcard given me by the (male) pupils of the Jesuits High School. It was entitled 'The American Dream' and showed an American flag but also, draped in it, a naked young woman. Jesuits seem to have different morals there . . .

My next rendezvous was with Phyllis Harmon in the northern suburbs of Chicago. I had already heard a lot about her. She had resurrected and managed the League of American Wheelmen in the thirties. Many cyclists I had met knew her by reputation and I had imagined her to be quite an old lady. I was therefore surprised when I was approached at the entrance to her street by a gorgeous blonde on a racing bicycle, who did not even look forty. As Phyllis had told me on the phone that she would ride out to meet me on the road, I thought this was her, and for a lady who was leading a cycling organization in the thirties, it was amazing.

'Hello,' she said, 'I am Lady Lafayette!'

Phyllis Harmon was host to a phenomenon. She herself was quite a phenomenon because at seventy she was still winning medals in cycling contests. But Lady Lafayette was another. Travelling around by bicycle, she was raising funds to resurrect the statue of Lafayette in Metz, France. It is a long story. The Marquis de Lafayette is a hero in the USA because, according to Washington, without him and his French troops, the Americans would never have won their independence. And in 1920 the Knights of Columbus donated a statue of him to the town of Metz where Gilbert de Lafayette came from. In 1944, the Germans melted the statue for arms, leaving only the stone pedestal. Carved on it, surprisingly, is a cyclist. That explains why a French cycling club from Metz had decided to re-erect the statue. Robin Radtke had met them while on holiday in France and became their American fundraiser. Nicknamed Lady Lafayette, she was cycling between all the American towns called Lafayette.

And here she was, also a lecturer-guest of the Wheeling Wheelers, whose secretary was Phyllis: a very busy Phyllis. On top of the two lectures, she was also organizing a Bike-a-Thon in aid of the local old people's home. Lady Lafayette and I were invited and the 50 miles we covered entitled us to a baseball cap and to enter a tombola. There were beautiful things to win, radio and TV sets, bottles of wine, bicycle computers. I would have been embarrassed to win the garden table, but fortunately I got a book about—long distance cycling!

Two more slide shows—with the Bike Psychos in southern Chicago and the Blackhawk Bicycle Club of Rockford—enabled me to leave Chicago 364 dollars richer.

Winfield, in southern Kansas, where the Walnut Valley Bicycle Club awaited me, is close to Wichita, the 'world capital' of light aviation. And a club member took me for a tour of the town from *above*, in his two-seater Beechcraft.

'Between a big plane and a small one,' explained the pilot, 'there is the same difference as between a car and a bicycle: you see much better and there are stronger sensations,' he added as he went into a dive.

Strong sensations indeed, I thought, my hands instinctively feeling for the brakes on the strange handlebar in front of me. And to hide my fright I asked a question: 'Since I entered Kansas, I have often come across small white planes painted on the road. Does that mean the road may be used as an airstrip?'

'No, not at all, it's for the traffic police. They check speeding cars from small planes. As the painted silhouettes are one mile apart, they just have to get a car's time between two planes to work out its speed . . .'

Thus, when I left Winfield, with an extra 114 dollars but pushed by a very strong east wind, I was very careful, the speed limit being 55 miles per hour, to go from one painted plane to the next in at least one minute . . .

California: 'Get Off the Freeway!'

'Do you read the *Deseret News?'* I asked the barmaid, thinking that it should be compulsory, here in Knolls, in the middle of the Great Salt Lake.

'No, because our mailbox is 40 miles away. We get there only once a week. So you see, a daily newspaper . . .'

'That's bad. I hoped you would recognize me, my picture was on the front page of the *Deseret News* two days ago. You see, I am a French cyclist and I've got a problem. It is already dark and I don't know where to sleep in this cold, and snow . . .'

Beside the counter there was an old juke-box from the fifties and the bar looked exactly like a bar in a western movie. Except that, being in Mormon territory, it didn't serve any alcohol, only coffee and doughnuts. The *Deseret News* was also Mormon territory and when they told my story, it was to their advantage. I had had a cyclist's address from the *Hospitality Directory* in the first town I came to in Utah. But the cyclist had moved and been replaced by a Mormon family. Not *any* Mormon family: the husband had been a missionary in France. They were fantastic: not only could I speak French but I had my laundry done and dried. And of course, I had to stay a bit longer for a press interview.

'Good heavens! On a bicycle you said?' The barmaid exclaimed. 'Listen, I've been here for 38 years and, as there isn't anything, and I mean *any*thing, except salt of course, for thirty miles around, you can be sure that any cyclist passing along stops here. In summer we see at least one per day, but I never saw a cyclist here in *winter!* Well, all I can offer you are the station-wagons parked in front. You've got a good sleeping-bag at least?'

I had had two since Salt Lake City. To reassure Millie, the secretary of the Bonneville Bicycle Club, I invested 20 dollars from the 75 I earned with the slide show, in an army sleeping bag. Since Colorado, where the Indian summer ended brutally for me, I had had more and more trouble sleeping outside. Every morning when I took the poles of my tent out, the tent stayed up, frozen stiff . . . And my arrival in Salt Lake City was marked by a terrifying snow storm. I couldn't reach my destination and kind passers-by took me home. Fortunately, since Chicago no more clubs had offered me baseball caps, but T-shirts in their colours instead. I had eight already. I put one on each time the temperature dropped five degrees. I had six on now, so there was still some margin: the temperature might drop another ten degrees . . .

'Listen now,' said the barmaid when I left, 'be sure you have enough water for tomorrow, because the next tap is 43 miles away.'

The next tap was in Wendover, on the border with Nevada. A spectacular border, marked to the inch by the wall of a provocative casino. On one side, Mormon monastic morals, on the other Las Vegas hedonism. On one side, even liqueur-chocolates are forbidden, on the other even prostitution is legal.

I went to the casino, just to look. The barmaids' skirts were so mini that I didn't dare to lower my gaze. I am not a gambler but when I saw one-armed bandits which cost only five cents, I thought what the heck, I can afford a nickel: just to try it. I put the coin in the slot, lowered the lever and could not believe my eyes, the machine went crazy, lights shining madly, and it began to play the American anthem while spitting out nickels just as if it was minting them.

Somebody came while I was trying to collect the coins in my hands. I felt so ill at ease that I apologized.

'It's not my fault. I'm no gambler. I just wanted to try, only once . . . the first time in my whole life and I put in only *one* coin!'

'Enjoy it, man!' came the answer.

I did enjoy it, but to spend the hundreds of coins laid by the machine, I needed the whole evening, feeding other machines, but being very careful to keep that very first nickel, just in case it would drive a machine wild again . . .

Millie, from the Bonneville Bicycle Touring Club, worrying about me as if I was her son, had called Paloma whom she knew in Oasis only 20 miles beyond Wendover. It took me the whole day to reach it, fighting a terrible blizzard, almost alone on the large freeway. Two drivers stopped to offer their help. I refused of course but I reached Oasis as thirsty as if it had been in the Sahara: I hadn't been able to drink a drop, my bottles were frozen.

Not only was the water frozen but my moustache too. Millie had given me a black cagoule which covered my whole face except for my eyes and mouth. My breath had frozen and before I could take off the cagoule, short of cutting off my moustache, I had to wait for it to thaw.

Paloma knew people in Wells, the next village. A phone call and I had the promise of another shelter for the next night. The Ericksens were dealers in heating devices. This was another piece of luck, because when I reached Wells I had a puncture which I could not repair until I had heated up my glue, which was also frozen stiff.

The Ericksens gave me a couple of addresses and called their family in Reno and a whole chain of friendly hospitality was set up along Interstate 80, including two lone women and a Park Ranger. Without them I would have had to spend a fortune in motels or been frozen stiff.

I arrived in San Francisco just as Eddy Constantine arrived in Godard's Alphaville: by night and by freeway. A freeway which looked unreal: 3 am, not a single car, I was alone with only my tiny yellow front light to light up the huge signposts.

It didn't last long. I suddenly heard a loudspeaker behind me: *'Make sure you take the next exit and get off the freeway!'*

And the police car waited for me at the next exit. When the policemen understood that I wasn't from L.A., or the USA at all, they were kinder and explained to me, as if I couldn't read the signs, that, unlike Nevada, California bans bicycles on the freeways.

'There is a cycle path to get to the Golden Gate bridge, look for it, we can't tell where it is, it's kind of complex, but if we find you on the freeway again, it'll cost you the maximum!'

This was bad luck for me. I had been cycling for almost 24 hours non-stop, because I was late. My appointment with the Santa Clara cyclists was for that night, Wednesday 4 December and that was in the southern suburbs of San Francisco. The delay was due first to the snow which kept me in Reno, 'the biggest little city in the world', for a whole day and then to a stupid ban on cyclists getting onto the Donner's Pass. I had to pedal a 120-mile detour and get into California through the Beckworth Pass.

On top of that, when I reached Davis, I found only freeways leading to Frisco. I asked the police, I asked passers-by how to get out of the trap. Nobody could tell me. Fortunately I came across a cyclist who showed me the way. A beautiful road, but a long one. It took me first to Napa, the capital of the Californian wine country, and, after dark, to the top of Cardiac Hill.

From there I discovered San Francisco on the ridge like a jewel shining with thousands of pinheads, from yellow to red, warm in the cold of the dusk, such a wonderful sight that I forgot my appointment and stopped for five minutes.

After my expulsion from the freeway, I spent the remainder of the night getting lost in the northern suburbs of San Francisco and didn't reach the famous bridge until 8 am: the right hand side of it. Unfortunately, on weekdays, only the left hand side is open to cyclists. I had to unload Rosinante II twice to get up the two flights of stairs on each side of the bridge. And Santa Clara, according to my map, was still 60 miles to the south . . .

I crossed the town in a state of torpor. To fight the sleepiness I stopped at a fast food restaurant every three hours. Since the day before I believe I had done all the chains, from the Napa McDonald to the Davis Jack-in-the-Box, including the Vallejo Karl Junior which was open at 1 am and the San Mateo Wendy's. In Sunnyvale, I even stopped at a Taco Bell, although I was tired of Mexican food. I fell asleep in my tray but I had to get back on the road: hateful road. I took the first which wasn't closed to cyclists: the Calle Real, the ancient Royal Way built by the Spanish and obviously not maintained since.

It was 4 pm when I reached my destination, after 220 miles non-stop with a 150-pound bicycle (with the luggage), and I was exhausted. I found a message from Joan, my new hostess. She said that night's slide show had been postponed but another one had been arranged for the following night in Berkeley—60 miles to the north!

My stay in San Francisco was made up of return trips up and down its bay. The Fremont Wheelers followed the Grizzly Peak Bicycle Club of Berkeley and the Manteca Bicycle Club brought to an end an impressive series of Christmas parties. By New Year, I was back on the road along the Pacific Ocean. I discovered there the best of all California's laws: in state parks, cyclists pay only one dollar to camp. I could afford it. I had already sold the 500 postcards I had had printed in New York and I was richer than a year ago . . .

Three other lectures still awaited me: one with the Orange County Wheelmen, another with the Cardiac Cyclists of Whittier and a third in San Diego, organised by Lady Lafayette, who lived there when she was not fundraising across the country. The three lectures largely provided for the plane ticket to Asia: I took the cheapest flight and the destination was a surprise.

The San Diego lecture, however, deserves some comment because it was to have been set up by Dr Clifford Graves. The first time I heard of Dr Graves was in the Darien Gap. Raymond was telling me about his south to north crossing of California. He was cycling in La Jolla when a car stopped and a smiling man introduced himself as the president of the International Bicycle Touring Club and invited him home. It was he too, who had been the first to answer my mailing the previous June.

But cancer moved faster than me and I learned of the doctor's death a week before I arrived in San Diego. I had just read in the mail I got in Santa Clara that he was the most senior member of *my* cycling club, over in France[1]. International indeed was Dr Graves, and the book he had just finished tells many fascinating stories, each one from a different country[2].

My stay in Los Angeles lasted much longer than planned. I was waiting for a new passport. My trip had begun more than five years ago. Something had gone wrong with the telexes because one month after my application I still had the same old passport and at the beginning of February a new problem arose: my American visa would expire soon.

To have it renewed I crossed the Mexican border. And after a week in Baja California, I again had to confront an American immigration officer. I hadn't had any problem so far but now if the officer saw that my passport didn't have the six-month validity usually required, I would have to go to Mexico City to apply for a new passport!

In front of me, a young Mexican declared, quite shamelessly, that he didn't even have a passport!

'Yes, I am a student in San Diego. I went to visit my parents in Mexico and forgot my papers in San Diego.'

'Very well,' the officer shrugged, 'if you are a student in the United States, you ought to be ready for a small test?'

'I am ready.'

'Tell me, what are the three colours of the American flag?'

'Blue, white and red.'

'All right, and now, sir, can you tell me the name of the first president of the United States?'

'Washington?'

'First name George, well done sir! You are admitted to American territory!'

I could not believe what I heard: this guy without papers had just been admitted simply because he knew the colours of the flag and the first president's name! But I didn't complain because immediately afterwards I was given a six-month visa, stamped on a passport which was valid only for the next eight days!

1 Cyclo Camping International, see Appendix I.
2 See Appendix I.

Part Three: Hong Kong to New Delhi

China: Entering Leshan.

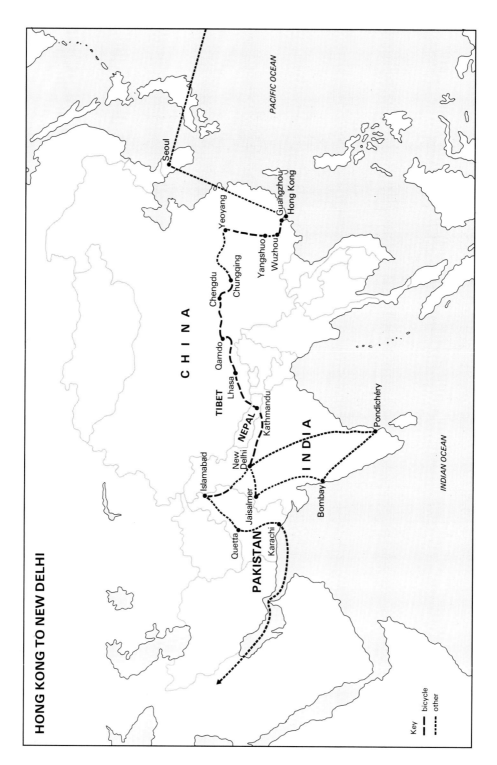

HONG KONG TO NEW DELHI

Seoul

PACIFIC OCEAN

Yeoyang
Guangzhou
Hong Kong
Yangshuo
Wuzhou
Chengdu
Chungqing

C H I N A

Qamdo

Lhasa

TIBET

Pondichéry

NEPAL
Kathmandu

I N D I A

Islamabad
New
Delhi

INDIAN OCEAN

Jaisalmer
Bombay

Quetta
Karachi

PAKISTAN

Key   bicycle
       other

Hong-Kong and Canton: Chinese Brainteasers

The cheapest flight from Los Angeles was to Hong Kong via Seoul by Korean Airlines. It was even cheaper than the Seoul flight! I don't know why, except that on my ticket the price was shown as $549, while I only paid $352. A ticket to Australia cost at least double so the decision was easy: I wouldn't include Down Under in my tour. Anyway I had met so many travelling Australians (they are certainly the most nomadic people I know) that I felt as though I had already lived among them—and it was extremely nice . . .

When I landed in Hong Kong and had to get Rosinante II out of her carton and rebuild her in the corridor after passing through customs, I hoped it would be the last time I had to do it. Bicycles the size of Rosinante II are definitely not to be taken on planes. This time I was lucky. In Los Angeles, in order to avoid extra charges, I had decided to take all my panniers as hand-luggage. Rosinante II alone weighed 22 kg. But I was told the flight to Seoul was a luxury one and allowed each passenger two 30-kg pieces of luggage. Unfortunately, that was not the case between Seoul and Hong Kong and I had to argue for a long time before they would skip the extra charges. That was after a night at Seoul Youth Hostel: my first contact with Asia. To get the right bus to the airport, at 6 am, I had to ask passers-by—by mime. And miming an airport is no easy business. I ended up miming a plane. It worked . . .

After three months I would be able to mime abstractions . . .

A stay in Hong Kong is a bit like an initiation ceremony. The mentors are the travellers on their way back. Those who have been *there,* those who have the knowledge. The others, the newcomers, the neophytes, listen to the masters' advice, often contradictory, without daring to smile and, hearts beating, they begin the introductory ritual to 'The Great Trip': a visa to be obtained here, a fake student card to be bought there and a few words of Mandarin to be learned in between.

'The Great Trip' is of course the individual visit to the mysteries of Communist China, possible only since 1981 and now completely free: no more permits are required and travellers report having been just about everywhere in the vast country.

In the Hong Kong Hostel in Kowloon, I was even assured that Tibet was open to foreigners and also the border with Nepal. This was such good news that I abandoned all my other Far Eastern projects to see if I could satisfy my trans-continental obsession and ride from Hong Kong to Kathmandu. Kathmandu, which used to be approached overland from Europe, before the troubles in Afghanistan and Iran, is now approachable from the opposite side. This would be the new road to Kathmandu . . .

But the details weren't easy to get: a German traveller swore that the direct route via Chengdu was closed, being subject to landslides and 'guerrilla attacks'. According to him, I should use the Golmud route, from northern China. It was surfaced but meant a formidable detour. A Canadian woman assured me that the Chinese would be intrigued by my ideas and would give me all the necessary permits. On the other hand, the German was very pessimistic and told several stories of Western cyclists being forbidden to use their bicycles outside the main towns. Confirming those stories, I found, in the hostel travellers' book, an account by a French cyclist of being expelled from China because he was using his bicycle to travel, after he reached Guiyang, 900 miles from Hong Kong.

I nonetheless was granted a three-month visa through a travel agency with the assurance that I would be allowed to travel by bicycle. And through an Australian girl I got my fake student card. It was made in Taiwan. Theoretically, the Chinese were obliged to recognize it because they consider Taiwan as part of China but they could not check its authenticity because in fact Taiwan is independent. That is how I like politics to be . . .

That card was very useful: in haggling over hotel prices and getting a third-class ticket on the Yangtse Kiang steamer. It was even to come in useful to get a 50% reduction on a train ticket in Pakistan and the student rate in Turkish museums! It eventually saved me ten times the 50 Hong Kong dollars (£5) it cost me. It also taught me how to write my name in Chinese ideograms, because everything on it, contrary to what the subsequent uses suggest, was written in Chinese. And I had to be warned: 'The first line is *not* your name, it is the subject you're supposed to be studying, History. And your name doesn't sound the same in Chinese, it is Wen Yu Lu. As a matter of fact, Lu is a very common name in China!' So I hoped I would pass unnoticed . . .

As for the Mandarin I discovered that it was completely useless as soon as

I crossed the border.

So far I only had one major problem and it was on the British side. They have a ten-mile exclusion zone just before the border and despite many efforts, I couldn't get a permit to cycle it.

'Take the train!' I was told.

'No bicycle on the train!' I was told at the nearest station. I insisted and finally had to pay ten times more for Rosinante II than for myself and reach Shenshen, the border town, among thousands of Hong Kongers going to visit relatives in Canton. The border crossing was easy, I just had to declare Rosinante II as a 'valuable' along with my wrist-watch, camera, radio and travellers' cheques . . . Outside I began to use my Mandarin Chinese to ask for a hotel, a *fandian*. It didn't work.

'Of course, everybody here speaks Cantonese,' said the bearded American I met in a kind of fast food restaurant serving chicken and rice for 8 yuans (£1.60) on cardboard plates. 'You'd better learn sign language if you want to travel in China. Otherwise you'd have to learn a number of different Chineses . . .'

'What kind of Chinese do *you* speak?' I asked, amazed, after hearing him answer a girl who was sitting at our table.

'Cantonese of course. I could only get a job here, as an English teacher, because I speak the language. It would have taken years if I had applied from the USA. Of course I am paid less but still three times more than my headmaster!'

'Do you know this girl?'

'Yes, she is one of my students, and one of my main problems here. She wants to marry me, or rather to marry my *passport* so that she can emigrate. Half of my female students want to marry me. Too bad, I want to marry only one, and she is from Peking, she doesn't speak Cantonese and we can only communicate by ideograms!'

'Do you know where the Overseas Chinese Hotel is?'

'You want to stay there? It costs a fortune! If you don't mind sharing a poor Chinese dwelling, I'll take you home . . .'

The 'dwelling' was a three-roomed flat with electricity and running water, which are luxuries in the Third World. In the afternoon, when another girl came to the flat, the teacher asked the first one to take me on a tour. He gave us two dictionaries: an English-Chinese one for me and a Chinese-English one for the girl, Deng.

She took me along miles of wide and well-kept streets, and eventually to the zoo. There I had my first experience of the curiosity of the Chinese towards Westerners: when I stepped in front of the monkey cage, all the spectators turned around and stared at me . . .

On the way back, Deng and I became quite good at using our

dictionaries to 'speak'. She was very pretty and I tried to tell her so. I showed her the ideogram for 'pretty'. She read too much into this, and after a feverish search showed me another ideogram. The translation was 'legal marriage' . . .

The idea required some reflection. I didn't want to be indelicate and suggest a 'one-night legal marriage'. That might not even exist . . . So I used the two Cantonese words I knew well: *tan-che* for 'bicycle' and *fa-guo* for 'France' and indicated that if she married me, she would have to follow me by bicycle all the way to France. She didn't insist . . .

The next day I managed to reach Canton. It was not only a 100-mile ride but a new brain-teaser. I soon realized that if I tried to pronounce the word *Guangzhou* (Canton) myself, nobody understood me. So I had to copy the two ideograms from my bilingual map and show them instead; or try to recognize them from the signposts.

On the other hand, cycling in China, after the mad traffic in Hong Kong, is a treat. To begin with, they drive on the right side of the road (Hong Kong drives on the *wrong* side). And then, it is a cyclist's paradise. At last I belonged to a powerful majority and didn't have to fight motorists any more. There, in towns, cycle tracks are provided to protect cars from cyclists! And when I was caught in a traffic jam, in the suburbs of Canton, eight lines of bicycles, mudguard to mudguard, I didn't suffer from exhaust fumes . . .

Another advantage is that here dogs don't chase cyclists as they so often do in other countries. First probably because there would be too many cyclists to chase, and then perhaps because the Chinese like their dogs so much that they . . . eat them. And, to be fattened, the dogs have to be prevented from running after cyclists . . .

In Canton I had to get used to another brain-teaser: money. I had already got Chinese currency on the border, but China is unique in the world as it has two kinds of currency. The tourist money, called 'FEC' (Foreign Exchange Currency) I was supposed to use always, even when I was given change in the other currency: the people's money, called *renminbi*.

In fact I was asked for FECs only in tourist hotels and there was a strong black market for them (which the Chinese use in Friendship Stores to buy imports). Near the Canton railway station, I got 130 *renminbi*-yuans for 100 FEC-yuans and from then on, I had to have two purses and two accounts: one FEC yuan is divided into 100 fennas, but with *renminbi* it is a bit more difficult: first the yuan is called kwei and one kwei is divided into ten jiao which are sometimes called mao. The most frustrating thing was when Chinese merchants, seeing that I didn't understand the price they were asking, showed me their abacus. I still didn't understand and they gave back my change in crumpled illegible notes. I soon learned to check because it seemed like a popular game to con tourists.

In Canton too, I realized that the Chinese can't understand that foreigners don't understand Chinese. I was eating in one of the numerous small and cheap restaurants set up on the pavement. It cost between 3 and 4 *renminbi*-yuans (60 or 70p) and could be delicious. A man approached me and seemed to be telling me a whole story.

Fortunately I was with a girl from Hong Kong. She came to Canton regularly to subcontract work subcontracted from Europe by her Hong Kong boss. She translated: 'He says he has beautiful mushrooms to sell to you.'

I indicated 'No', and the man pulled out a piece of paper and a pen. He drew an ideogram.

'He has written "mushrooms",' said the girl. 'It is very common, he realized you didn't speak Cantonese but he thinks, like all the Chinese, that the entire world understands ideograms. It works between Chinese from different regions, who wouldn't understand one another without the ideograms.'

Meanwhile, as I had repeated my 'No', the man pulled out a bigger sheet of paper and wrote several ideograms.

'I would like to have the honour to sell you mushrooms,' the girl translated again.

And before I could say 'No' again, the man gave me the paper and the pen so that I could write my answer!

I did as he wanted—but in English of course. And the poor man gave up, telling his partner, according to the Hong Kong girl, that I was pretending not to understand and to pretend better, I had scribbled meaningless signs . . .

China: The Chinese Bicycle is a Sorry Sight

'Foreigners may *not* travel in China by bicycle, that is the *rule!*' The interpreter stressed, 'You must leave Wuzhou by *bus,* and I want to see your bus ticket before you can collect your bicycle!'

'Why haven't I been arrested so far? I have already covered 300 miles since Guangzhou!'

'Because the policemen who saw you leaving Guangzhou probably thought you were just touring the town. This, you have the right to do. Here for instance, you may visit Wuzhou on your bicycle but you must leave your luggage in the hotel.'

I would have liked to insult him, the small smiling interpreter who spoke so politely and who was bothering me with all the politeness in the world. Come on, I wanted to say, you talk bullshit: I wasn't let out of Guangzhou with my loaded bicycle because they thought I was visiting the suburbs!

I was convinced that even if it was officially forbidden to travel by bicycle, the law was not enforced in most places. Just here where the small interpreter in the huge Ho-Bin Hotel believed he was Deng Tsiao Ping himself and had sworn that not a single white cyclist would leave his town pedalling. So he called the police as soon as he saw Rosinante II, and I was just settling into my room—shared with two Swiss, 6 yuans per head, including the colour TV, the teapots and the thermos—when he introduced a policewoman and began to preach at me. He didn't have to, because the policewoman had all her Chinese texts translated into English. It was so well done that all the questions I could have asked had been anticipated and answered in English. But I was stubborn.

'If I cannot go on my bicycle, I am no longer interested in visiting China, may I ride back to Guangzhou?'

'No, forbidden!'

'All right, then I shall take a boat to Yangshuo.'

'You may *not* because Pinguo, the town where the boat stops, is not open to foreigners. *You must leave by bus* Sir! Tomorrow morning, I shall

176

USA: Camping along Lovelock's Lake in Nevada, December 1985.

China: In Sichuan the road signs are brain teasers, March 1986.

go with you to buy the ticket. See you at nine o'clock!'

The two Swiss couldn't believe their ears. So, the country where the bicycle is king is a segregated country: if your skin colour is wrong, you are not allowed the same means of transport! One has to be Chinese to bicycle in China!

As Rosinante II's freedom of movement was in the balance, I complied with the small interpreter's orders and went by bus to Yangshuo, 130 miles away. There I remounted Rosinante and in Guilin, a major tourist town fifty miles further on, I went to the local daily newspaper to be interviewed, hoping that a press cutting would in the future give me more status when confronted with other zealous civil servants.

The interview was conducted through another interpreter, more pleasant than the Ho-Bin one, but much less efficient in translation. I had the article translated by another American who spoke Chinese. It said that when I embarked on a bicycle trip around the world, it was to follow the example of Mr Poon, a Chinese who did the same years ago. The Chinese, obviously, as far as egocentrism is concerned (in Chinese, China is the 'Middle Kingdom') have no lessons to learn.

After Guilin, I avoided the hotels. But the area was so densely populated that I had to wait for dark before I could pitch my tent. One evening I chose a dry rice-paddy. It rained all night and at dawn, I felt as though I were in a dinghy. To avoid Guyang and its province, Guizhou, I cycled due north and in Yeoyang, to complete the detour, I bought myself a cruise up the Yangtse Kiang to Chungqing. It meant 5 rest days, away from the Chinese crowds which I was beginning to hate.

For all my meals, I had an average of 30 spectators. A flat tyre usually brought between 70 and 100 curious onlookers and if I opened a book in a restaurant, there was a rush to look over my shoulder at the strange Western ideograms. It happened often in restaurants that customers came up to examine me closely, and because their toilets are communal, I was the most popular show even there! After a while though, Rosinante II attracted more attention than me. My toe-clips were a hit with the Chinese and made them laugh a lot. Then somebody found my horn and everybody wanted to try it. Chinese bicycles only have bells: the same bell for millions of bicycles, and it has become completely useless because everybody rings them at the same time. Urban noise is nothing but a continuous ringing of bicycle bells. So my horn was very effective and very popular, until I finally took it off, driven crazy by its repeated use.

It was interesting when somebody noticed the three chain wheels and the two derailleurs because they impressed them. A tourist told me, 'When the Chinese had invented paper and gunpowder, they thought, well we've done a good job here, let's rest! And they're still resting!' This is certainly what Chinese bicycles suggest. They are as far removed from ours as the ox-cart is from the motor car.

When finally they sat down on their heels to discuss at length the comparative merits of a pair of derailleurs, I could eat in peace, thanks to Rosinante II.

As I have said, the Chinese ride on the right side of the road. But I came across a cyclist, on the hilly road between Chungqing and Chengdu, who seemed to have forgotten: he emerged from the crowd on my right while I was speeding down the road. I smashed into him with my left pannier, but managed to stop without falling. Rosinante appeared to be all right, but the Chinese bicycle looked a sorry sight: the front wheel was bent into a figure of eight, the front fork was broken and the tyres were flat. The cyclist came up to me, and grabbed Rosinante. He shouted vehemently and mimed 'money'. He probably wanted me to pay for the damage. What a nerve! Wasn't he riding on the left? I shouted back in French. The crowd surrounded us and listened to us shouting alternately in Chinese and French. And the crowd agreed with me, especially when I mimed my arguments. The crowd agreed that in China one has to ride on the right side of the road. I could proceed unhindered . . .

Whether as a direct result of this accident or not, Rosinante II let me down two weeks later, when I left Emei Shan for Tibet. A broken free-wheel. I had to walk half a day to reach Ya'an where I finally found a bicycle shop. It was a typical shop in a country with a planned economy: the less the shopkeepers sell, the better it seems to them. By sheer tenacity, I managed to buy a free-wheel, in the naive hope that it would fit my French wheel. It was impossible of course, and just as well because it was a one-gear free-wheel with which I would probably not have got very far in the Himalayas. But I am a stubborn imbecile and, before the crowd which had invaded the shop, I decided to buy a back wheel to mount the free-wheel on.

'*Meyo* (There isn't one),' I was told.

'*Meyo?*'

'*Meyo!*'

'Well, what the heck, give me all the necessary spare parts to build a back wheel.' I pointed out the corresponding parts on Rosinante and I successfully got a rim, a tyre, an inner tube, 38 spokes, 38 spoke-nipples, an axle and then *meyo,* no more back hubs. Front hubs there were aplenty, but back hubs, *meyo!*

Which was just as well for me, stubborn imbecile that I am, because to fit a Chinese back wheel on Rosinante II, I would probably have had to buy a new frame! Instead I bought a bus ticket back to Chengdu where I planned to phone home and have a free-wheel sent as soon as possible. But

Tibet: The giant prayer wheel can just be seen inside this building near Đégé, April 1986.
Below left: At Kangding in Tibet, Rosinante meets her first yaks, April 1986.
Below right: Near the Cho-La in Tibet, a pilgrim monk tries Rosinante.

Right: A shepherdess stands on top of Karo La (5045m), poised with a sling in Tibet.

Far right: A spinning shepherdess.

Tibet: The author near Toba with a team of female road menders.

Tibet: Roadmenders at Bayizhen with heavy machinery.

before I went to the trouble of finding a phone, I had a look at the broken free-wheel.

In fact, nothing was broken, it had just opened and, in the process, had lost its bearings, pawls and springs in the dirt of the road. Then I had a brilliant idea: replace the lost pieces with those of the Chinese free-wheel I had bought in Ya'an. Instead of changing the whole free-wheel, the wasteful instinct of industrialized countries, why not react as they would in Africa or South America, why not repair it?

It cost 4 kweis in a bicycle repair shop and it worked. It even worked all the way to France. And it showed that these two kinds of bicycle, so obviously different and incompatible, nevertheless have surprising similarities . . .

Tibet: Sky Burials

On the first bend the road-mender's house appeared at last. Hail was battering my helmet. Good old helmet—one of my Californian hostesses had given it to me. Americans can't ride a bicycle without a helmet. I used to laugh at that and was taken to task for not wearing head protection. I accepted the gift because I reckoned I always had something on my head, to protect it against the sun or against the cold. So why not a helmet?

Under this hail, I wasn't sorry I'd accepted—except maybe for the noise it made. It was the noise which prevented me from hearing properly the strange incantation coming from a small conical tent, two yards from the dirt road. A pilgrims' tent! In front of it, on smoking embers, a big black kettle also resounded under the hail. This was the traditional kettle for making *tsui,* the Tibetan tea made from salted Chinese tea, yak butter and roasted barley flour, an excellent soup! In the tent, there were four pilgrims singing mantras and striking minute cymbals as the Krishna devotees do, except that these pilgrims were black with dirt and covered in many layers of heavy clothing. They had probably set up their tent here so as to have a whole day to scale the pass. It was an example I should have followed, but as there were still two hours before sunset and as the hail had stopped abruptly, I decided to continue.

This pass was my eighth since China proper. Down there, passes are called *Shan Cau, Shan,* 'mountain' and *Cau,* 'door'. Chinese poetry knows no limits! In Tibetan, a pass is *la:* an easier word which shows that the Tibetans are more used to passes than the Chinese. I would soon be just as used to them because I had to climb ten more to reach Lhasa and seventeen more to reach Kathmandu. The passes before Lhasa were the most difficult as the dirt road crossed three major Asian rivers, the Yangtse Kiang, the Mekong and the Salween, and had to get close to sea level before climbing again over 13,000 feet. After Kathmandu, it never went below 11,000 feet.

It took one mile to realize my mistake: the melting hail had transformed

Tibet: At last complete happiness is found at Lhasa, 25 May 1986.

Tibet: It isn't a French flag but a prayer flag!

the dirt road into a quagmire and I now had to push Rosinante II. Next it began to freeze and the mud became like cement to block my wheels. I didn't have any alternative: I had to spend the night there, in a curve of the narrow road which barely clung to the slope, ten feet from the tyre tracks. The tent was ready and dusk was falling when a lorry came on its way down. It stopped. The Chinese driver looked flabbergasted.

'You are not going to sleep here,' he mimed, 'it will be freezing. Hop in my lorry! I'll take you down to the valley.'

'*Down?* You're kidding! Then I will have to climb back tomorrow!' And, still with mime, I tried to reassure him. He came to inspect my tent. He frowned at my sleeping bag, it was so thin, and didn't understand the space blanket. I realized then that I didn't have any water left and began to collect unmelted hailstones. That was stupid again: how could I turn them into water. I didn't have any heater. But it had a helpful effect on the driver: he took me to his lorry. Next to the cabin, there was a tank with a tap. I filled a bottle with the rusty water. It was probably destined for the lorry's radiator . . .

Before he left, he gave me his store of food: enormous red beans, coated with sugar and pepper. I was glad to have some water. Although it was cold, I usually did not need to heat my water because one of the consequences of the Chinese colonization of Tibet is the road-menders' house every ten kilometres. And the Chinese, when they invented paper and gunpowder, did a bit more and invented hot water!

Of course they didn't 'invent' it, but it is true that the Chinese, always and everywhere, have very hot water with them, in very big thermoses. They have it for their tea of course but also for their daily foot baths. And the consequence for me was a comfort I wouldn't have dreamed of in the Sudan or Bolivia: I was certain to find hot water waiting for me every six miles, whatever the difficulties in between.

That night it snowed, and my sleep wasn't exactly comfortable, but contrary to the driver's predictions, I did survive. Around 9 am I reached the summit of the pass and there I made another mistake. I tried to pump up my back tyre. But the valve would not work. I had to change the inner tube, in the mud and the snow. And Rosinante II had hub-brakes which made the job extremely awkward.

I reached the valley in a very sombre mood but rather than hurrying to make up the delay, I now had to take advantage of the sunshine to dry my tent and sleeping bag.

I headed for one of the numerous shelters dug by the road-menders in the slope, in which they shelter from the wind. I scattered my things all around, gathered twigs and started a fire. I had Australian Nescafé bought with FEC in the Chengdu Friendship Store.

When I lifted my head, I noticed an old man staring at me. With a hand gesture I discovered in Africa, I asked what he wanted. He answered by pulling his tongue out! This is sheer politeness in Tibet: it means something like 'I am your humble servant'. My coffee didn't interest him but I was interested in the tobacco he sniffed: he took it out of a hollow goat horn. I took out my camera, and he asked for money. A Chinese would have taken up a dignified pose and asked for a print . . .

The next village was called Qu'nyido. There was not a single shop, but the police chief invited me to eat *tsampa*. Served in a bowl, it consisted of one third boiling *tsui* with a chunk of yak butter and was filled to the top with roasted barley flour. You are supposed to mix it all up with your right hand without burning yourself. Apart from that, you need a lot of experience to keep everything in the bowl. The police chief, having ostentatiously washed his hands, mixed the *tsampa* for me and it filled my stomach for the day.

When I left Qu'nyido, the road started climbing again to the next pass. I met a Chinese cyclist. On his back carrier he had a cassette player box. Our conversation was limited by the thirty words (including numbers!) of my Chinese vocabulary, but he learned everything about me and I learned everything about him: he was a road-mender and he was on his way back from Qu'nyido where he had bought cigarettes.

We came to a road-mender's house but it was not my companion's. He stopped, however, and pulled out five packets of cigarettes from the cassette player box. He sold them to the four men who had come out. Yang Tsiao, as my companion was called, told me that he was now heading for the next road-mender's house and that I would be welcome to sleep there, ten kilometres away.

Yang Tsiao was already looking tired when the snow began to fall. And he had to push his bike when I just had to gear down. There were only three kilometres to go, as far as I could see by the milestones, when the storm became wild. At that altitude, between 10,000 and 12,000 feet, it was terrifying.

Yang Tsiao seemed to be suffering. I urged him on but I was beginning to worry. We were moving in a stinging white blur. White with snow and stinging because the blizzard was in our faces. Not only did the density of the flakes and the depth of the snow prevent us from seeing the road clearly, but it was painful just to look for it. And suddenly, when I glanced back, my Chinese cyclist had disappeared.

I thought he was yards behind. I thought he had stopped to put on his hood. Up till then, he had been playing Mister Tough and stayed bareheaded, confident in the thickness of his hair. But then I saw him

India: Near Agra, I found this camel easy to pass! (photo: Françoise).

folded in two over his bicycle. I called, but he didn't move. I retraced my steps. He was arched against the wind and he was crying.

He held his hands under his armpits. I gave him my gloves: I still had the protection of devices I had had a skilled shoemaker sew on my handlebars in Ganze. Yang Tsiao refused and this time I became angry. I treated him like a child, and forced him to put gloves and hood on, and zip up his anorak. This was no joke. *He* was the only chance for *me* to find a shelter tonight!

The blizzard hadn't abated and while I was taking care of Yang Tsiao, snow was getting under my cape and my back was frozen white. Yang Tsiao noticed this and it seemed to give him renewed courage. I told him to stay close behind me, and started off. I was puzzled by his weakness and lack of stamina. I suppose he came from one of the southern Chinese provinces . . . It was a hard fight against the blizzard, foot by foot. I knew we had won when I heard the dogs barking. Everybody came out when we entered the yard and Yang Tsiao gave a victorious smile. In the narrow flat that he shared with two other young road-menders, he prepared not *tsampa,* but delicious Cantonese dishes.

At dawn it was still snowing but after a typical Chinese breakfast (rice soup with pickles) it calmed down and Yang Tsiao wrote down his address (well, *drew* it) so that I could send him the photo I had taken. Then I left.

Near the first bend, some nomads were camping. Tibetans don't like dogs the same way as Chinese do, and since entering Tibet I had often been chased by sheep dogs. I was now watching a woman fighting to prevent an enormous, I mean *enormous,* dog from rushing at me. Unlike the Tibetan women I had seen before, this one didn't wear one of the red undershirts which every Chinese seemed to wear. And as it was fashionable for Tibetans not to put on the right sleeve of their thick dark robes, it meant that this woman had her naked arm, naked shoulder and naked breast exposed to the extreme cold.

The most surprising thing about my crossing of Tibet by the southern route was its illegality. Swedish birdwatchers I had met in Chengdu had applied for a permit to come to this region and had been refused. I just didn't apply for permission but stayed on my guard and camped as long as I could bear the cold. Now when an army jeep passed me, I slowed down, my heart beating. It stopped 200 yards further on and several green and red uniforms got out, pointing black things at me. Cameras! They were young army officers and all they wanted from me were autographs!

So I became more confident, kept the road-menders' houses for the most deserted parts and began to stop at lorry drivers' resthouses. In fact I was getting tired of having the hairs of my legs plucked out whenever I visited road-menders with my shorts on. Chinese and Tibetans don't have

190

any hair on their legs and arms and to discover some on mine excited them. And to check if they were real, they plucked them out. After that they were confirmed in their belief that the hairy white man is closer to the ape, and therefore less evolved, than the yellow man.

A lorry drivers' resthouse meant a bed in a dormitory for two or three kweis. It meant eight or twelve lorry drivers, tireless smokers and spitters, it meant electricity until 10 pm and no running water, but it meant warmth! Many of these resthouses were run by the army, like the first I slept in, in Bamda. The officer in charge invited me to his table and he tried to show off his education to his soldiers.

'Fa-Guo, Fa-Guo (France) . . . hum Napoleon!'

I congratulated him on the extent of his knowledge but the soldiers didn't agree. One of them summarized the general feeling:

'Fa-Guo: Platini, Meesal Platini!'[1]

In Qamdo, on the Mekong River, I met my first two 'Westerners' in three weeks: a Danish girl and a Japanese man.

They had been stuck there for a whole week. No lorry would give them a lift. Now they had found a solution: the postal van would take them one by one. The girl left that afternoon, and the Japanese and I went into town together for dinner.

We were in the heart of Tibet, but there were only Chinese restaurants and with our experience of China, we behaved in these just as if we had been Chinese. Habit had given us some dexterity in handling chopsticks, we were able to understand the prices immediately and anyway the Japanese had also learned the abacus at school. He was even able, thanks to his dictionary, to give the English names for what were eating. This put a new light on months of Chinese meals for me.

Three young Tibetans sat down at the table next to us. They were ill at ease and I was afraid for a moment that they would be expelled. They didn't speak a word of Chinese and could only eat with their fingers, completely lost with a pair of chopsticks. And these three Tibetans were treated as immigrants, in the middle of their own country!

After the tropical Nu Jiang valley (the river which is called Salween when it reaches Burma), after Baxoi where the soldiers at the resthouse were entertaining the village with a movie projected onto a sheet hung in the backyard, after the pass which follows Zhaxize, at Kilometre 781, I rolled through impressive gorges, down into a bizarre valley: green with pine trees. The river itself, born in a lake near Dawu, had such a pure crystal blue-green colour that I christened it 'Emerald River'. But because it was a wet valley, quite unlike the desert ones I had crossed so far, it was subject

Nepal, and Rosinante claims 42 countries visited, June 1986.

Nepal: With Françoise in the Thamel Quarter, Kathmandu, June 1986.

India: Spectators crowd round to watch a puncture being mended at Benares (photo: Françoise).

to landslides and the more spectacular 'glacier-slides' on the left. The road had been built on the right side of the river and I should have felt safe but every time I heard an explosion, I looked anxiously to see how far the piece of glacier which had broken off would reach. Sometimes they actually crossed the river and my route cut across mountains of ice.

The day I reached Bomi, the main village of the valley, also called Bowo, I came to the end of my food reserves. I had only had *tsampa* for the last few days and I thought that it was playing tricks with my mind when I saw in the road ahead a replica of myself. I began to blow my horn as loud as I could. Another Doctor Livingstone? Right, a German cyclist who had been cycling all the way from Germany, he said, including Iran! He had left Lhasa only ten days before and had bad news; he told me that I shouldn't plan to return to Europe: a Russian nuclear plant had exploded, he said, and the whole continent was radioactive!

He explained that all the travellers in Lhasa had cancelled their plans and were thinking of heading for the Pacific islands rather than for Europe. My God, I thought, how can I complete the circle if they destroy the starting point?

In the Bomi resthouse next morning I could not get up. I was as sick as anything. I wondered how old the pork was that I had eaten when I reached the village the day before. My illness was exactly like 'giardia'. I had to stay in bed for three nights and two days, reading Mary Shelley's *Frankenstein* between painful expeditions to the toilets, which were downstairs, at the end of a muddy yard. I had to be good at anticipating my needs if I didn't want to do my business before I got there.

At the pass before Nyingchi, I broke my derailleur in two. It had got into the spokes. And I had to shorten my chain by several links so that I could still use my lowest gear. Anyway the road had become so bad that I didn't need higher gears. It was very sandy along this tributary of the Yarlung Zangpo Jiang (called the Brahmaputra in India) and the road-menders had covered it with pebbles. For me it was like pedalling in a bag of marbles . . .

After thirty-three days of roasted barley flour and yak butter, after 1500 miles of very bad dirt road, after enchanting names like Gongbo'gyamda and Maizhokunggar, after eighteen passes between 10,000 and 12,000 feet, floating over the valley bed, the white and yellow structure of the Potala appeared.

Lhasa, at last!

In the middle of another hail-storm, going up the Cho La, one of the few passes where I had difficulty breathing because of the altitude, I had passed a pilgrim who prostrated himself every three steps, chanting *Om Mani Padme Oum*. He had a sort of leather smock and wooden gloves to protect him, but he was really sweeping the dirt road with his body. I asked if he was going to Lhasa, which was still 1200 miles further, and he answered, 'Yes, Dalai Lama'. The Dalai Lama, I knew, means more to Tibetan Buddhists than the Pope to Roman Catholics, but I had wondered for a long time whether this pilgrim had meant that he wanted to visit the Dalai Lama, who doesn't live in Lhasa but in exile in India, or if his outstanding feat would enable him to become the next Dalai Lama . . .

In Lhasa, I began to understand it all: Tibetans are just as fanatically religious as Sudanese Muslims or Ugandan Christians and around the Jockang, the most sacred temple in Tibet, pilgrims prostrate themselves every *inch*. Most of them, however, didn't prostrate themselves and were satisfied with walking clockwise around the temple, chanting mantras and turning prayer-wheels. The most spectacular prostrating pilgrims received quite large sums of money from the others.

And I wondered if, under the surface there is such a difference between the Tibetan pilgrim who prostrates himself every three steps for 2000 miles on his way to Lhasa and the European cyclist pushing on his pedals every couple of yards for 40,000 miles around the world.

Is religious piety the real motivation for the Tibetan? Isn't it more general—a kind of social pressure, or the force of tradition? And isn't it exactly the same for the European?

To go around the world has become, for young Westerners, the social and cultural equivalent of a pilgrimage to Jerusalem for medieval Christians, to Mecca for present-day Muslims and to Lhasa for Tibetans. This thirst for travel, it seems to me, is a new form of initiation, a new set of atheistic rituals . . .

Speaking of rituals, it was also in Lhasa that I saw the most impressive ritual of the whole trip: the sky burials.

The ground is too hard to allow normal burial of the dead and wood too expensive for cremation. So the dead are carefully dismembered on a large flat rock outside Lhasa, the bones are smashed with hammers, the skull is crushed between stones and it is all mixed with *tsampa*. Then the *domdens* (caretakers) utter peculiar cries to call the vultures. The huge birds soon cover the rock to clean up the red and white mess.

What could be a more efficient way to go up to Heaven?

I couldn't find a derailleur in Lhasa and I had to repair mine, African style, with wire and string. I made a 100 per cent improvement: instead of one gear, I could now use two! But of course the road between Lhasa and

Kathmandu was almost flat!

There were two passes over 13,000 feet and two over 16,500 feet but the slopes were gentle; so gentle that on the bends of the last pass before Nyalam, for instance, the tourists' four-wheel drive Toyotas didn't bother to follow the road—they cut straight through. This might explain why on this stretch, between Lhasa and Kathmandu, I met more Western cyclists than in the previous four years of travel!

There were two English cousins heading for the Gobi Desert. They didn't have much time and could only stop two nights in Lhasa. They rode racing bikes and had reduced their equipment to a pair of panniers. They had even cut their T-shirts off at navel level to save a few ounces.

'What do you do when it gets cold?'

'We just go faster!'

There were two Americans on 'mountain bikes', which ought to be called all-terrain bicycles, their superiority being not on mountain roads but *off* roads . . . There was a New Zealander, an Irishman and two girls, a Canadian and a Dutch girl, both by themselves.

All were cycling from Kathmandu to Lhasa. But I had been told in Qamdo that a Belgian cyclist was ahead of me. Every time I reached a place he had just left it. After Lhasa I gained ground and I was soon able to distinguish his tracks in the dirt. I met up with him just after Xegar. Tired of being told by other tourists that the French cyclist behind him was going to win the race, he had just stopped to wait for me. He was washing his socks under a bridge when I came upon his machine. Another mountain bike curiously loaded, just as if the rider was a hitch-hiker suddenly converted to cycling. One bag was clumsily fixed to the back carrier and the rest hung from the handlebars.

The cyclist himself looked weird. He was dressed Chinese style in an army-green overall and red starred cap. Marc had already been cycling in China for eight months. His itinerary was amazing. He cycled all the way from Canton to Peking via Shanghai, then took a train to Chengdu and resumed his cycling. He didn't follow my route, however, and went through Markam, a more direct way which I had avoided for fear of the police. But Marc wasn't afraid of the police, he had never been bothered by them in his whole stay.

He was a professional photographer and I left him in Tingri waiting for the perfect light to capture the magnificence of the Qomolangma Feng. The Qomolangma Feng is famous under its English alias: Mount Everest.

The last pass before Nepal was a double one with two summits separated by almost ten miles. The altitude was 17,100 feet and I had to get down into Nepal, to as low as 1600 feet. It took me two whole days. A two-day descent! No wonder it gave to me a view of Nepal which was just the opposite of its stereotype. For decades, Nepal has been reached from India and is therefore depicted as the Mountain Kingdom. But reached from Tibet it just looks like the bottom of a very deep valley!

Khasa, the last village before the Friendship Bridge between 'China' and Nepal was a Tower of Babel.

Mingling in the mud were long-haired and dark-skinned Tibetans with braids mixed with red wool, turquoises hanging from their earlobes, dark robes and heavy boots. There were Chinese settlers, fair-skinned, their trousers rolled up to their knees because of the heat but still wearing their red underpants, women dressed exactly as men.

There were Nepalese women, looking sexy with their tiny blouses leaving their stomachs completely naked and sometimes their breasts too. The Tibetan women, on the other hand, had their stomachs armoured with large belts with enormous silver buckles. There were Nepalese men, looking fragile and naked by comparison as most of them were only wearing dhotis.

There was also a fourth ethnic variety in Khasa, difficult to describe. Its representatives shied away from any kind of uniformity. A German boy sported a pony-tail, an Indian shirt and black leather trousers. A French girl wore a tiny Nepalese hat embroidered with golden threads. A Swedish couple looked as though they had come straight from San Francisco in the sixties, with flowered robes. Finally, the Americans, all clad in Goretex . . .

In the minute restaurant perched on the slope, the change of culture for me took the shape of a Coca Cola bottle. The famous name was written in two alphabets: Roman and Indian. But the trade mark registration was only in English. I ordered a soup and told the waiter, 'No thank you. I didn't order a Coke!' He didn't understand and taking the bottle I realized it contained only soy sauce. I was definitely still on Chinese territory and the Coca Cola bottle had only reached it empty!

The next day in Nepal, at the top of Dhulikhel pass the change was much more complete. In the Dhulikhel Lodge, I cried with joy at the luxury: individual rooms, a carpet in the corridor, hot showers, kind English-speaking staff and a restaurant with more than twenty items on the menu. I remembered the Tingri restaurant where I had gone with Marc: a dark smoky hole in which the question was not 'What's on the menu?' but 'Do you have *any*thing to eat?' It was potatoes and nothing else, but that was a treat compared to *tsampa* . . .

1 Michel Platini: Famous French football player.

Nepal, India: A Month as a Regular Tourist

When, in my rear-view mirror, I saw Françoise and the Indian cyclist crash in the middle of the road with a bus coming at them at full speed, I thought this is it, the Indian adventure is over and it will not be a happy ending. I also thought that it could have happened hundreds of times already, with the Indian cyclists' mania for believing we were racing every time we passed them and gathering round us, impeding our progress. And right now, the young cyclist who had been following us for more than an hour, passing us and letting us pass him alternately, had fallen on Françoise while trying to get back onto the tar after a lorry had frightened him off.

Françoise had joined me again for her summer holidays. She flew to Kathmandu where I was busy regaining the 20 pounds I had lost in Tibet. I was eating only in European restaurants. The Nepalese capital, which has seen generations of alpinists, hippies and trekkers, is remarkably well equipped with Western comforts. There are restaurants for every cuisine, from Mexican to Tibetan. They have tablecloths, clean cutlery and purified water, but their prices are still Nepalese. In Kathmandu, I tried a new restaurant at every meal, four times a day, and still wasn't spending more than five dollars a day.

And Françoise didn't understand at first: she hadn't come all the way from Paris to buy croissants every morning at the Pampernickel and drink café-au-lait at the Bistro. She wanted something more typical, so she could really feel far from home.

I took her then to the Shere Punjab where we had *dal bhât*, the Indian and Nepalese staple food: a divided tray, generally of stainless steel, containing white rice, mashed lentils, potatoes drowned in chilli, an ultra-hot sauce, a sliced onion and an entire pepper. To extinguish the fire, the most effective drink was lassi, a kind of liquid yoghurt. And very soon Françoise pleaded for mercy and we went back to Italian lasagnes.

India, at first, reminded me a great deal of Egypt and China: Egypt because of the squalor and the turbaned heads; China because of the millions of bicycles and because here too people were spitting everywhere. However, if the Chinese made a lot of noise to clear their throats, which gave a warning as to where the danger was coming from, Indians spat in silence. But, probably to compensate, they spat red: so red that some streets were completely coloured crimson by the spittle. This was because of the betel nuts and leaves which adults chewed all day and which gave them sympathetic vampire smiles.

The big difference between India and China, however, was the toilets—or lack of them. In China, toilets can be found just about everywhere and especially along country roads just as if the peasants coveted the stools of the passers-by. Among travellers there was even the delicious story of a Westerner, crouching over a country cesspool, who suddenly noticed a woman waiting at the bottom, her shovel at the ready.

In India, nothing of the kind: everybody defecates where the need takes them. When we left at dawn, our incredulous eyes took in the eerie spectacle of hundreds of Indians, of both sexes, defecating together, lined along the streets, scattered in the wastelands, crouching over gullies or, to have water close at hand (toilet paper doesn't exist, one has to use one's left hand), around ponds and puddles . . .

The tourist pamphlets and official information had not prepared us for this major component of the Indian landscape but it didn't bother us; except when we wanted to stop by the side of the road for a break—no way could we sit down! What really bothered us was something else: the choking curiosity of the crowds. In India as in China or Egypt, cyclists don't get the same impression of the country as regular tourists. The latter hop from tourist town to tourist town, where people are used to seeing foreigners. In between, they are not and it is frantic.

It was impossible for us to stop anywhere without attracting crowds. First pedestrians, then rickshaws, the tricycles which are the taxis of India, and soon the traffic was jammed and it was our fault.

As in China, nobody knocked before entering our hotel room and when we locked it, they knocked it down, as though it was our duty to satisfy their curiosity day and night.

When we were offered tea, which was rare, it was in the same way one offers peanuts to an elephant: to watch it use its trunk. But one day near Manpuri, a lady began to talk to Françoise and they discovered that they were both school headmistresses. The lady invited us to her house for tea. But what she didn't expect was that the whole village would follow and the poor lady had to preside over tea, a polo stick in her hand, to fight back the curious and prevent them from stampeding us . . .

The worst thing of all was to ride a bicycle in the overpopulated Ganga plain. The traffic laws in India seem to be that might is right. Lorry drivers expected cars, and *a fortiori* bicycles, to leave them in sole possession of the narrow strip of tar. It was common to have them passing in front of us, or even pulling over to their right just for the pleasure of forcing us off the tar.

Not wanting to break my rims, I came to a desperate solution: I kept a stone in my handlebar bag and I brandished it, threatening to smash the windscreen of any encroaching lorry. Nine times out of ten it worked, the lorry drivers were not used to rebellious cyclists; but when it didn't work, I didn't aim for the windscreen, of course, but for the radiator to avoid worse problems.

In Billiaur however, after I had dented a radiator in this way, a taxi driver sent a policeman after us. I was scared, as the rapidly gathering crowd began to look like a lynch mob. The policeman probably feared the same thing because he suddenly told us to get away.

On top of all that, India was expensive. The year before in the richest country on earth, Françoise and I had kept our budget to under five dollars a day per head, all-inclusive. Now on a much lower standard of living we were spending more than seven dollars.

In North America of course, we were mostly camping and cooking outside or were looked after by the locals. In the Ganga Plain, we learned quickly how foolish it would be to camp out. One single night outside, in the compound of Dohrighât police station, cured us of the idea. The long police questioning, the dubious behaviour of the men towards Françoise and a continuous flow of curious onlookers definitely ruined our sleep.

Indian hotel rooms are outrageously expensive, when you compare them with what you get for the same price in Nepal. In India of course there is always electricity. But it is invariably cut as soon as night falls!

As for food, it was possible to fill our stomachs for 2 dollars per day, per head, but it would mean eating only *dal bhât,* where only the pepper power counts and our stomachs soon went on strike. So we had to rely on restaurants for tourists, where spices don't obliterate the natural taste of the ingredients, and they were more expensive again.

Another example of the expensiveness of India: in 1986 it cost 5 rupees (25p) to send an air letter from India and 36 cents (22p) from the USA. And American aerograms have two advantages over their Indian counterparts: they have colour pictures on them and to close them one has only to moisten the gummed flaps. In India, one has to find some glue!

Françoise's accident, between Agra and New Delhi was therefore a kind of apotheosis of India as we saw it. But the bus stopped in time, probably to allow the passengers to have a good look at us, and Françoise got up with only scratches. The young Indian begged for mercy as I was threatening him with capital punishment. But the bicycles didn't get up . . .

The impact must have been considerable because I needed five good minutes to disentangle one from the other, among the babbling crowd. And even then, Françoise's bicycle refused to move; the Indian's saddle cover was still stuck between the tyre and the mudguard . . .

In New Delhi, the French Embassy did not improve our feelings about India. From time to time, they said, they had to take care of French tourists who had been poisoned before being robbed, and lately a young traveller had been beaten to death in a Delhi backstreet.

So, as Françoise was flying back from there, we decided to give up the bikes for the second month of our holiday and to do as everybody does in India; travel by train, from one tourist town to another.

With a First Class Indrail Pass in our pockets, we were then able to visit the India celebrated by the tourist pamphlets, without the crowds, and it did a lot to improve our opinion of this definitely fascinating country. But we also missed our bicycles.

First we went to Rajasthan where, in the Thar desert, determined to behave like regular tourists we bought a two-day camel ride. Less than two miles out of Jaisalmer, it began to rain cats and dogs. Desert, it is well known, is ill-equipped for torrential rains and we were soon surrounded by new-born rivers. The camels too, were badly equipped for this kind of weather. Our camel driver explained that the camel's feet, too well adapted for dry sand, are useless on mud. He became so worried ('If they slip, they break their legs!') that I feared the moment when he would ask us to carry the camels!

On to Bombay then where I worked out that the train's average speed was no better than that of our bicycles. Finally on the beaches of Mahabalipuram where, at 47°C, we missed the natural breeze of a cruising bicycle.

Then the happy reunion with the bikes which we had left in the bicycle park of new Delhi railway station. After an afternoon's short ride to the airport, Françoise left for France and I stayed alone in the racket, the jostle and the stench, waiting for the Punjab situation to improve so that I could cycle into Pakistan. I took advantage of the delay to have a tooth extracted in the Main Bazaar of Pahar Ganj in old Delhi.

There was an old shop selling frames in the middle of the vegetable market. In the shop, there were also two tailors with their sewing machines and a lottery hawker. All in barely 80 square feet. In the back, just beside the artist who was painting landscapes to fill the frames, there was the dentist's swivel chair. It faced a cupboard full of dusty flasks, a stained mirror and a spittoon filled with cigarette butts.

The dentist looked very old although he had dyed his hair with henna and I wondered if he wasn't senile when I felt his shaking hands. His anaesthetic must have been just as old as he was because I needed five injections to numb my molar. But I had only one fear, that he would extract the wrong tooth. It happened to an English girl I met in Lhasa.

Over there, the Chinese dentists are a show; they work in the street and work their drills with their feet (imagine for a moment your dentist pedalling to bore into your tooth) . . . And the Chinese dentist, when he realized his mistake, told the English girl: 'Whoops forgive me, but don't worry, I'm going to replant it!'

And that is exactly what he did. He replanted the tooth as if it were a lettuce, but of course it became infected and the girl lost two teeth in the incident.

I was therefore much relieved when my Indian dentist wrapped the correct tooth in a newspaper together with some permanganate powder for rinsing my mouth.

Epilogue: The World is not Round

Crossing the Punjab didn't improve the bad opinion I had of Indians. Three weeks in advance and with a deposit of 50 rupees, I had reserved a seat in a supposedly British Magic Bus, with an assurance from the Tourist Camp Travel Agent that I would be registered as the extra driver and therefore exempt from the special permit needed by foreigners to enter Punjab.

On D-Day, the bus was Turkish and already contained seven 'extra drivers', four Turks and three Westerners. The Turks revealed the trap only at the border: as we didn't have permits, we had to pay double the price, thirty dollars, to bribe the Indian border officials. The choice was between that and a direct confrontation with the Indian police, in a perfectly illegal situation. Everybody paid, and after such a conclusion, Pakistan didn't have much of an effort to win my vote over India. However I didn't expect such a difference.

In Pakistan, when somebody was kind and courteous to me, it didn't mean he had something for sale, it was natural. I again met the Muslim hospitality which was such a feature of the beginning of my trip and therefore I almost felt at home. In Pakistan I recognized the typical trait of the true Muslim: he tries to please the foreigner and to give him the best image possible of his country and religion. As in North Africa and the Sudan, it often happened that, when the moment came to pay for my tea, I was told that somebody had paid for me and had left! It often happened that asking a simple question brought a series of kind services. That happened with some civil servants I asked for the address of an hotel: they paid for it!

Of course, sometimes the country was a bit too Muslim. I decided to relearn my Arabic alphabet and somebody gave me a page from a school book. It contained all the Arabic letters with their different styles. Beyond Rawalpindi, I broke Rosinante's pedal block. I could not repair it there and had to take the train to Karachi. And in the train I asked the people around to help me practise the alphabet. Soon, the whole compartment was around me and my page. At that moment a middle-aged man began to object quite angrily in Urdu, the Pakistani language. An animated discussion followed, obviously about me and my alphabet, but I could not understand a single word. As the protagonists kept pointing their fingers at me, somebody explained.

'On your alphabet page, at the top of it, it says *Bismillah El Rââman El Rââmin* and this is a sacred phrase for a Muslim. It comes straight from the Koran and must begin all the prayers. Moreover it sanctifies every object on which it is written and so your page is sacred. According to this man, we should not leave it in your hands because you are not a Muslim. It would be a sacrilege.'

Several fanatics had taken the side of the first objector. However the group who were defending me was composed of older men and they all came to a compromise.

'Here it is, you may keep your page, but you must understand it is sacred and swear not to mistreat it in any way, just as though it was the Bible of the Christians!'

Reading the newspaper in Karachi I realized that I had been in great danger. The Pakistani government had just passed a law introducing the death penalty for anybody committing sacrilege against a Koranic text, like my page. And before the episode on the train, I was all ready to use it as toilet paper, in a country where that commodity is scarce.

If I had been Swiss or German, I could have cycled across Iran. I would have needed only a couple of days to get a visa, and it would have been a thirty-day one. Unfortunately I am French and that, to the Iranians, was not much better than being American: I had to wait forty-five days to get a ridiculous seven-day visa, with a compulsory charge of 150 dollars at the extortionate official rate.

Waiting in Pakistan for forty-five days was another problem. At the Pakistani Embassy in New Delhi, on 6 September, I was told that French citizens didn't need visas to enter Pakistan and indeed in Lahore, on the 24th, I was given a one-month visitor's permit.

So when I learned in Islamabad that I needed 45 days at least, I began to look for an official who could give me a visa extension. Looking for administrative offices in Islamabad is no easy task. The new capital, 10 miles from Rawalpindi, was obviously built for the year 2000, when the average Pakistani has his own car. This makes it a weird town in the 1980s, a town without a soul, scattered along miles and miles of deserted streets. Eight-lane avenues, populated only by donkey carts, cross districts which are not yet built. Some of them are occupied by shanty towns but most of them are still wastelands. It took me two days to find the right office, only to be asked: 'How did you obtain this visitor's permit? You French have needed visas since 1 September! All right, I don't want to know, but don't expect me to extend a suspect permit!'

What was I supposed to do? Go back into India? Which way? Through the forbidden Punjab or through Tibet and Nepal? But then I would have to get a Chinese visa, and how long would that take?

At this point my patience broke down, and I was reduced to buying a ticket on a direct flight to Turkey. But there is only one international airport in Turkey, at the furthest point from Pakistan, Istanbul. So I was now waiting to be rudely propelled to Istanbul, which means, dreadful thought, to Europe!

My journey had started long before I left Europe, and it was over before I returned. I knew exactly where and when it was over. In the French Embassy in New Delhi. I had frozen in front of an aerial photo of Vézelay, a village which looked so clean and so quiet; where houses were built of stone and covered with tiles; where streets were paved, where I couldn't see a single hut with plastic sheets for a roof, a single open sewer, a single stray cow. There were no animal droppings every few yards, no crowds whenever a foreigner appeared even if he was a cyclist arriving from the moon!

And from that moment, I began to read the tourist pamphlets of only one country, promising myself to take a holiday there very soon. That country was France.

In the French embassy, at four o'clock of a windy afternoon, without warning or good-bye, my journey disappeared and left me stranded far from home. I tried to call it back, to catch it up—a foolish and hopeless attempt, because it was definitely and permanently over.

From Istanbul, I had decided to cross eastern Europe and bring the number of countries visited on this journey to fifty. I had even got a Bulgarian visa for ten dollars. It was wasted, for I had forgotten what a European winter was like. Thrace, in the north-west of Turkey, was a cruel reminder. Under a miserable sky, there was such a cold strong wind, straight from Siberia it seemed, that I chose to have it at my back, rather than facing it. So instead of crossing the Bulgarian border, I crossed the Greek one. They are so close together that the Greek officials, seeing the Bulgarian visa, thought that I had mistaken one for the other . . .

Rosinante II's pedal block, badly repaired in Istanbul, worried me again and I headed for Thessalonica to have it repaired. I wanted to have the tread remade, a delicate operation which a Zambian cycle repairer did on Rosinante in 1982, in a shop which was only a square yard of dust under a mango tree. But in 1986 in Thessalonica, I could only get the whole thing welded together. This, added to everything else, encouraged me to shorten my route back and continue under the Greek sun, which was agreeably warm. It also enabled me to make a detour full of emotion: to the village near Amphilochia.

Vassili and One-tooth had made me promise to stop 'on the way back'. They were convinced that when I arrived at the end of the world, I would have to turn around and come back.

Nothing had changed, my rendering hadn't a wrinkle. But the policeman's house was closed and so was Vassili's café. I was told that he had left for Athens. I could see One-tooth in the distance, wandering with his hands in his pockets. It took him several seconds to recognize me.

'Pente kronia, Bernardo, pente kronia! (Five years, Bernard, five years!)' he repeated as he took me to his farm. His wife prepared a meal and we went to inspect the barn I had plastered. It hadn't moved. On the other hand, I learned through the few words of Greek which I still remembered after five years that all the village's youth had left. Maria was a lawyer in Athens, Andriana was married in Arta, her sister was also married in Amphilochia . . . But my Greek wasn't good enough for me to disillusion One-tooth: when I left, he still believed that the earth wasn't round because I was finishing my journey by the same route by which I began it, only backwards . . .

There were female customs officers to welcome Rosinante II on the French border at Menton. They asked me to tell them some of my stories and allowed me to take pictures. It was the first border where I was allowed to do so. But in the youth hostel, the welcome was very different.

The warden came to open the gate. Besides me, there was only one young Dutchman. As the warden didn't say anything about Rosinante, and as it was drizzling, I took her into the hostel hall. Thirty seconds later the man shouted: *'Ouh la, sortez-moi ce vélo, et plus vite que cela! Non mais vous vous croyez où?* (Get this bike outside, and on the double! Where the hell do you think you are? There is a small shelter near the gate, leave your bloody bike there!)'

I took Rosinante outside, parked her where I was told without uttering a single word, while the warden kept on raving. When I went back in, I heard him tell the Dutchman: *'Ouais,* it is always the same with these Americans, they land and *crac* they're at home. Especially the cyclists, they expect us to bow to them! *Non mais,* these barbarians, they would use my living room as a garage if I let them!'

I remarked that I was not an American but he yelled even louder that I didn't have to bring my dirty bike inside. I eventually lost my temper and shouted even louder than him. I was careful not to insult him, but his reaction was immediate.

'Get out of here! I don't want you here anymore. *Non mais,* he should apologize and he shouts at me! I'll teach him!'

'You started it, didn't you? I have stayed in maybe one hundred youth hostels all around the world, without any problems, in more than twenty different countries, and here, back in my own country, I am expelled from a youth hostel! No, I'm going to sleep on this couch here, and if you don't like it, you can call the police!'

'Ah, *monsieur* wants to play the *caïd*[1], but I'll get you out with my dog, yes *monsieur*. Ah, he wants to play the *caïd* but he is afraid to go out at night!'

'At playing the *caïd*,' I could not help saying, 'you are better than me, at least you've got the accent!'

I thought he was Italian. Unfortunately he was North African . . .[1]

'And racist as well.'

'I'm not talking about race but accent.'

'Everybody has an accent, haven't you?'

It was getting out of hand. I kept quiet but settled down on the couch. The young Dutchman was sorry for me and tried to intervene on my behalf. But it didn't work, at least not immediately. But after half an hour of quarrelling, the warden seemed to repent.

'*Allez, amenez-moi votre carte.* (Come here, and bring your card.)'

Phew, I had a chance of being accepted back . . .

---

1   *Caïd:* Big shot in the French mafia, but a *kaid* is a civil servant in North Africa.

Appendices

These appendices are intended to provide the international cyclist with practical information about the countries I have been through. They do not pretend to take the place of guidebooks but to complement them with specific cycling information.

Appendix I: General Advice

Bibliography

Bicycle Travel Stories

Full Tilt: Ireland to India with a Bicycle by D. MURPHY/Penguin.

Into Remote Places by Ian HIBBEL/Robson Books Ltd. (Tierra del Fuego-Alaska inc. Darien Gap, North Cape-Cape of Good Hope, Trans-Peru)

Riding the Mountains Down by Bettina SELBY/ V. Gollancz Ltd. (Karachi-Kathmandu-Darjeeling by lone woman)

Riding to Jerusalem by Bettina SELBY/Sidgwick & Jackson. (London-Palestine along pilgrim routes and history)

Bicycles up Kilimanjaro by Nick CRANE/Oxford Illustrated Press.

My Life on Two Wheels by Clifford GRAVES/Manivelle Press. (Very entertaining stories by cycling Californian surgeon)

Le Tour du Chili à Vélo by Pierre DEVAUX/Manufacture. (Round Chile on Chilian bikes without using the same road twice)

Trois Roues pour Timbouctou by Jean NAUD/Albin Michel. (Self supported bike ride through Tanezrouft desert—amazing)

Seul à Bicyclette de Paris à Saïgon by L. BRANS/Amiot-Dumont. (Paris–Calcutta ride in the 1940s)

La Chevauchée vers l'Ouest by Suzanne BOJ/Boj. (Around North America, incl. Alaska by retired French couple)

Les Coureurs des Déserts by Joël LODE/PAC. (Cycling the great deserts of the world)

A Pedaller to Peking by C. HOUGH/Methuen. (London to Aleppo and Bombay to Madras and Hong Kong to Peking)

Journey to the Centre of the Earth by Dick & Nick CRANE/Bantam. (from Bangladesh to the centre of western China through Tibet)

Journey to the Sources of the Nile by N. SANDERS/Sanders. (Album of photos: Across Egypt, Sudan, Uganda, Rwanda-Burundi)

Keith's Incredible Journey by K. JACKSON/Jackson (Alaska–Tierra del Fuego including Darien Gap)

The Wonderful Ride by G. LOHER/Harper & Row (S. Francisco–New York by cycling butcher in 1895)

The Impossible Ride by L. SUTHERLAND/Sutherland (Trans-Amazonian journey by lone Kiwi Woman)

It's all Uphill by K. DUNSTAN. (Along the Trans-America trail in 1976)

The Great Bicycle Adventure by N. CRANE/Oxford Illustrated Press (Western Europe, Mediterranean islands, Lapland, Kenya)

Cycling to X'ian by M. BUCKLEY/Crazy Horse Press. (Across Tibet in summer 1986, by guide-book author)

Een Fietstocht van Boston naar Lima by B. AARDEMA

Mit dem Velo von Kanada nach Chile by M. KIENHOLZ/Mondo Verlag

Round-the-World Bicycle Stories

Miles from Nowhere by Barbara SAVAGE/Mountaineers Seattle. (In two years, mostly by plane but funny)

The Long Ride by Lloyd SUMNER/Hemrock Waters. (In four years, lots of planes)

La Terre sur Deux Roues and *Deux Vélos pour le Bout du Monde* by Alain GUIGNY/Flammarion (also in German and Spanish).
(First tour alone, second with girlfriend and backwards)

La Planète à Vélo and *Amistad* by J.P. VUILLEMENET/André Eisele

Les Aventures de Rossinante by B. MAGNOULOUX/Magnouloux (In 5 years, 45 countries, 77000 km pedalled)

Maps

Very few maps are published specifically for cyclists and those that are, are only of developed countries (cf. Appendix X). Among ordinary maps, the best are probably the **Michelin** maps, as they show clearly the state of the roads. They are also the cheapest. Unfortunately they only cover western Europe and Africa. I have therefore indicated in each appendix which map I think is the best for that area. MICHELIN: Lyon Road, Harrow, Middlesex, HA1 2DQ.

Guidebooks

Although I know of none intended specifically for cyclists, I found the **Lonely Planet** guidebooks the most interesting and comprehensive for Africa and Asia. For South America, the *South American Handbook* is a must, although it is heavy.
LONELY PLANET: PO Box 88, South Yarra, Victoria 4141, Australia.
SOUTH AMERICAN HANDBOOK: Trade and Travel Publications, England.

Youth Hostel Handbooks

These are necessary to be sure that a particular youth hostel exists, its real location and when it is open. There are two, one for Europe and Mediterranean countries and the other for the rest of the world. They are updated every year and are usually available around February and March. They can be bought at any youth hostel or direct from:
INTERNATIONAL YOUTH HOSTEL FEDERATION, Midland Bank Chambers, Howardsgate, Welwyn Garden City, HERTS. Tel (0707) 332487.
NOTE: You can usually pick up free in any youth hostel a list of other hostels in the same country.

Two Useful Addresses

In England: Cyclists' Touring Club, Cotterall House, 69 Meadrow, Godalming, Surrey GU7 3HS. Tel (04868) 7217.
In France: Cyclo-Camping-International, 20 rue Saint Sauveur, 75002 PARIS. Tel (33-1) 4233 8082.

Equipment

The Bicycle

If I had to do it again, I would choose an all-terrain bicycle ('mountain bike') equipped, of course, with mudguards, luggage carriers and lights. Most of the roads I had to use were in such a bad state that it would make little difference if one were riding off the roads. Even New York City is famous for its pot-holes.

Have at least 15 gears including a granny (one pedal stroke equalling less than a wheel turn) which is useful on soft sand, rocky tracks and high altitude passes.

If you have 26 x 1³/₈ tyres, you will find spares everywhere, except in France and 'French' Africa where the corresponding standard, 650A, is scarce (unlike the very common 650B).

A rear derailleur, a chain and of course inner tubes are essential spare parts to take along. Don't count too much on local bicycle repairers, although some of them are very good. Most of the time the difference in standard, between your bike and the bikes they are used to, will disconcert them.

Consequently the ideal tool-kit would include every tool you need to take your bike apart. In practice get rid of the heaviest. And don't forget string and wire for temporary repairs.

Bedding

I prefer a large mosquito-net to a tent, except for temperate and rainy countries. And I hate hammocks.

Most of the time I didn't need a warm sleeping bag (in tropical countries only a sheet is necessary) but I suffered so much from the cold in the Andes, the Rockies and the Himalayas that next time I'll take a very warm down sleeping-bag.

A space blanket is light to carry and can always be useful.

Cooking

I don't like paraffin stoves because they stink and are usually quite complex to operate. I love gas stoves (such as Camping-Gaz). It is now possible to find the cylinders almost everywhere and where it's not, it is usually a country where you can light wood fires safely and easily, or, more often, find a restaurant every ten miles (China and India for instance).

A couple of bicycle-bottles are enough for keeping water in 'wet' countries. In dry areas, you can buy extra containers on the spot. I never needed more than a gallon a day, light washing included, even in deserts.

Clothing

Clothing is only a problem in bad weather (or for delicate skin: keep it covered!) For rain I like a cycle cape better than Gore-tex. In any case, since the real problem in rain is the *luggage* getting soaked, I always thought the best solution was to find a shelter, make some coffee and read until the rain stopped.

In cold conditions feet and hands are the most difficult to keep warm on a bicycle. I used cellophane bags (bread bags for instance) between socks and shoes and over gloves. It was very efficient.

212

Security

Violent encounters are scarce and the large majority happen in or near towns. In the countryside, I encountered problems only with dogs and North African children. The danger is not great: keep dogs at bay with a club or pebbles (if you're good with a sling, take it along), never let yourself be surrounded by several children without an adult in sight and concentrate on the only *real* security problem for the cyclist: the traffic accident.

Bicycles on Public Transport

The general rule on planes is that a bicycle is a piece of luggage. It must be put in a box and the total luggage shouldn't exceed 20kg.

But I soon realized that most airport employees preferred a bicycle they could wheel rather than a box they couldn't carry. It is better anyway to take out everything which could be ripped off. The pedals should also be taken off and the handlebars should be turned in line with the bicycle to diminish its bulk. But it is not necessary to let the air out of the tubes, luggage holds are pressurized nowadays.

I encountered very different attitudes towards the weight problem. South African Airways didn't bother to charge my extra weight. Avianca employees, in Colombia, applauded Raymond and me when we checked in with our bikes and didn't bother to weigh our luggage. American companies on the other hand are becoming more and more difficult to deal with. Some of them charge a 'bicycle tax' of between 20 and 50 dollars. Note that American Airlines sell handy plastic bicycle bags.

Turkish Airlines were just as strict on weight and I had to share my luggage out with fellow travellers to avoid extra charges.

There is usually a set charge for bicycles on boats. I paid almost as much for Rosinante as for myself in China (The Yangtse Kiang steamer) Egypt (Lake Nasser ferry) and Greece (Crete ferry) and I refused to pay on the Lake Tanganyika steamer. It was free on the Italian ferries between Tunisia and Italy and Greece, and also on the Danish ferry between Crete and Egypt.

On buses the price and trouble are usually not worth any benefit. In Mexico after my mugging, Rosinante cost only a tip to the conductor but in China it was quite a lot. On the other hand, bus stations in China are best equipped for bicycles: they are two-storeyed and luggage is loaded from the first floor.

It is possible to take bicycles on the underground. In New York City, they are free and you only have to learn how to control your bike standing on its back wheel, like in hotel elevators. In San Francisco, where the underground can be a great help in crossing bridges closed to bicycles, you need a special authorization, as you do in Hong Kong. In Mexico City on the other hand, I was refused entry just because I was carrying a bicycle wheel.

Bicycles at Borders

Bikes either simplify things, because they create sympathy, or they complicate them because they create suspicion.

An official receipt from your bicycle dealer, specifying the serial number of your bicycle's frame, might ease things.

Health

The cycle-tourist is, at one and the same time, the most exposed to diseases (because his living conditions are precarious) and the least vulnerable (because he has time to acclimatize, and because the exercise makes him fitter).

My advice would again be basic: have the compulsory vaccinations (i.e. yellow fever, smallpox and cholera for Africa) plus the ones that are useful everywhere (tetanus, diphtheria, polio and perhaps meningitis), but forget the others. Vaccines won't protect you against the most common ailments, which are all due to parasites (e.g. malaria, amoebic and other dysenteries, bilharzia).

So take your quinine tablets, purify or disinfect your water whenever you can (hydroclonazone pills, or drops of iodine or bleach—iodine has the extra advantage of stopping common diarrhoea—or filters). Wash your hands as often as possible and do not bathe in stagnant water in Africa. Don't try to catch the rare snakes you'll see and don't put on your shoes in the morning without checking: a scorpion might be inside. And don't bother carrying around a snake-bite kit.

Money

If you have enough of it

Carry a variety of sorts: travellers' cheques, very handy everywhere; cash which provides hard currency for the black market; and a credit card, which is becoming more and more handy (I could use my Master Card in China!) and, unlike travellers' cheques, may allow you to get dollars in cash from the bank and then go to the black market.

214

If you want to travel for long, you'd better use the black market. You can do it with a clear conscience, as through the black market, your money goes directly to the people who need it. Through the bank, it goes to the élite. But beware, the black market should be treated with care. It can be dangerous. Try never to change money in the streets and get good information first from fellow travellers (The best info always comes from experienced fellow travellers, never from the locals).

Sometimes I changed travellers' cheques on the black market (the Sudan, Argentina, Nepal and Guatemala) but dollars in cash work better elsewhere. And in India only large denomination notes (from $100) are worth the trouble.

There are a few exceptions to the dollar's supremacy in black markets: The French franc in Morocco and Algeria, and sterling in Egypt and the Sudan; and in China the double monetary system favours a black market where one exchanges 'tourist' money for 'people's' money, both of them Chinese.

If you don't have enough of it

Hide a small amount inside your bicycle frame for a really desperate situation and earn some more in rich countries (i.e. Western Europe, USA, Canada, Australia, New Zealand, South Africa, Japan, Hong Kong and Singapore) or, if you are experienced, between rich and poor countries (selling Nepalese jewellery in Australia, Zaïrian malachite in South Africa, Guatemalan cloth in the USA). This however could be risky.

I know of three temporary jobs for which a cycle traveller is particularly suited: bicycle repairer anywhere, bicycle messenger in New York, Montreal or San Francisco and bicycle instructor at a Club Med in a tourist country . . .

Appendix II: Northern Africa—Morocco, Algeria, Tunisia, Egypt

Maps and State of Roads

Michelin maps (169-153-972-953 & 154 for Egypt) show clearly which roads are tarred. This is most important for a cyclist.

In North Africa, most roads are tarred and pretty good by African standards. The traffic is heavy but, except in Egypt, not as crazy as in India.

Accommodation Between Major Cities

Morocco and Tunisia being very touristy, the cyclo-camper will find plenty of campsites and cheap hotels. I have very often been invited home by people. French helps even if the youngsters are willing to learn English. There are several youth hostels in tourist areas, although the one in Gabes (Tunisia) doesn't allow bicycles inside while the one in Marrakech (Morocco) doesn't permit early starts, the warden being a late sleeper.

Northern Algeria is another problem. After the good campsite in Tiemcen, I had to rely on people's hospitality and camp out. Another solution here could be the *hamman,* the public baths which every village has. But they can be expensive, filthy and a lot of trouble . . .

Egypt presents very special problems, as it is *impossible* to camp out except perhaps on the Red Sea coast and deep in the desert. However I managed it twice: in the garden of the Aluminium Hotel (five stars!) in Nag Hammad between Abydos and Luxor and in the YMCA campsite at Aswan.

Fortunately, if there are not enough youth hostels to provide a shelter at each stage of a bicycle trip up the Nile Valley, there are almost enough and they are by far the best places to stay.

Food Supplies

You will need food for no more than a day at a time. These four countries are well equipped with cheap small restaurants and markets. Again, however, this does not apply to the remote desert regions of the south.

Bicycle Repairers

'French-speaking' North Africa uses Western-type bicycles, Egypt the Indian type. Hence the repairers have their different expertise. I had my carriers rewelded in Cairo but couldn't find a new axle in Sohag—curiously I found one in southern Sudan.

Most Suitable Season for Cycling

Summer is best for the northern mountains of 'French-speaking' North Africa, but if you head south, wait for the autumn. The same applies to Egypt. Nights are still very cold in winter, and in the north it can be as harsh as in Europe. Don't forget, Algeria has ski resorts too!

General Impressions

Good, except for stone-throwing children. Try to ensure that an adult is present when confronted with a group of children. Sometimes it will be necessary to call the police. Don't hesitate to ask for help, a friend of mine had an arm badly injured by stones.

On Djerba Island, Tunisia.

Appendix III: Sudan

Maps and State of Roads
Michelin map 154 is reasonable, but not enough for the cyclist. The following 3 maps of Wadi Halfa to Khartoum, Khartoum to Malakal and Malakal to Kapoeta offer some more details.

Accommodation Between Major Cities
You will mostly have to camp out in the desert or the savannah. There is need for a tent in the dry season. A mosquito-net is only necessary in the south along the Nile. A warm sleeping-bag is necessary in the northern deserts.

There are also police compounds and stations if you are following the railway. At one place, the Akoka police station, the policemen even fed the local travellers. As everybody took the sorghum porridge from the same dish and everyone else was much faster than me, the policemen served me separately to give me a chance to eat something.

Food Supplies
You will need enough for up to a week most of the time. I solved the problem by buying large reserves of bread which I dried in the sun in small pieces. Light to carry, they needed only to be soaked in water to provide food. I was also given a couple of tins by local employees of UNICEF. Food is scarce, and even fruit may be expensive.

Bicycle Repairers
Most bicycles are Chinese. Don't count on getting spare parts. I did find an axle but I kept the original bearings and they bored into the cups . . .

Most Suitable Season for Cycling
The dry season, our winter, is best, from November to March. Rains may start in the south as soon as February. There is no rain in the north of course.

General Impressions

Very good. The hospitality is fantastic in the Muslim north. The primitive south is very difficult but very impressive. Note that the south is closed to foreigners at present because of the civil war, but not to determined cyclists: Bettina Selby crossed it on her way to the Mountains of the Moon.

Generally it is physically a very difficult country to cycle in.

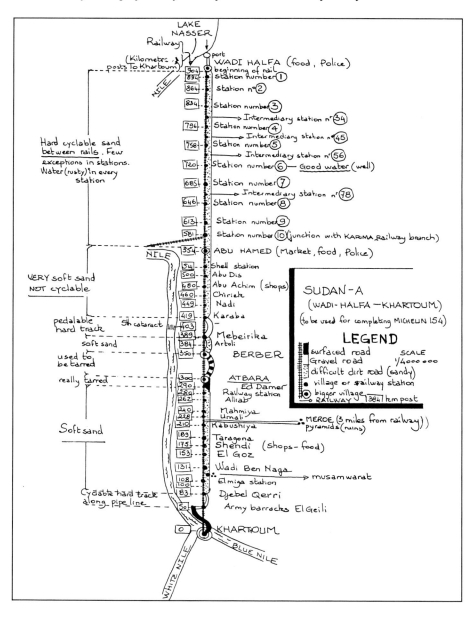

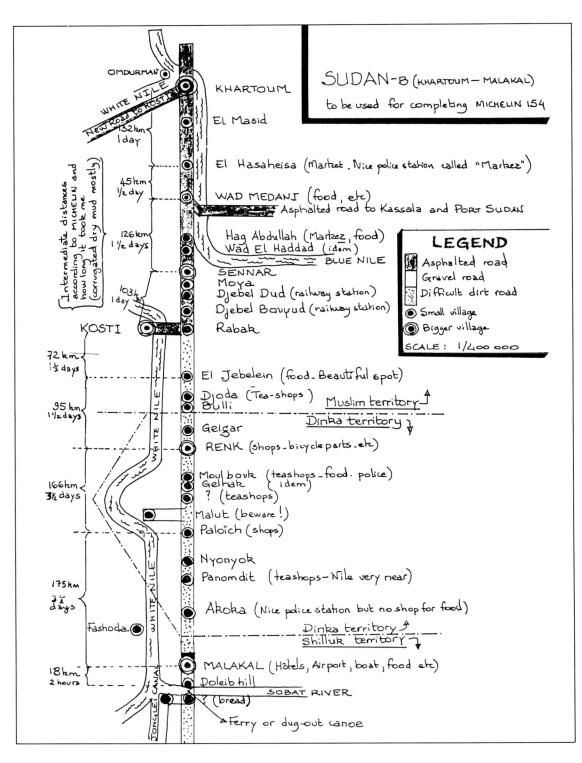

SUDAN-B (KHARTOUM — MALAKAL)
to be used for completing MICHELIN 154

OMDURMAN
WHITE NILE
New Road to Kosti
132 km 1 day
KHARTOUM
El Masid

El Hasaheisa (Market. Nice police station called "Markez")

45 km ½ day
WAD MEDANI (food, etc)
Asphalted road to Kassala and PORT SUDAN

Intermediate distances according to MICHELIN and how long it took me (corrugated dry mud mostly)

126 km 1½ days
Hag Abdullah (Markez, food)
Wad El Haddad (idem)
BLUE NILE
SENNAR
Moya
Djebel Dud (railway station)
Djebel Bouyud (railway station)
Rabak

103 km 1 day

KOSTI

LEGEND

	Asphalted road
	Gravel road
	Difficult dirt road
◉	Small village
◎	Bigger village

SCALE : 1/400 000

72 km 1½ days
El Jebelein (food. Beautiful spot)

WHITE NILE 1

Djoda (Tea-shops)
Bulli
Muslim territory
Dinka territory

95 km 1½ days
Geigar
RENK (shops-bicycle parts etc)

166 km 3½ days
Moulbouk (teashops-food. police)
Gelhak (idem)
? (teashops)
Malut (beware!)
Paloïch (shops)

Nyonyok
Panomdit (teashops—Nile very near)

175 km 3½ days
WHITE NILE 3
Akoka (Nice police station but no shop for food)
Fashoda
Dinka territory
Shilluk territory

18 km 2 hours
JONGLEI CANAL
MALAKAL (Hotels, Airport, boat, food etc)
Doleib hill
(bread)
SOBAT RIVER
Ferry or dug-out canoe

220

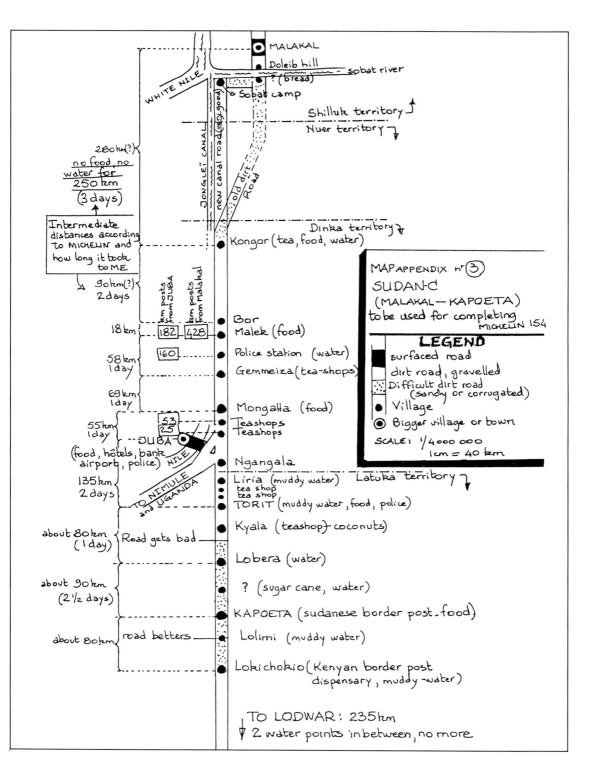

MALAKAL

Doleib hill

? (bread) ── sobat river

⊙ Sobat camp

Shilluk territory ↗

Nuer territory ↘

WHITE NILE

JONGLEI CANAL

new canal road (very good)

old dirt Road

280km(?)
no food, no
water for
250 km
(3 days)

Intermediate
distances according
to MICHELIN and
how long it took
to ME

Dinka territory ↘

● Kongor (tea, food, water)

90km(?)
2 days

km posts from JUBA

km posts from Malakal

18 km |182| |428|
● Bor
● Malek (food)

58 km
1 day |160|
● Police station (water)

69 km
1 day
● Gemmeiza (tea-shops)

55 km
1 day |53|
|25|
● Mongalla (food)
◐ Teashops
◐ Teashops

──JUBA─⊙
(food, hotels, bank,
airport, police) NILE
△
● Ngangala

135 km
2 days

TO NIMULE
and UGANDA

● Liria (muddy water)   Latuka territory ↘
● tea shop
● tea shop
● TORIT (muddy water, food, police)

about 80km
(1 day)   Road gets bad ───
● Kyala (teashop) coconuts)

● Lobera (water)

about 90 km
(2½ days)
● ? (sugar cane, water)

● KAPOETA (sudanese border post_food)

about 80km   road betters ───
● Lolimi (muddy water)

● Lokichokio (Kenyan border post
dispensary, muddy water)

TO LODWAR: 235km
↓ 2 water points in between, no more

MAP APPENDIX n° ③

SUDAN-C

(MALAKAL — KAPOETA)
to be used for completing
MICHELIN 154

LEGEND

■ surfaced road
▨ dirt road, gravelled
▦ Difficult dirt road
(sandy or corrugated)
● Village
⊙ Bigger village or town

SCALE: 1/4 000 000
1cm = 40 km

Appendix IV: Eastern Africa—Kenya, Uganda, Rwanda, Burundi, Tanzania

Maps and State of Roads

Michelin map 955. The roads are good in Kenya where secondary roads are sometimes better than the main highways. (For instance the Nairobi-Murang'a-Nyeri-Nyahururu-Nakuru-Molo-Kisumu route is better tarred than the direct route between Nairobi and Eldoret).

The roads used to be surfaced in Uganda and you might still find some tar between the potholes, if you try hard . . . The French and the Chinese were busy surfacing the main roads of Rwanda and Burundi when I was there, and might have finished. Non-surfaced roads in these countries are a big problem when it rains: if they stay hard, they are slippery as ice and if they don't, the mud clogs your wheels.

One drives on the right hand side of the road in Rwanda and Burundi but on the left in the other countries.

Accommodation Between Major Cities

Because of the rain and the insecurity, I didn't sleep out much. I generally used schools, but also Sikh temples, Christian churches, Belgian missions in Rwanda, a Catholic seminary in Uganda, cheap hotels and virtually all the Kenyan youth hostels.

It is not difficult to get permission from a small restaurant or a transport café to sleep inside after a meal.

Food Supplies

You need no more than one or two days' supply. There are numerous markets and small cafés.

Bicycle Repairers

There is a good one in Nairobi. It might even be the only one. I even found French standard tyres there. He is a very competent mechanic. However, the Indian pedal that I bought there worked for only a month and only the

222

axle remained afterwards—as is the case with most local bicycles. Absolutely no spare parts are available in Uganda and Western-type spares can only be obtained on the black market in Rwanda and Burundi.

Most Suitable Season for Cycling
In theory the best time is between the rainy seasons, but there are two rainy seasons a year (roughly from February to May and October to November) and anyway I didn't find the rains a real problem: it pours for a couple of hours but is hot and sunny for the next ten. One only has to be patient.

General Impressions
Very good. No real difficulty except, at the time I was there, in Uganda.

Appendix V: Southern Africa—Malawi, Zambia, Zimbabwe, Botswana, RSA

Maps and State of Roads

Michelin map 955. All major roads are tarred and pretty good except in Malawi. There the M'bala-Nakonde-Chitipa road is bad after Tunduma. Beware, it can be confusing. The white posts no longer show the distance to Chitipa in kilometres but the distance to Chisenga in miles. The only food found along this road is bananas and bananas and bananas. You should stock up in Nakonde. The dirt road between Nkhata Bay and Nkhotakota is also long and difficult, and to be avoided during the rainy season. But there are villages where you can get food.

They drive on the left hand side of the road in all these countries.

Accommodation Between Major Cities

Schools are best again and large farms in the Republic of South Africa. There are very few youth hostels, and hotels are usually very expensive.

Camping out is no problem in Malawi where one can also use the several government rest houses. The one in Nkhotakota is very unusual. It seems to float on Lake Malawi where the level has suddenly risen and submerged most of Nkhotakota itself. It is built with pieces of cars and boats. It is a kind of African Venice.

In Zambia I found only one campsite, in M'pulungu (M'bala Rest House) but there were gaboon vipers there. Sikh temples are also a good idea.

In Zimbabwe, I again tried police stations, and got a good reception.

Food Supplies

These countries are quite sparsely populated. It is better to have a three-day food supply and sometimes a one-day water supply.

Bicycle Repairers

There is one in Lusaka in the 'African Market' on Independence Avenue near the Railway Station. But, as in the bush, it is rather basic and the parts would fit only Chinese and Indian bicycles. 26 x 1^3/$_8$ tyres are very common though.

In South Africa, however, Western-type bicycles are better known. And Peugeot RSA has helped other cyclists for nothing. Look for their address in the phone book. They are very nice people.

Most Suitable Season for Cycling
The dry season, roughly from May to September. In South Africa, the best time is during their summer (European winter).

General Impression
Very good except for the murderous behaviour of drivers. No real difficulties.

Appendix VI: Argentina and Chile

Maps and State of Roads
Kummerly & Frey map 4252 (1:8,000,000), or, better, *Instituto Geographico Nacional* map 1 (1:2,200,000). I was satisfied with the maps distributed free by tourist offices.

These two countries, being the richest in South America, have the best roads. In Chile, there are not many, apart from the Panamerican Highway. However, Pierre Devaux and Regine Bienvenue managed to cycle around Chile without using the same road twice. They had to carry their bikes more than once.

Accommodation Between Major Cities
You will mostly have to camp out. Large estates *(haciendas)* are very hospitable in Patagonia and there is a lot of room in the Atacama Desert.

There are permanent youth hostels in Buenos Aires but others are open only in summer.

Food Supplies
One day's supply is enough in the populated parts (e.g. the Argentine Pampas), and also along the Panamerican Highway in the desert—one comes across a town every day. But you will need up to a week's supply in the south. Water is not a problem except when one leaves the Panamerican Highway for the desert.

Bicycle Repairers
They are well equipped and trained to deal with Western bicycles. They are in every major town.

Most Suitable Season for Cycling
Their summer (European winter). In any case, Argentina is a pretty wet country and northern Chile a very dry one, whatever the season. It is very

cold in Tierra del Fuego, and the winds are well known for discouraging cyclists.

General Impression

Very good. People are very hospitable and thanks to the depreciation of local currencies, one can enjoy luxuries there at cheap prices. One exception as regards hospitality was the Pampa where I was often refused permission to camp out.

I should add that this applies to British citizens even in Argentina. I was there just after the Falklands affair and I met British travellers visiting Argentina without any problem.

Argentina: A bike is converted into a knife sharpener.

Appendix VII: Bolivia, Peru, Ecuador, Colombia

Maps and State of Roads

Kummerly & Frey 4252 and IGN. I found the *South American Handbook* maps satisfactory, as well as those distributed free by tourist offices which I complemented with the following three maps: Ollagüe to Epizana, Epizana to Juliaca and Juliaca to Nazca.

Good roads are extremely rare. Even the Panamerican Highway has literally been washed out near Piura in northern Peru. Away from it, there are only difficult dirt roads.

Accommodation Between Major Cities

Camp out—there is plenty of room . . . Cheap hotels and basic rented accommodation with locals are available in the tourist areas. Hospitality is scarce.

Food Supplies

Stock up for between three and five days depending on your speed. Markets are far apart in the mountains. Water can, however, be found more often in streams. The area is a paradise for cooking on wood fires . . .

Bicycle Repairers

Again, Chinese and Indian bicycles are most common, except in Colombia of course, where there are plenty of good repairers, accustomed to sophisticated bicycles.

Most Suitable Season for Cycling

The dry season, between May and October. It is their winter, and nights are cold. There is a big difference in climate between dry Bolivia and Peru (in the Andean areas) and wet Ecuador and Colombia.

General Impressions

Very good with regard to the amazing landscape, quiet life in the wild and difficult but almost deserted roads, but disappointing in relations with the locals. Colombia is an exception, with friendly, hospitable people.

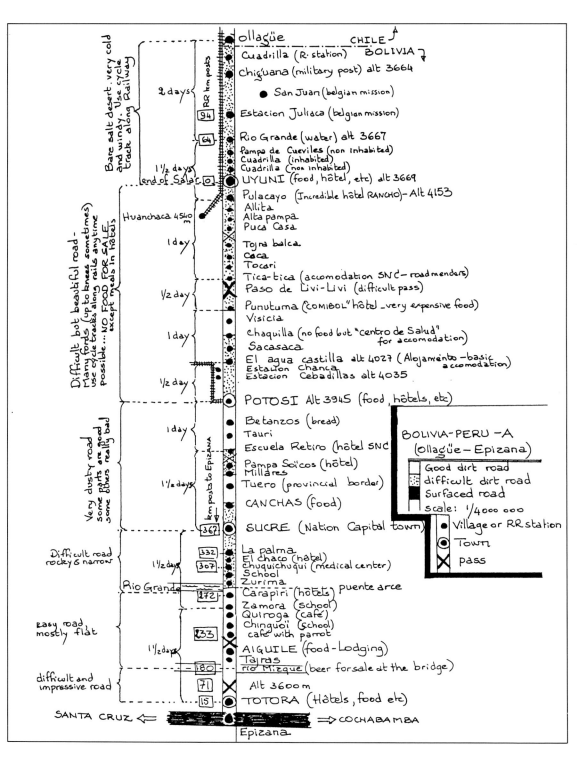

229

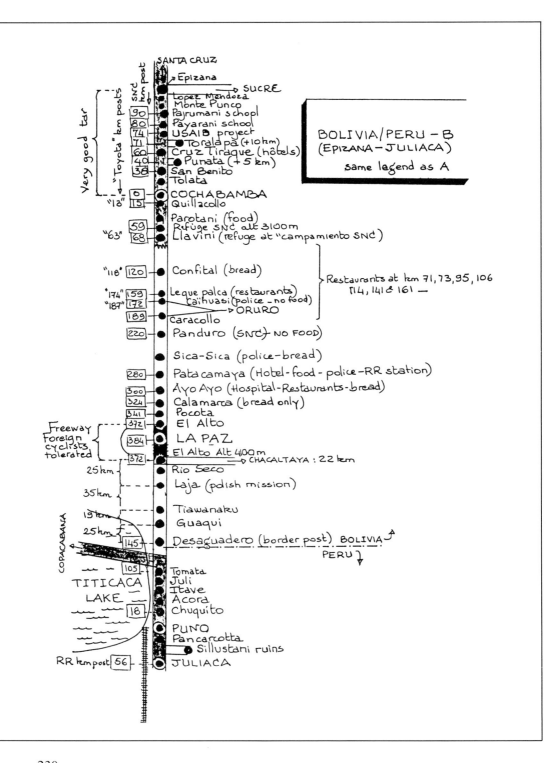

SANTA CRUZ

→ Epizana

→ SUCRE

Lopez Mendoza
Monte Punco

90 Pajrumani school
80 Payarani school
74 USAID project
71 Toralapā (+10km)
60 Cruz Tiraque (hôtels)
40 Punata (+5 km)
38 San Benito
Tolata

"12" 0 15 COCHABAMBA
Quillacollo

Parotani (food)
59 Refuge SNC alt 3100m
"63" 68 Llavini (refuge at "campamiento SNC)

"118" 120 Confital (bread)

"174" 159 Leque palca (restaurants)
"187" 172 Caihuasi (police - no food)
→ ORURO
189 Caracollo

220 Panduro (SNC) NO FOOD

Sica-Sica (police-bread)

280 Patacamaya (Hotel-food-police-RR station)
300 Ayo Ayo (Hospital-Restaurants-bread)
324 Calamarca (bread only)
341 Pocota
372 El Alto
384 LA PAZ
372 El Alto Alt 4100m
→ CHACALTAYA : 22 km

Freeway
Foreign
cyclists
tolerated

25km Rio Seco
35km Laja (parish mission)

19km Tiawanaku
25km Guaqui
145 Desaguadero (border post) BOLIVIA
PERU

105 Tomata
Juli
Itave
Acora
18 Chuquito
PUNO
Pancarcotta
Sillustani ruins
RR kmpost 56 JULIACA

TITICACA
LAKE

COPACABANA

BOLIVIA/PERU – B
(EPIZANA – JULIACA)

same legend as A

→ Restaurants at km 71, 73, 95, 106
114, 141 & 161 —

snc km post

"Toyota" km posts

Very good tar

230

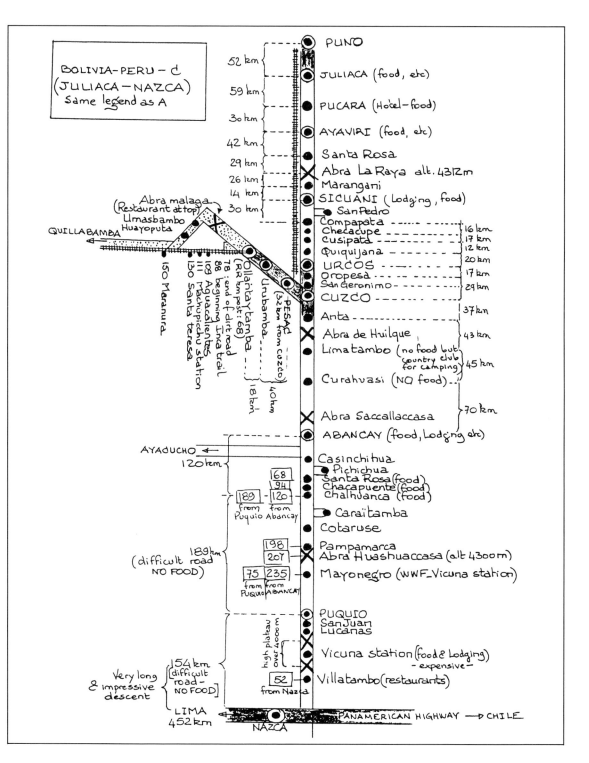

BOLIVIA–PERU – c
(JULIACA–NAZCA)
Same legend as A

PUNO
52 km
JULIACA (food, etc)
59 km
PUCARA (Hotel–food)
30 km
AYAVIRI (food, etc)
42 km
Santa Rosa
29 km
Abra La Raya alt. 4312m
26 km
Marangani
14 km
SICUANI (Lodging, food)
30 km
San Pedro
Compapata ---------- 16 km
Checacupe ----------- 17 km
Cusipata ----------- 12 km
Quiquijana --------- 20 km
URCOS --------------- 17 km
Oropesa ------------ 29 km
San Geronimo --------
CUZCO ---------------
Anta ----------- 37 km
Abra de Huilque 43 km
Lima tambo (no food but country club for camping) 45 km
Curahuasi (NO food)
Abra Saccallaccasa 70 km
ABANCAY (food, Lodging etc)

AYACUCHO ←
120 km
Casinchihua
Pichichua
Santa Rosa (food)
68
94
Chacapuente (food)
189 - 120
Chalhuanca (food)
from   from
Puquio Abancay
Caraïtamba
Cotaruse
198
Pampamarca
207
Abra Huashuaccasa (alt 4300m)
75 235
Mayonegro (WWF_Vicuna station)
from   from
PUQUIO ABANCAY

(difficult road NO FOOD) 189 km

QUILLABAMBA

Abra malaga (Restaurant at top)
Umasbamba
Huayoputa
150 Maranura
130 Santa teresa
III Machupicchu station
109 Aguascalientes
88 beginning Inca trail
78 (end of dirt road)
Ollantaytambo (RR km post: 68)
Urubamba (32 km from cuzco)
PISAC
18 km
40 km

high plateau over 4000m

PUQUIO
San Juan
Lucanas
Vicuna station (food & Lodging) - expensive -
154 km (difficult road – NO FOOD)
52
from Nazca
Villatambo (restaurants)

Very long & impressive descent
LIMA 452 km

NAZCA
PANAMERICAN HIGHWAY → CHILE

231

Appendix VIII: Darien Gap

This is a highly unsuitable place for cycling but there is a great temptation to try to overcome this short obstacle if one is cycling from Alaska to Tierra del Fuego. To my knowledge, only one man has 'overlanded' the entire distance, carrying his bicycle across the Darien Gap, and his name is Ian Hibbel. In *Into Remote Places* he tells of the gruelling expedition. There were three of them (the two others gave up as soon as they got out), and they had to hack their way through with machetes. The water was up to their waists and, when they cooked, one of them had to hold the stove over the water. They slept in hammocks hanging over the sludge.

But this was only as far as Traversia (also named Puerto America), after which it seems to have been easy for them. In other words, they looked for unnecessary difficulties. Everybody admits that crossing the Darien Gap overland includes the necessity of a boat trip up or down the Atrato river, since the road on the Colombian side reaches as far as Turbo on the mouth of the Atrato.

Hence, following the directions of *Backpacking in Central America,* the bicycle crossing of the Darien Gap is not as difficult as Ian Hibbel describes it.

Hurry up, *you* could still be the second person to 'overland' entirely from Alaska to Tierra del Fuego.

Appendix IX: Central America and Mexico

Maps and State of Roads
Bartholomew map 941. Only one road in Central America is tarred and that is the Panamerican Highway, ranging from very good but overcrowded in Panama to quite bad and still overcrowded in Mexico.

Accommodation Between Major Cities
I camped out. A mosquito-net is a vital necessity. I was never invited into people's homes, except once in Panama and by Americans in Costa Rica.

When it rained I asked for shelter in schools and was always made welcome. I also tried a new idea: fire stations. A cycling colleague of mine is an ace at it, he asks to stay with the night-duty firemen. He has a whole book of letters of recommendation from one lot of firemen to another and is never turned down. I wasn't either in Panama and Costa Rica, but it just became difficult to find fire stations further on.

I must add that, when staying with firemen, you are *not* supposed to help them with their duties in the middle of the night!

Food Supplies
One day's supply is all you need.

Bicycle Repairers
A good address in Mexico City is: Guiseppe Grassi, Balboa 916A, Colonia Portales, Mexico 13. He is a former world champion cyclist. He helped several of my cycling friends.

Most Suitable Season for Cycling
The dry season (European winter).

General Impression
Very good in Panama and Costa Rica, which are non-touristy countries.

Moderate in Nicaragua, not very good in Honduras and Guatemala, where foreigners are seen primarily as purses to be emptied. Finally, good in Mexico, despite the mugging or perhaps because of the mugging. Knowing my story, Mexicans made a lot of effort afterwards to help me forget it.

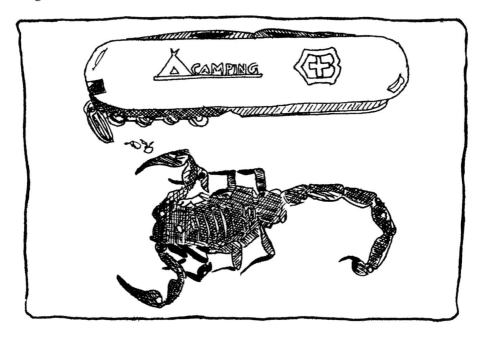

In Nicaragua I am stung by a scorpion; the scorpion dies.

Appendix X: USA, Quebec

Maps and State of Roads

Rand McNally or Exxon maps free from the Exxon main office, on the corner of 50th Street and Avenue of the Americas, New York. One map per state.

Each state transportation department also distributes very useful maps free.

The cycle tourist needs a lot of maps here. Cycling across the main North American conurbations for instance would be very difficult without the help of the bicycle routes that American clubs have set up and tested. Below is one I mapped for myself.

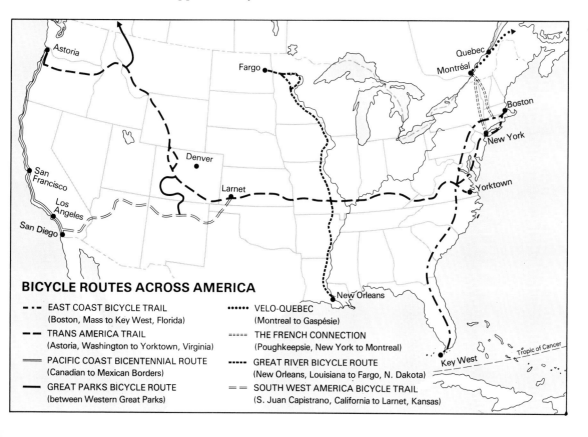

BICYCLE ROUTES ACROSS AMERICA

- ▪ ▪ EAST COAST BICYCLE TRAIL
  (Boston, Mass to Key West, Florida)
- ▪▪ TRANS AMERICA TRAIL
  (Astoria, Washington to Yorktown, Virginia)
- ══ PACIFIC COAST BICENTENNIAL ROUTE
  (Canadian to Mexican Borders)
- ▬ GREAT PARKS BICYCLE ROUTE
  (between Western Great Parks)

- •••• VELO-QUEBEC
  (Montreal to Gaspésie)
- ═════ THE FRENCH CONNECTION
  (Poughkeepsie, New York to Montreal)
- ▪▪▪▪ GREAT RIVER BICYCLE ROUTE
  (New Orleans, Louisiana to Fargo, N. Dakota)
- ══ SOUTH WEST AMERICA BICYCLE TRAIL
  (S. Juan Capistrano, California to Larnet, Kansas)

Cyclists' maps can be bought from:
League of American Wheelmen, 6707 Whitestone Road, Suite 209, Baltimore, MD 21207, USA.
American Youth Hostels, 1332 'I' Street NW, Suite 800, Washington DC 20005, USA.
Bikecentennial, PO Box 8308 Missoula, MT 59807 USA.
Vélo Québec 4545, Ave P de Coubertin CP 1000 succ. M Montreal, H1V 3R2 Canada.

Other very useful maps are:
San Francisco Bay Area Bicycle Route Guide from Caltrans Bicycle Unit PO Box 7310 San Francisco CA 94120.
California Aqueduct Bikeway from Department of Water Resources, Southern District, PO Box 65898 Los Angeles CA 90055.

Note that freeways are open to cyclists in many western states (from Texas to Nevada), but not in California (except the US 5 between the most southern suburbs of San Francisco and the most northern ones of Los Angeles).

Montreal has a north–south cycle track, not easy to use (from Vélo Québec).

Accommodation Between Major Cities
The cheapest motels cost between 16 and 25 dollars. Campsites in most parts are expensive (6 dollars or more) as they don't differentiate between a whole family in two campers and a poor lone cyclist with his small tent.

California is the exception: in state parks, cyclists are only charged one dollar.

Camping is allowed for one night in roadside parks in Kansas. In other states, it is expressly forbidden, but policemen would probably be tolerant towards cyclists camping for a single night. Youth hostels, finally, are very fond of cyclists, and there are seventy-five in the continental USA. Some of them even reserve their services for 'bikers & hikers only'. Check with the guide to the AYH.

Salvation Army centres can be of great help in large towns. They provide a bed, two meals and only ask a prayer in exchange. In some towns (as I found in Fredericksburg, Virginia) accommodation is not provided directly by the Salvation Army: I had to ask for a voucher at the police station and spent the night free in a designated motel.

I described in the relevant chapters how I spent a few nights in unusual ways. In summary, I have often been invited home straight from the road, even by women on their own, something I never experienced in any other country.

Food Supplies
No more than a day except, of course, for Alaska . . .

Bicycle Repairers
Available in any major town. They are indicated on the bicycle trails mentioned above.

Most Suitable Season for Cycling
May–October in the north and the mountains. All year round in California and the southern states. (A popular winter ride is San Diego–Miami).

General Impressions
This was *the* most hospitable country on my tour. But car drivers are much less used to cyclists than in Europe and may be unconsciously dangerous. (In Louisiana and Florida, it may be consciously . . .)

In Indiana, Rosinante is introduced to a strange sport.

Appendix XI: China

It is officially forbidden for foreigners to travel by bicycle in China, unless of course they are on an organized tour under Chinese authority, with a lorry in front carrying the luggage, and a car behind with an interpreter and a policeman. You are then allowed only expensive restaurants and hotels, you never have to fend for yourself. This is definitely not my cup of tea nor what I have been describing in this book.

Foreigners are allowed to use bicycles, even their own, within towns and their suburbs, but shouldn't cycle between towns. The idea behind this rule is not to hide what's between the towns, but stems from a respectful concern to keep tourists where there are tourist facilities such as five-star hotels. The Chinese are also concerned, and I can understand this, about letting fragile Western cyclists risk their lives on their very poor roads.

However, this rule is seldom enforced. I have heard that the legal system has not been properly reconstructed since the Cultural Revolution. It appeared, in 1986 and 1987, that roughly half the Western cyclists in China didn't have any problems, while the other half had considerable problems: most of them were fined and expelled from China altogether. Some had to spend a week in prison.

Most of these problems occurred near Peking and in the southern provinces, bordering Vietnam and Burma. There have even been reports recently of foreigners being obliged to sell their bikes on the spot before their expulsion.

A couple of friends of mine on the other hand cycled around China for eight months on their own, without permission but with the support of the Chinese press. Followed by the Chinese national TV, they became so famous that the police, and even, according to their reports, the Ministry of Tourism, didn't dare to enforce the law!

Maps and State of Roads

The only useful map is the one published by the Chinese themselves and specifying the names in Chinese characters and 'pinyin' transcription into the Roman alphabet. European maps usually alter the pronunciation of names so far as to make them unrecognizable.

I bought a Chinese map in Canton (Guangzhou) Youth Hostel (behind the five-star White Swan Hotel); it is a very large map which I cut into pieces to make it more handy. But every single Chinese word in it is translated into English and it helps. It is called the Map of the People's Republic of China, number 12014-1341, is published by the Cartographic Publishing House in Peking and its scale is 1:4,000,000.

Note that the Recta-Foldex map 328 shows roads and altitudes better than any other, including the Chinese ones, but it has not been updated for a long time.

In the towns, the cyclist can thoroughly enjoy the large avenues and wide cycle paths, but outside, roads are narrow, poorly tarred and overcrowded. I encountered a 100-mile stretch, between Zhaoqing and Wuzhou, which was not surfaced.

Accommodation Between Major Cities
This is difficult. I shied away from hotels after my problem with the police and camped out. There is not much room but, with practice, it is quite possible. If you hide, nobody will disturb you; if you don't you might have to show your passport and you may be invited home. I was never invited home by Chinese in China proper, only in Tibet.

There is moreover, a difficult barrier to cross in China proper. Hotels are like money: some are intended for tourists and they are scarce and expensive; others are intended for the Chinese only and they can be found in every town. With persuasion, patience, diplomacy and shrewdness (this is a lot to carry on a bike!), it is possible to stay in hotels intended for the Chinese; it is even possible to bargain over tourist hotel prices. Thanks to my fake student card, I was able, one rainy night, to get my room price reduced from 54 yuans to 22 yuans . . .

Food Supplies
I hardly ever carried any supplies; small restaurants are to be found everywhere. There is plenty of food (good and usually cheap) in China.

Bicycle Repairers
See 'The Chinese Bicycle is a Sorry Sight': the title says it all!

Most Suitable Season for Cycling
Summer is probably best, especially in the north where winters are very fierce. The far south can be visited in winter, especially the island of Hainan, but autumn and spring are also rainy.

General Impressions
It is an impressive country, which I'd like to see more of. But it is difficult on a bicycle, and I suffered a lot from the crowds' curiosity.

Appendix XII: Tibet

The same remarks apply here as for China proper, except that no one has been forbidden to cycle in this remote part of the People's Republic. This is strange, as Tibet is actually more difficult than China proper: food is scarce, the roads are terrible, and altitude can be a dangerous problem for some people . . .

Maps and State of Roads
Use the same map as in China, with this essential addition for the Chengdu-Qamdo-Lhasa-Kathmandu road: Chengdu to Gamtog, Gamtog to Nyingchi, Nyingchi to Xegar and Xegar to Kathmandu.

Accommodation Between Major Cities
There is plenty of room to camp out, but it is very cold. Road menders' houses, every ten kilometres, may be of help. And every average-sized town has a lorry drivers' resthouse.

Food Supplies
A three- or four-day supply is recommended unless you like *tsampa* enough to live on it! There is plenty of water.

Bicycle Repairers
Everything, down to the spokes, is Chinese-made and the local repairers, although good at, say, building a wheel from 38 spokes, a rim and a hub, are hopeless when confronted with a Western bicycle.

Most Suitable Season for Cycling
Summer is best but winters, although colder, aren't too snowy. Tibet is very dry.

General Impressions
Extremely good. It is like China without the crowds and it was only in Tibet that I began to enjoy the company of the Chinese. There were exceptions between Lhasa and Kathmandu where the sudden influx of tourists and cyclists had had a corrupting influence on people: I was refused water twice and the military truck stop at kilometre 582 tried to make me pay ten times the usual price—I had to camp out . . .

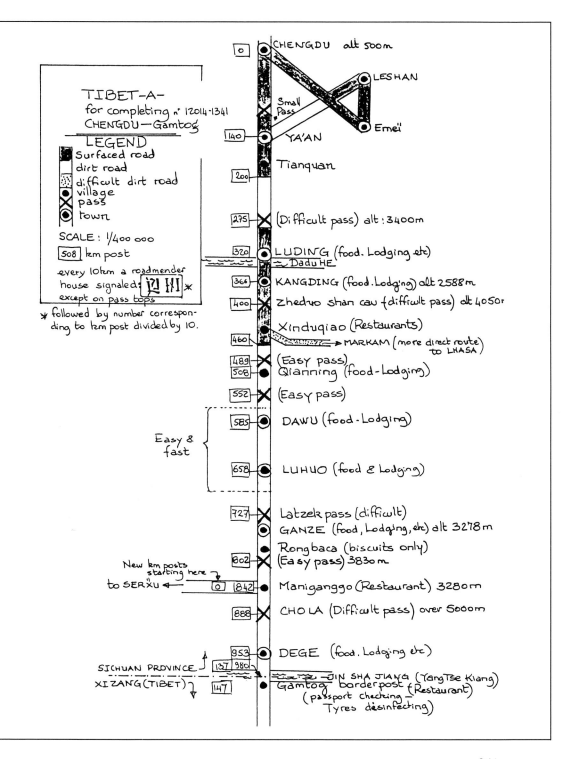

TIBET —A—
for completing n° 12014-1341
CHENGDU — Gamtog

LEGEND
■ Surfaced road
▨ dirt road
▨ difficult dirt road
● village
✕ pass
◉ town

SCALE : 1/400 000
[508] km post

every 10km a roadmender
house signaled: [川] [川] ✱
except on pass tops

✱ followed by number corresponding to km post divided by 10.

[0] ◉ CHENGDU alt 500m
◉ LESHAN
✕ Small Pass
◉ Emeï
[140] ◉ YA'AN
[200] Tianquan
[275] ✕ (Difficult pass) alt : 3400m
[320] ◉ LUDING (food. Lodging etc)
Dadu HE
[366] ◉ KANGDING (food. Lodging) alt 2588m
[400] Zheduo shan cau (difficult pass) alt 4050r
● Xinduqiao (Restaurants)
[460] → MARKAM (more direct route) to LHASA
[489] ✕ (Easy pass)
[508] ● Qianning (food - Lodging)
[552] ✕ (Easy pass)
[585] ◉ DAWU (food - Lodging)
Easy & fast
[658] ◉ LUHUO (food & Lodging)
[727] ✕ Latzek pass (difficult)
◉ GANZE (food, Lodging, etc) alt 3278m
● Rongbaca (biscuits only)
[802] ✕ (Easy pass) 3830m
New km posts starting here
to SERXU ← [0] [842] ● Maniganggo (Restaurant) 3280m
[888] ✕ CHO LA (Difficult pass) over 5000m
[953] ◉ DEGE (food. Lodging etc)
SICHUAN PROVINCE [137] [980]
XIZANG (TIBET) [147] JIN SHA JIANG (YangTse Kiang)
● Gamtog borderpost (Restaurant)
(passport checking - Tyres desinfecting)

241

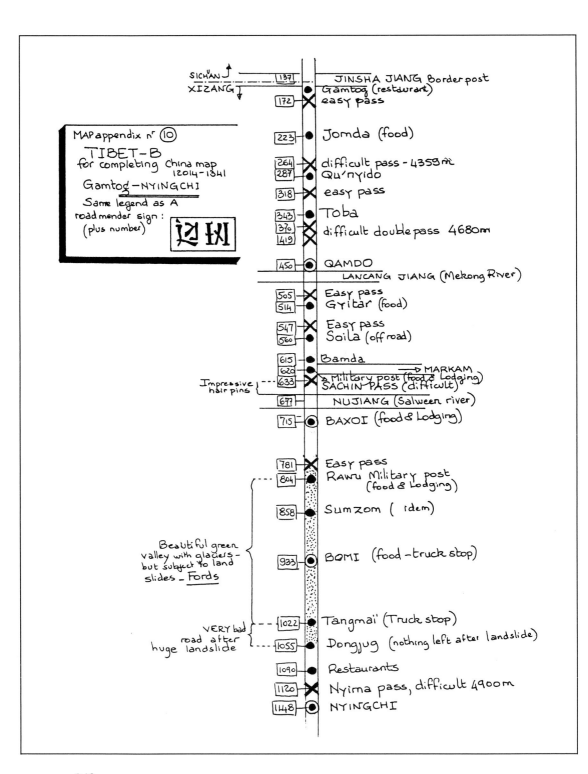

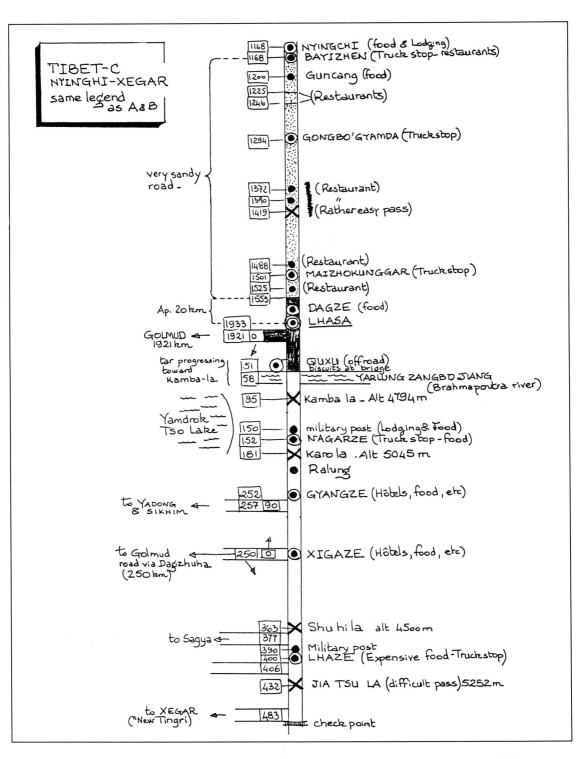

TIBET-C
NYINGHI-XEGAR
same legend
as A & B

1148	⦿ NYINGCHI (food & lodging)
1168	⦿ BAYIZHEN (Truck stop- restaurants)
1200	● Guncang (food)
1225	
1246	(Restaurants)
1294	⦿ GONGBO'GYAMDA (Truckstop)

very sandy road –

1372	● (Restaurant)
1390	● "
1419	✕ (Rather easy pass)
1488	● (Restaurant)
1501	⦿ MAIZHOKUNGGAR (Truckstop)
1525	● (Restaurant)

Ap. 20 km
| 1555 | ● DAGZE (food) |
| 1933 | ⦿ LHASA |

GOLMUD ←
1921 km
| 1921 | 0 |

tar progressing toward Kamba-la
51	⦿ QUXU (offroad) biscuits at bridge
58	YARLUNG ZANGBO JIANG (Brahmapoutra river)
95	✕ Kamba la - Alt 4794m

Yamdrok Tso Lake
150	● military post (Lodging & Food)
152	⦿ NAGARZE (Truckstop-food)
181	✕ Karo la . Alt 5045 m
	● Ralung

to YADONG & SIKHIM ←
| 252 | ⦿ GYANGZE (Hôtels, food, etc) |
| 257 | 90 |

to Golmud road via Dagzhuha (250 km)
| 250 | 0 | ⦿ XIGAZE (Hôtels, food, etc) |

| 363 | ✕ Shu hi la alt 4500 m |
to Sagya ←
377	
390	● Military post
400	⦿ LHAZE (Expensive food -Truckstop)
406	
432	✕ JIA TSU LA (difficult pass) 5252 m

to XEGAR ("New Tingri") ←
| 483 | ▭ check point |

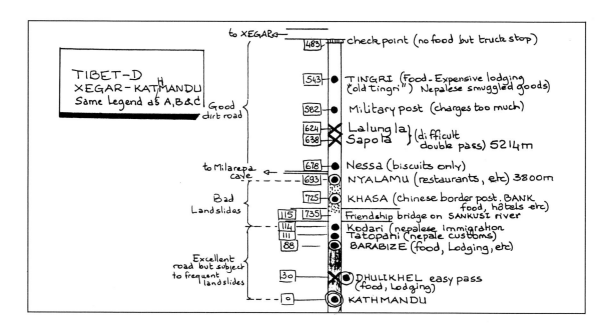

TIBET-D
XEGAR - KATHMANDU
Same Legend as A,B&C

to XEGAR ─────

| 483 | check point (no food but truck stop)

Good
dirt road

| 543 | ● TINGRI (Food - Expensive lodging "old tingri") Nepalese smuggled goods)

| 582 | ● Military post (charges too much)

| 624 | ✕ Lalung la } (difficult
| 638 | ✕ Sapola } double pass) 5214m

to Milarepa
cave ←

| 678 | ● Nessa (biscuits only)

| 693 | ◉ NYALAMU (restaurants, etc) 3800m

Bad
Landslidas

| 725 | ◉ KHASA (chinese border post. BANK
food, hotels etc)

| 115 | 735 | Friendship bridge on SANKUSI river

| 114 | ● Kodari (nepalese immigration
| 111 | Tatopahi (nepale customs)
| 88 | ◉ BARABIZE (food, Lodging, etc)

Excellent
road but subject
to frequent
landslides

| 30 | ✕◉ DHULIKHEL easy pass
(food, Lodging)

| 0 | ◉ KATHMANDU

TO SUMMARIZE :

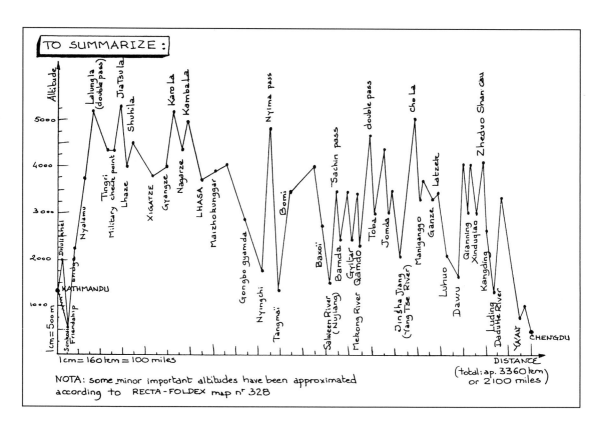

NOTA: some minor important altitudes have been approximated
according to RECTA - FOLDEX map n° 328

DISTANCE
(total: ap. 3360 km)
or 2100 miles)

1cm = 160 km = 100 miles

244

Appendix XIII: Nepal, India, Pakistan

Maps and State of Roads

Bartholomew's *Indian Subcontinent,* scale 1:4,000,000. There is one made in plastic and it is very durable. Unfortunately, and this applies to all Bartholomew maps, although it shows relief and altitude very well, it doesn't give much detail of the roads themselves. It doesn't show any difference between surfaced and non-surfaced roads, for instance, or one- and two-lane highways.

In Nepal, there are very few roads, but nearly all are surfaced. The surface rarely exceeds a couple of yards in width but it is better than dirt. Unfortunately, many of these roads are prone to landslides.

Indian roads are more numerous and in a better state. They are however much more crowded than in Nepal. It should of course be less dangerous in the southern and central parts of the country than in the overcrowded Ganga valley.

Accommodation Between Major Cities

Camping is out, of course, but there are small hotels and, if not, you may be accepted in inspection bungalows and dak bungalows if they are not occupied by civil servants. If you want to stay in these, it would be very useful to obtain a letter of recommendation from an Indian official, even from, say, a tourist office clerk in New Delhi or Bombay. Wardens may have difficulty taking decisions on their own. Small useful maps are distributed by tourist offices and specify where to find the government bungalows.

Sikh temples are also a good idea . . .

Food Supplies

None are necessary as there are plenty of small restaurants and tea shops. An exception is Rajasthan, where distances between villages are greater: there you should carry one day's supply.

245

Bicycle Repairers

The area has one advantage over China: there are Indian bicycles with gears. Repairers are therefore not puzzled by a derailleur. Otherwise, standards are not the same. One might nevertheless be able to count on a natural mechanical genius to find a solution in desperate cases. There are, of course, plenty of bicycle shops . . .

Most Suitable Season for Cycling

I was there during the officially unsuitable season: the monsoon. But it didn't bother me much. When it rains, it pours for a couple of hours, but that is followed by several days of burning sunshine. One problem might be the extreme heat but again, all bicycles have a built-in air conditioning system . . .

General Impressions

The same problems in India as in China, but it was much better in Nepal and Pakistan.

Appendix XIV: Southern Europe—Greece, Italy, Spain, Portugal, European Turkey

Maps and State of Roads
Michelin map 990 for Spain and Portugal, Centato 1:500,000 in four parts for Italy, Pocket Map 782 for Greece and Kummerly and Frey map 1177 for Western Turkey.

Roads are pretty good in Greece and Italy, less good in Spain and even worse in Portugal and Turkey. I love the Greek tar, which is very smooth, and hate the Italian motorway system: suddenly a national highway becomes a motorway closed to cyclists and there is no sign to say what cyclists are supposed to do.

Accommodation Between Major Cities
Camp out. There are several youth hostels in Italy, which are expensive, and in Greece, which are very nice. Spanish youth hostels are usually only open during summer holidays . . .

Food Supplies
No more than one day's supply is necessary.

Bicycle Repairers
In Istanbul, they are all grouped together in Sirkeci, around Ankara Caddesi. In other countries they are not difficult to find.

General Impressions
I didn't like cycling in northern Spain and in Sicily but loved Greece, western Turkey and central and northern Italy.

Appendix XV: Statistics

Money
On this trip I spent a total of 72,000 French francs (roughly £7200) and this included *everything* I needed in *five* years' travelling, including plane fares between continents (about £1000), slide films and camera (another £1000), passport and visa expenses (£350), bicycle repairs, clothing and stamps. That didn't leave much for food and lodging (about £2 per day) and proves that anybody can afford this kind of adventure . . .

I would, however, advise anyone to allow for another pound a day . . .

Mileages and Spares
I cycled 76,988 km (about 48,000 miles), of which less than 2 per cent (1500 km or 950 miles) were pushing, and about 10 per cent (8000 km or 4800 miles) were on unsurfaced roads. I used other means of transport (mostly planes to travel from one continent to another) over 17,000 km (10,600 miles), less than 20 per cent of the total distance covered (93,988 km or 58,742 miles).

I wore out twenty-seven tyres, repaired 199 punctures, broke two wheels, three derailleurs, four carriers and stopped counting my broken spokes after the 145th. My chains and chain wheels wore down very quickly when sand or mud mixed with their grease to make a kind of abrasive paste.